PERSONALIZING THE STATE

CLARENDON STUDIES IN CRIMINOLOGY

Published under the auspices of the Institute of Criminology, University of Cambridge; the Mannheim Centre, London School of Economics; and the Centre for Criminology, University of Oxford.

General Editors: Loraine Gelsthorpe and Kyle Treiber
(*University of Cambridge*)

Editors: Alison Liebling
(*University of Cambridge*)

Robert Reiner, Tim Newburn, Jill Peay, and Coretta Phillips
(*London School of Economics*)

Mary Bosworth, Carolyn Hoyle, Ian Loader, and Lucia Zedner
(*University of Oxford*)

RECENT TITLES IN THIS SERIES:
Common Enemies: Crime, Policy, and Politics in Australia-Indonesia Relations
McKenzie

Embodying Punishment: Emotions, Identities, and Lived Experiences in Women's Prisons
Chamberlen

Professionalizing the Police: The Unfulfilled Promise of Police Training
Fielding

Getting Out: Early Release in England and Wales, 1960–1995
Guiney

Sentencing Policy and Social Justice
Henham

Cold Case Reviews: DNA, Detective Work and Unsolved Major Crimes
Allsop

Justice, Mercy, and Caprice: Clemency and the Death Penalty in Ireland
O'Donnell

Young Criminal Lives:Life Courses and Life Chances from 1850
Barry Godfrey, Pamela Cox, Heather Shore, and Zoe Alker

Personalizing the State

An Anthropology of Law, Politics, and Welfare in Austerity Britain

INSA LEE KOCH

OXFORD
UNIVERSITY PRESS

Great Clarendon Street, Oxford, OX2 6DP,
United Kingdom

Oxford University Press is a department of the University of Oxford.
It furthers the University's objective of excellence in research, scholarship,
and education by publishing worldwide. Oxford is a registered trade mark of
Oxford University Press in the UK and in certain other countries

© Insa Lee Koch 2018

The moral rights of the author have been asserted

First Edition published in 2018

Impression: 1

All rights reserved. No part of this publication may be reproduced, stored in
a retrieval system, or transmitted, in any form or by any means, without the
prior permission in writing of Oxford University Press, or as expressly permitted
by law, by licence or under terms agreed with the appropriate reprographics
rights organization. Enquiries concerning reproduction outside the scope of the
above should be sent to the Rights Department, Oxford University Press, at the
address above

You must not circulate this work in any other form
and you must impose this same condition on any acquirer

Crown copyright material is reproduced under Class Licence
Number C01P0000148 with the permission of OPSI
and the Queen's Printer for Scotland

Published in the United States of America by Oxford University Press
198 Madison Avenue, New York, NY 10016, United States of America

British Library Cataloguing in Publication Data

Data available

Library of Congress Control Number: 2018952416

ISBN 978-0-19-880751-3

Printed and bound by
CPI Group (UK) Ltd, Croydon, CR0 4YY

Links to third party websites are provided by Oxford in good faith and
for information only. Oxford disclaims any responsibility for the materials
contained in any third party website referenced in this work.

General Editors' Introduction

The *Clarendon Studies in Criminology* series aims to provide a forum for outstanding theoretical and empirical work in all aspects of criminology and criminal justice, broadly understood. The Editors welcome submissions from established scholars, as well as excellent PhD work. The Series was inaugurated in 1994, with Roger Hood as its first General Editor, following discussions between Oxford University Press and their criminology centres. It is edited under the auspices of the Institute of Criminology at the University of Cambridge, the Mannheim Centre for Criminology at the London School of Economics, and the Centre for Criminology at the University of Oxford. Each supplies members of the Editorial Board and, in turn, the Series Editor or Editors.

Insa Koch's *Personalizing the State* presents a unique book-length treatment of the ethnography of state-citizen relationships on UK council estates. Encapsulating a long-term ethnographic project that began in 2009, *Personalizing the State* analyses the impact of daily encounters with agents and agencies of the state on council estate residents, who often receive the brunt of these social institutions and their policies. In doing so, Koch contributes to our understanding of post-war British society and especially the socio-political experiences of those who are often marginalized, bringing to light experiences at a local level which help to illuminate and explain contemporary socio-political phenomenon at a much broader national and international level. In particular, the book focuses on the seemingly paradoxical rise of support for punitive populism amongst these marginalized citizens, despite the fact they experience the greatest repercussions. *Personalizing the State* goes beyond previous commentary that stops short of considering people's daily lives and experiences and how communities appropriate state powers on their own terms. It also goes beyond a purely descriptive ethnography to analyse the unique perspective and experiences of those living on council estates and how this can explain their support for illiberal policies that legitimize the very practices of state control to which they are particularly subjected.

Personalizing the State considers the disconnection between estate residents' expectations for a personalized state that answers to local needs and rewards hard work and good citizenship with adequate support, and their day-to-day experience of marginalization and subjugation to state control, and explores how this can lead both to their support for increasingly punitive policies towards those seen as breaking local norms, and subsequently narratives of victimhood as these responsive state policies serve to further marginalize and exclude them, fuelling the rise of political parties like the British National Party (BNP) and the UK Independence Party (UKIP).

Personalizing the State presents a strong overarching narrative drawing synergies across criminology, anthropology, sociology and other socio-legal fields, while at the same time being designed so that its chapters are also self-contained treatments of underlying issues relevant to experiences of citizenship and life, both day-to-day and in terms of its socio-political nature, on UK council estates. These include historic insights into the impact of the reconstruction of the welfare state and housing policies in post-war Britain, followed by a unique depiction of life on UK council estates informed by extensive ethnographic research. This hones in on a window into family life and the struggles of single mothers to manage their home environments, and then expands to examine neighbourhood social dynamics, with a special treatment of residents' experiences of the police and policing. This builds to an analysis of residents' avenues for expressing their discontents and the implications for liberal democracy on a much wider scale.

As Editors, we feel that Insa Koch's book has much to offer in terms of understanding the lives of those on the social margins and how their day-to-day experiences of citizenship and relation to the state can have socio-political repercussions at a national level, and how these repercussions are shaping UK politics, leading to insights into the current political climate around the world. We therefore warmly welcome *Personalizing the State* to the *Clarendon Studies in Criminology* series.

Kyle Treiber and Loraine Gelsthorpe
University of Cambridge Institute of Criminology
October 2018

Acknowledgements

This book would not have been possible without the generosity, support, and time of others. Most of all, I would like to thank the people in Park End (which is not the real name of the estate). Reasons of confidentiality prevent me from mentioning any names here—but you know who you are. It has been a huge honour to be welcomed into your community and I continue to learn from you. Without the numerous cups of tea, shared meals, and pints of beer, as well as our chats in the community centres, pubs, homes, and the streets, this book would not have been written. This book is not intended as a representation of your lives, but rather as an ongoing conversation that I hope will continue long into the future. I will always be grateful for your generosity, friendship, inspiration, and time.

I first began thinking through the ideas presented in this book as a PhD student at Oxford. There, I am indebted to the support of my supervisors David Gellner and Bob Parkin. My college mentors Laura Hoyano and Jeffrey Hackney offered me support with their wisdom and wit. Nicola Lacey and Catherine Alexander were the kindest and most rigorous PhD examiners that anyone could hope for and continue to be of great intellectual and personal support to me. David Pratten, Fernanda Pirie, and Phil Clark provided helpful feedback on earlier drafts. Friends and colleagues in Oxford helped me in many ways. Without Sasha East, Saul and Nabila Goode, Christine McDermott and Paula Williams, I would not have done the PhD that I did and the book would have never been written. Charlotte Bruckermann, Olly Owen, Marco di Nunzio and Matthew Wilhelm-Solomon were my fellow PhD companions and friends, and provided me with much intellectual and emotional support.

At the LSE, I have been fortunate enough to continue developing my ideas across the departments of anthropology and law. Many thanks to Catherine Allerton, Rita Astuti, Mukulika Banerjee, Fenella Cannell, Katy Gardner, Yan Hinrichsen, Tom Hinrichsen, David Graeber, Deborah James, Nick Long, Mathijs Pelkmans,

Alpa Shah, Michael Scott, Charles Stafford, Hans Steinmuller, Harry Walker, and Gisa Weszkalnys. I am also grateful to Michael Blackwell, Jacco Bomhoff, Jeremy Horder, Emily Jackson, Niki Lacey, Linda Mulcahy, Jill Peay, Meredith Rossner, and the late Mike Redmayne. Peter Ramsay has supported me from the beginning of my journey, first as my lecturer, then as de facto supervisor, and as a friend. Bev Skeggs has been a big source of inspiration and a hugely supportive colleague. Thank you for intellectual support and for friendship to Max Bolt, Zelia Gallo, Ana Gutierrez, Ryan Davey, Matt Wilde, Jess Jacobsen, Anna Tuckett, and Alice Tilce. I have benefited from many conversations at the LSE Mannheim centre, the International Inequalities Institute, the Criminal Law and Criminal Justice Theory forum, and the Anthropology of Economy writing group. Thank you also to all my students, from whom I continue to learn a great deal. Further afield, I gratefully acknowledge fruitful exchanges with members of the Anthropology of Britain Network and with Maja Hojer-Bruun.

I am grateful for the financial support received through collaborative projects and the intellectual benefits that I have derived from them: first, an ESRC-funded project entitled 'An Ethnography of Advice: Between Market, Society and the Declining Welfare State'. The Grant ES/M003825/1 funded part of this book. Thank you also to Deborah, our PI on the project, for nurturing our team so wonderfully and taking us on intellectual and real adventures. The IGA's 'Research and Impact Seed Fund' supported by the Rockefeller Foundation has funded another collaborative project on 'Challenging Urban Decline Narratives'. Headed by PI Mike Savage and David Soskice, this project has provided a wonderful opportunity to work with inspiring and supportive colleagues and to continue thinking through some of the ideas that I present in this research. I continue learning huge amounts from Sasha East, who has been the best research assistant on this project that anyone can hope to have. During my PhD, the German Academic Scholarship Foundation and Wadham College generously funded my research.

I could not have written the actual book without the support of many people. The academic board and staff at Clarendon Series at Oxford University Press have supported this project from start to finish. Tim Newburn and Jill Peay were the editors of Clarendon Series when I first committed to this project, and they have supported me with enthusiasm and valuable feedback throughout. Without Jill's support, this book would not be what it is now. I thank her for that. I am also grateful to Mohith and to Amy Baker for their patience and support along the way. Cheryl Prophett has done a wonderful job of copy-editing my manuscript. Beyond OUP, Eleanor Bush has edited my manuscript with huge sensitivity, intelligence, and grace. I could not have wished for a better critic and kinder audience, and I will always be indebted to her for that. Tom Grisaffi has been my intellectual companion, and supported me with patience and humour throughout. Without him, the book would not be what it is now. Of course, all remaining errors are mine. Finally, George Shaw kindly granted permission to reproduce his painting on the cover of the book. I am very grateful to him and his agent.

Most of all, it was my family and friends, many of whom have already been mentioned, that sustained me in writing this book. The process of finishing this book was overshadowed by the illness and death on 5 August 2018 of Eleonora Schinella. She was the first friend I made when I moved to England in 2005 and we stayed close ever since. Her courage and positivity in the last few months of her life have also given me strength to finish this work. Marthe Achtnich, Rita Astuti, Sasha East, Katja Fuder, Tom Grisaffi, Hannah Hoechner, and Clara Weinhardt have supported me especially through this period. Eleanor Bush, Adam Etinson, Clare Grisaffi, JP Hayes, Sarah Hegenbart, Adam Lacy, Andrew Littlejohn, Rebecca Small, Marie Tidball, Andreas Schmidt, Rebecca Thomas, Sorana Toma and all my school friends from Münster have been wonderful friends over the years.

Finally, my Korean and German family in Münster, Munich, Sankt Augustin and Hagen have been important to me in so many ways. My grandmother, Hanelore Koch, and my grandfather, Manfred Koch, when he was still alive; my uncle and aunts; and my cousins have always looked out for me. I thank them for that. Above all, in Münster, kimschi and spicy sauces have nourished me through these years. Thank you to my parents, Chun-Kyung Lee and Olaf Koch, and to my twin sister Mia Lee Koch and her family.

Insa Lee Koch,
September 2018

Table of Contents

Introduction: Questioning the Punitive Paradox   1
    Prologue   1
    A Punitive Paradox   3
    Liberal Democracy's Illiberal Turn   7
    Explaining the Punitive Turn   10
    Ethnographic and Historical Revisions   13
    Personalizing the State   17
    Doing Fieldwork in a Marginalized Place   19
    The Ethics of Fieldwork   23
    Chapter Outline   26

1. **A Political History of Council Estates: Council Estates as State-Building Projects**   31
    The Punitive Turn Revisited   36
    The Citizen–Worker and Post-War Paternalism   39
    The Citizen–Consumer and the 'Iron Law of Liberalism'   44
    The Vulnerable Citizen and the 'Law-and-Order-State'   50
    Conclusion   55

2. **The Good Person and the Bad Citizen: History, Class, and Sociality**   58
    History, Class, and Alternative Personhood Values   61
    A Fragile Moral Union Between Citizens and the State   65
    A Moral Union Under Attack   71
    Alternative Processes of Value Accrual   76
    Conclusion   82

3. **Precarious Homes: Encounters with the Benefit System**   85
    Women, the Benefit System, and the Citizen–Consumer Revisited   88

Precarious Homes 92
'The State has Replaced the Man' 97
Personalizing the Benefit System 103
Conclusion 107

4. **Troubled Neighbourhoods: Encounters with Housing Authorities** ... 110
   Material Homes, Nuisance Disputes, and the Vulnerable Citizen ... 113
   Troubled Neighbourhoods 117
   'They Become Part of the Problem' 122
   Personalizing 'Anti-Social Behaviour' 128
   Conclusion 133

5. **Dangerous Streets: Encounters with the Police** 136
   Policing, Crime, and Security as a Collective Public Good ... 139
   'You Do or Get Done' 143
   'The Police are the Biggest Gang of All' 148
   Personalizing 'Law and Order' 153
   Conclusion 159

6. **Political Brokers: Active Citizenship** 162
   Active Citizenship, the Third Way, and Alternative Politics ... 165
   Responsibilization and Participatory Governance 169
   Community Champions as Political Brokers 174
   Personalizing Politics 180
   Conclusion 186

7. **Democracy as Punishment: Brexit and Austerity Politics** ... 188
   Brexit, Popular Authoritarianism, and the Crisis of Democracy ... 192
   Austerity Politics 196
   State Failure 202
   Democracy in Crisis 207
   Conclusion 213

Conclusion: A Different Kind of Paradox 216
Citizenship as Punishment: Moving Beyond the Criminal Law 220
On Popular Punitivism and State Authority: Bringing Down the Leviathan 224
From 'Law and Order' to Post-Democracy? Reconnecting Moral and Political Statecraft 228
Epilogue 232

References 237
Index 255

Introduction: Questioning the Punitive Paradox

Prologue

It was an overcast day in the autumn of 2009, my first day on a council estate I call Park End, a large government-built housing development on the edge of a city in the south of England, and one of the biggest estates in the country. Tracey, a local black woman in her late thirties, had been running the estate's community centre with great charisma, and offered to let me volunteer alongside her for purposes of my research. I was sitting at the large, round table in the centre of the room, when Lindsey—a mother of three teenage children, a local white woman in her thirties, and a long-standing resident who I would soon get to know as a central pillar of the estate community—walked in. She and Tracey had known each other for years; we got talking and I explained to her that I was interested in studying local experiences of 'anti-social behaviour' and policing on Park End. Having listened politely to my explanation of the research project, Lindsey said she would like to take me on a walk around the estate and show me the daily challenges that residents face.

We set off together, leaving the community centre, a 1960s-concrete block located in the middle of what I would get to know as the 'old' part of the estate, next to a church, pub, and opposite a row of shops, and headed down the main street of the estate, past rows of uniform brick terraced houses that were typical of the housing provided by local authorities for industrial working-class families in the post-war decades. Close by, I could see two high-rise towerblocks that had been built more recently by the local authorities to house 'vulnerable people'. A sign had been pinned up on the wall: 'no ball games'; it was one of the innumerable signs that local authorities put up on council estates telling residents how to behave in public spaces: where they are not

Personalizing the State: An Anthropology of Law, Politics, and Welfare in Austerity Britain. First Edition. Insa Koch. © Insa Koch 2018. Published 2018 by Oxford University Press.

allowed to step, to cycle, to feed pigeons, and to walk their dogs. Lindsey and I continued down the road, onto the 'new' part of the estate, built in the early 1990s. As we progressed, the streets began to grow narrow and winding, branching off into a labyrinth of cul-de-sacs. Lindsey navigated our way through the maze of flats, terraced rows, and maisonettes, long after I had lost my orientation. Residents say that the design and one-way road system of the new housing development was no accident: concerned about joy riding on Park End, urban planners had designed the estate in a manner that made escape from police chases virtually impossible.

Our destination was a long cul-de-sac on the edge of the estate. Lindsey got visibly upset as we entered the close. 'Look over there', she instructed me, pointing at a small brook nearby and what looked like an unfinished attempt to pave it over. Bricks lay scattered around amidst broken bottles and litter. The council had started building a footbridge, Lindsey explained, but given up after some damage had been done to it. The council had blamed the young people for it, when the damage had actually been caused by flooding. 'They would never say that about young people if it was in a different neighbourhood!' Lindsey commented. As we walked along the close, past an old people's home and an abandoned playground, Lindsey drew my attention to various fences and walls. There was a security fence with spikes on top that had been built around a pitch that the kids used to play football on. A few steps down, there was another fence, over 2m tall around a small patch of empty land. Some plastic bags and broken toys lay scattered on it. Lindsey explained that local people used to dump their rubbish here. One day, the council had come and built the wall to stop people from leaving their refuse there, instead of providing them with proper refuse collection.

We continued our walk down the close. Lindsey pointed out a small metal gate that had been installed along a footpath that led to the local bingo hall in the distance. I could see the hall from where we were standing, a big bulky building on the edges of an industrial complex that also accommodated some restaurants, a gym, and a cinema. The metal gate was so narrow that residents of the old people's home could not pass through on their wheel chairs and had to take a taxi to reach the bingo hall—a £6-ride to get somewhere that was right on their doorstep. The young people on the close were more mobile: they would cut across the disused land and railway tracks at the end of the close to get to the local school, in order to avoid a much longer detour around the whole estate. But they also risked being run over by the train. Lindsey explained that the only times there were trains coming through was when the children started and finished school. Lindsey turned to me. 'How does it make people feel, to be locked in like that, with fences and brick walls everywhere, day in and day out?'

When I first started doing fieldwork, my idea had been to study the then New Labour government's turn to 'law and order'. As I had explained to Lindsey before we had gone for our walk, I was particularly interested to understand the expansion of the government's 'anti-social behaviour' policies into the country's post-industrial neighbourhoods that were commonly portrayed as areas of high disorder and youth crime. And yet, while I had intended to study one particular type of 'anti-social behaviour'—that of young people causing havoc, mayhem, and distress—the tour that Lindsey took me on had painfully drawn my attention to a different kind of 'anti-social behaviour': that of the authorities who treated estate residents like Lindsey herself as 'other', as suspect, and by implication, as less worthy of state services and support than their wealthier counterparts. But I also learned over the following months, indeed years, that repressive governance was not the whole story. Park End residents also brought their own moral and political understandings to their engagements with the authorities that challenged their claims to legitimacy in multiple, sometimes contradictory, ways. This book aims to tell this double story of both top-down control and bottom-up attempts to personalize the state on a council estate at a time of deep democratic crisis. But first, let me sketch in more detail the contours of the problem.

A Punitive Paradox

For many, liberal democracy is in crisis. In Britain, signs of a growing malaise abound. At the turn of the twenty-first century, criminal justice policies have taken an ever more punitive outlook. From anti-social behaviour laws and mandatory sentencing, to expanded policing for the poor, the last few decades have seen 'law and order' policies encroach into areas traditionally insulated from its reach. Perhaps less notice has been paid to how the crisis extends beyond the criminal justice system, where it hits the lives of marginalized citizens the hardest. Means-tested welfare policies are now the order of the day, as the post-war settlement of so-called universal social insurance is fast becoming a thing of the past. Social benefits of all kinds are being cut, a drive reinforced under the shift to 'austerity politics' and public-sector cuts since 2010. The political ramifications of these various processes are making themselves felt. From widespread voter withdrawal, to a growing mistrust in elected representatives, to the 2016 referendum result on leaving the European Union, commentators decry the downward path that democracy has taken. Everywhere, it seems, the freedoms and rights once protected by the state, and supported through civic participation in political processes like elections, have come under attack.

What makes these developments worrying for many is that they are not just autocratic or top-down measures: the drive towards more coercive modes of governance seems to have been supported by the masses from below. This, at any rate, is the thesis put forward in at least some strands of the liberal media and scholarship. Criminal justice scholars have identified what they call both a punitive *and* a populist turn within criminal justice policies. The 'mob rule' thesis (Miller, 2016) presumes that the public are retributive and indiscriminately support tougher law and order interventions, no matter what. Some scholars have even called for more technocratic governance, or 'bureaucratic insulation' from direct democratic input, in a manner akin to approaches adopted with respect to monetary policies. From this perspective, the criminal justice system needs to be protected from the anti-democratic will of the people. Images of a punitive citizenry also loom large in recent explanations of the EU referendum. 'Leave' voters are frequently presented as being characterized by their support for 'popular authoritarianism' or 'authoritarian populism'. This is expressed in a series of related assumptions, including their support for anti-immigrant policies, for more punishment and anti-human rights rhetoric, as well as their consent for stronger defence policies.

The images invoked in these portrayals are not novel or unfamiliar. Since the inception of liberal democracy in the nineteenth century, political leaders and thinkers from Alexis de Tocqueville onwards, have warned of the tyranny of the masses that results from too much democratic participation. But the contrast that is drawn between the 'people' and the 'state', between those who constitute a threat to democracy's even-handed workings and those who are able to protect against it, needs to be critically unpacked. State policies and practices have never been free of coercion in the manner assumed by democracy's own self-image of progress and freedom. The British state has always supported the workings and institutions of liberal capitalism, favouring possessive individuals (MacPherson, 1962) over those who do not own property and land. Even in the post-war period, frequently upheld as the 'golden age' of British social democracy, working-class citizens were exposed to forms of social governance that did not apply to their middle-class counterparts (Joyce, 2013). This classed coercion has been interwoven with other axes of power, including those of race and gender. Racialized legacies that once justified colonial endeavours and white supremacy were carried into the practices of domestic statecraft (Gilroy, 1987). And the patriarchal nuclear family model has been central to liberal policies, even as these have come to be framed in more gender-neutral terms (Lacey, 1998).

This book is an ethnography of mostly British-born white and non-white working-class tenants who live on the housing estate in England that I call Park End. It asks: how do Park End residents' experiences bring into focus a different understanding of the state, and of democracy writ large? How does an ethnography of popular punitivism uncover a legacy of state coercion in the lives of working-class citizens in general, and of working-class women in particular? And what happens when we take as our point of departure not the crisis of the people but that of the state? Starting with the current turn to 'law and order', this book moves between different areas of governance that are not often brought into conversation: those of criminal justice and policing and the supposedly 'softer' arms of the welfare state, including the benefit system and social housing policies. It decentres the narrative of liberal democracy in crisis, popular among those who have critiqued its illiberal turn, by linking contemporary governance to a broader history of state control. And it uncovers how coercive policies impact and reconfigure everyday relations in intimate and often unexpected ways, as they play out in the homes of some of Britain's most destitute and socially abandoned neighbourhoods.

But top-down governance is only half of the story. Citizens at the receiving end of repressive policies also come to engage with, act upon, and sometimes passionately embrace the state's coercive powers on their own terms. This book then also tells a much less familiar story of how citizens make sense of their own dependence upon the authorities in their daily struggles for security and survival. Going into people's homes, community spaces, and neighbourhoods, it uncovers voices that are too easily collapsed in a singular narrative of the 'authoritarian' citizen by top-down accounts of punitive control. Citizens at the margins relate to, and incorporate, state institutions, officials, and images of the state into their daily lives in myriad ways. They subvert the official rules of the system to make them fit their own requirements and needs, draw local officials into intimate disputes with kin, lovers, and neighbours, use the language of punishment as an arena for articulating their own understandings of justice and fairness, and appropriate electoral politics to make it more accountable to their daily lives. Sometimes, everyday attempts to personalize the state dovetail with official rationalities and policy logics. More often than not, however, they open discrepancies between those who govern and those are governed, ultimately putting the state's ability to command consent for its policies of 'law and order' into question.

Offering an ethnographically grounded and historically informed account of state–citizen relations, this book pursues a broad question: how do marginalized citizens negotiate their own dependence upon what they experience as a coercive system? I argue that quotidian forms of engagement with the state are best understood as bottom-up attempts to 'personalize' the powers of the state. Personalization captures a particular mode of vernacularization, which has been used to describe how the meanings attached to particular concepts, like human rights law, travel between cultural contexts (Merry, 2006). I use the term 'personalization' to refer to the various ways in which people appropriate political, legal, and bureaucratic processes to fit with their understandings of what it means to be a good person. On a council estate in England, people make their own efforts to be a good person a basis for entitlement to citizenship claims; they appropriate local state officials and politicians as brokers who act like ordinary persons; and they expect policies to enforce localized logics of loyalty and care. And just as 'personalization' captures a variety of processes, so the term 'state' refers to a range of actors that make up the body of authority figures, including 'traditional' state agents like the police, social workers, and local politicians but also private and third sector bodies to which the government has outsourced its responsibilities.

The book offers empirically grounded attention to larger questions, questions about how citizens come to engage with, and even show support for, illiberal practices and policies in a liberal democracy. This constitutes, in part, a methodological inquiry, one that brings ethnography and political and legal anthropology to bear on criminology and criminal justice, and furthers a nascent interdisciplinary endeavour. This innovative methodology in turn generates new and, crucially, more nuanced insights into the material reality of relations between working-class citizens and the state, one which dispenses with both the romanticization of past patterns of engagement and the centring of the state as the principal actor defining the forms and the terms of the relationship. Everyday forms of engagement with the state, including at times popular support for its authoritarian powers, reflect a broader legacy of state coercion towards its most marginalized citizens, and the homes and neighbourhoods that they inhabit. They call for a very different political theory of state–citizen relations to that which has been assumed by defenders of liberal democracy. Ultimately, *Personalizing the State* demonstrates that how we make sense of the punitive paradox—the illiberal turn that liberal democracy has taken—hinges on how we want to view democratic citizenship itself; and suggests that for those at the margins, liberal democracy's promises of freedom have never been fulfilled.

Liberal Democracy's Illiberal Turn

The twenty-first century has seen a global turn to discourses and practices of 'law and order'. From the United States (Wacquant, 2009) to Latin America (Auyero, Bourgois, and Scheper-Hughes, 2015) to Africa's post-colonies (Comaroff and Comaroff, 2006) to Europe (Fassin, 2013), democracy has taken on punitive dimensions. The United Kingdom has been at the forefront of this trend. In 2006, it spent more per capita on 'law and order' than any other country in the Organisation for Economic Co-operation and Development (OECD), with a total spending for public order and safety amounting to £29.5 billion that year (Cabinet Office, 2006). Under the New Labour government, imprisonment rates reached unprecedented levels, making England and Wales the most prolific incarcerator in western Europe (Newburn, 2007). Imprisonment rates were matched by an ever-tougher drive to generate legislation dealing with petty crimes and low-level nuisance behaviour. Furthermore, this legislative pursuit of crime control was accompanied by a growth of a policing apparatus on the ground, including the introduction of 'neighbourhood policing' initiatives (Reiner, 2010) and the expansion of novel penal sanctions and powers, ranging from Anti-Social Behaviour Orders (ASBOs) to gang injunction orders, and curfews within and beyond the police force. The idealized citizen, the citizen on behalf of whom the government should act, was reconceived as the 'victim of crime' who was vulnerable from the threat of attack by others (Ramsay, 2012). And while there are signs that the tide of preoccupation with 'law and order' has been ebbing since 2010 (see Miller, 2016; Morgan and Smith, 2017), the overall trend towards 'law and order' has yet to be reversed.

The shift towards 'law and order' occurred at a time when crime levels had already reached their peak and had in fact started to decline. Yet, as Newburn (2007) has pointed out, a significant proportion of the public continue to believe the opposite to be true (ibid.: 226) and, when given the opportunity, express the demand for harsher punishment (Duffy et al., 2008). It is here, then, that we encounter what Lacey describes as one of the 'most troubling empirical paradoxes of contemporary democratic criminal justice': the paradox that 'criminal justice policy has been driven in an exclusionary direction with—or *perhaps even because of*— popular and *hence literally democratic* support' (2008: 8 my emphasis). By this account, while democracy is a contested term, a central attribute of the democratic aspirations of the criminal justice system includes the capacity to respond even-handedly and effectively to the harms and rights violations represented by criminal conduct, without resorting to measures which, in effect, negate the democratic membership and entitlements of offenders (Lacey, 2008: 7–8). Policies such as harsher sentencing and the increased use of imprisonment, mandatory minimum-sentencing laws, retribution in juvenile court, and the resort to civil/criminal hybrids erode precisely the grounds for democratic membership demanded by an inclusive criminal justice system.

What explains, then, the genesis and workings of this 'penal populism' (Pratt, 2007) or 'populist punitiveness' (Bottoms, 1995)? How do we make sense of the changes that have occurred in policy-making not simply on their own terms but as processes that seem to have commanded, at times, popular support from some of the most marginalized citizens, indeed the very citizens marked by these policies as targets to be vigorously corrected? What, in short, explains democratic support for anti-democratic measures? Scholars of punishment have offered a range of answers, from cultural explanations to those that favour more institutional and political economy-inspired accounts. These have tried to isolate various macro-reasons to explain the paradox of illiberalism in liberal democracy, whether these are to do with broader social and cultural transformations (Comaroff and Comaroff, 2016; Garland, 2001; Pratt, 2007; Simon, 2007; Young, 1999), institutional and political economy factors (Lacey, 2008; Reiner, 2007), or with political ideology and the hegemony of neoliberal power (Ramsay, 2012, 2016; Reiner, 2010; Wacquant, 2010). This book adopts a different perspective, one which shifts the focus from the 'why' to the 'how' and the 'what': from why liberal democracy has taken an illiberal turn to how we can understand its workings in the first place. Thus, I ask: how does liberal democracy maintain its self-image of progress and freedom in the face of its own violence? What experiences are silenced in the process? How does an ethnographic account of state–citizen relations complicate given narratives of the punitive turn?

Judged from the perspective of those at the margins, the narrative of a recent 'punitive turn' needs to be urgently rethought. While undoubtedly important changes have taken place at the level of policy, society, and the economy in the decades of the twentieth century, working-class citizens have always been subject to forms of control not known to their middle-class counterparts. Whether this was in the post-war decades, so often upheld as the 'golden decades' of social democracy, or more recently with shifts to 'neoliberalism' and the 'law-and-order state', class coercion has been an integral part of governance in the liberal state. State policies have intervened in, and modulate precisely those areas of life that the liberal state allegedly deems to be 'private' and hence 'off limits' for governmental involvement, such as people's homes and their most intimate relations with kin, family, and friends. But behind the walls, working-class citizens have also appropriated state powers on their own terms, as they have bypassed, acted against, and importantly, personalized the authorities into their daily lives. In so doing, their own understandings of what makes a good person and by extension a good citizen have at times dovetailed with, but more often than not, diverged from, official policies and rationalities, producing complex patterns of state desire and its rejection. In what follows, I will first return to the criminological literature on the punitive turn before discussing the ethnographic and historical arguments put forward in this book. Finally, I will outline my conceptual framework and methodology. Readers less interested in theory can also go straight to the later sections on the methods and the ethics of doing fieldwork and the outline of the chapters.

Explaining the Punitive Turn

While the arguments advanced in criminal justice scholarship are varied and nuanced, most accounts have started from the assumption that the contemporary landscape of policy-making needs to be understood within broader shifts in governance (Garland, 2001; Lacey, 2008; Ramsay, 2012; Reiner, 2007; Simon, 2007; Wacquant 2009; Young, 1999). But within these accounts, authors have offered widely different interpretations as to what factors to prioritize, whether these are cultural, ideological, or grounded in particular institutional developments. One of the best-known examples of a cultural account is Garland's *Culture of Control* (2001). Garland explains the analytic challenge of the punitive paradox: 'if masses of people are now emotionally invested in crime control issues and supportive of tougher legislation, casting their votes and spending their taxes in support of these laws, then this is a phenomenon that requires explanation' (ibid.: 146). His account is primarily concerned with the middle classes and the body of professional civil servants who acted as the architects and enforcers of policy reforms in both the United States and the United Kingdom. Garland starts from the premise that key to the changes have been 'shifts in social practice and cultural sensibility' in the wake of 'late twentieth-century modernity' (ibid.: 139) that have fundamentally changed the outlook and tolerance of contemporary society. The 'culture of control' is grounded in broader cultural, social, and economic changes that will be further explored in Chapter 1.

To briefly summarize here, Garland suggests that in the decades immediately following the Second World War, the criminal as the prototypical outsider was portrayed not as an external enemy so much, but as someone who must be socialized and cured. These policies were actively supported and protected by the 'welfarist consensus' espoused by what Loader (2006) has called the 'platonic guardianship' of a professional elite. This body of middle-class civil servants (including social workers, psychologists, and clinical and educational experts) believed in the liberal ideals of rehabilitation and progress through governance through the 'social'. But as crime became a 'normal social fact' (that is to say, as crime both increased and came to be accepted as a normal and expected occurrence by large sections of the middle classes) from the late 1960s onwards, and society became more porous, transient, and divided, so the ethos of welfarist decision-making has been undermined. Coupled with a marked decline in deference towards professionals and experts, this has resulted in a climate where the deviant 'other' has become a generalized object of internal social threat: an object that is vital to root out rather than reform in order to preserve social health. It is precisely this collective sensation of exposure to risk that feeds into policy-making and results in the punitive outcome we witness today. Policy-makers and politicians, faced with widespread insecurity and a crisis of authority, come to govern through a focus on 'law and order'.

Garland's account of the punitive turn in terms of the cultural conditions of late-twentieth-century modernity finds powerful resonances in other meta-narratives, including Ericson's 'Insecure Society' (Ericson, 2007), Young's 'Exclusive Society' (Young, 1999), and Simon's 'Governing through Crime' (Simon, 2007). But these cultural and social accounts of 'late modernity' have not gone uncontested. A second and alternative perspective approaches the punitive turn in terms of political ideology and power; or, in Gallo's (2018) words, 'as a set of ideas which partially reveals and partially obscures existing power relations'. This approach will be further explored in Chapters 5 and 6, but briefly, the turn to 'law and order' typically signifies the triumph of neoliberalism over post-war social democracy, and the broader crisis of state legitimacy that this has provoked (Ramsay, 2012; Reiner, 2007; Wacquant, 2012). As the hegemony of the economy and the insecurities of neoliberalism are becoming more prominent, we are also experiencing a weakening of the relationship between representatives and represented (Ramsay, 2012). In *The Insecurity State*, Ramsay argues that it is precisely this 'legitimacy gap' (ibid.: 102) that has been filled by the idea of 'vulnerable autonomy', which sees 'representative citizens as vulnerable in their interdependence, and, therefore, required to be active in their attention to others' needs for reassurance' (ibid: 84).

A third perspective prioritizes questions of political economy and institutional factors in explaining penal developments (Barker, 2009, 2017; Cavadino and Dignan, 2005; Gallo, 2015,

2017; Lacey, 2008, 2010; Lacey and Soskice, 2015; Miller, 2008, 2016). Like the political ideological accounts, this perspective shares a rejection of the linearity imposed by cultural and social accounts of 'late modernity', and the possibility of conceiving alternatives to it. Yet, closer attention is paid to comparative perspectives. An excellent account of such an approach is Lacey's *The Prisoners' Dilemma* (2008). Her starting point is the difference between 'coordinated market economies' (CME) and 'liberal market economies' (LME) developed by Hall and Soskice (2001). On her account, the 'culture of control', both on the level of policy and in terms of its popular support (Lacey, 2008: 8), is 'a product of the dynamics of liberal market economies' (ibid.: 110), such as we find in the United Kingdom or the United States. LMEs, unlike their CME counterparts, 'are typically more individualistic in structure, are less interventionist and depend far less strongly on the sorts of coordinating institutions which are needed to sustain long-term economic and social relations' (ibid.: 59). They tend to rely on majoritarian electoral systems in contrast to the proportional representation that is prevalent in CME countries. All things being equal, the strategic advantages of flexibility prioritized in LMEs generate harsher criminal justice policies.

Cultural, ideological, and institutional perspectives all provide important insights into the genesis and workings of punitive policies, whether this be by looking at society's internal developments, the state's political crisis of legitimacy, or its 'practical capacity to meet the normative demand for re-integrative inclusion' (ibid.: 8). But by prioritizing questions of cause and effect, meta-narratives do not bring the actual experiences and views of citizens into focus. On the contrary, as Steinberg (2016: 522) has remarked with respect to Garland's (2001) account, the heart of his narrative 'concerns the institutions of the state and high politics and the cultural practices of the middle classes. It excludes the sentiments and practices of those who actually vote for the governing party'. Or rather, the electorate's punitive dispositions and their consent for more 'law and order' are taken for granted (Miller, 2016), despite evidence from the restorative justice literature (Rossner, 2013) that offers more complicated views of public attitudes. This tendency to deduce broader generalizations about 'the public' from the state's own logics of punitiveness (and its middle-class inflections) is perhaps not surprising. It reflects a pervasive idea central to much political and social theory that the state is necessary for the maintenance of order and that, in the absence of a strong government, society will further descend into chaos (Roberts, 2013).

This book goes where much of the dominant commentary has stopped short: to the lived experiences of citizens at the margins. My focus on council estate residents is no accident. Rather, it is among the 'common people' that what Narotzky (2017) refers to as 'similar anti-liberal and anti-capitalist popular mobilizations scattered throughout European history' can be found. While social scientists have distinguished 'exclusionary' (i.e. 'bad') populism from 'inclusionary' (i.e. 'good') populism, Narotzky suggests that this moralization of discourses and practices obscures 'the actual issues that push reasonable people to mobilize against a particular social system, either seeking restitution of past forms of obligation, or proposition of new forms of social responsibility' (ibid.). This resonates with E. P. Thompson's account (1971) of eighteenth-century peasant crowds in revolt—commonly seen as an example of the 'dangerous mob'—but who were defending an old moral economy of customary grain prices and fair market transactions against the encroachment of modern-day capitalism. This book takes these criticisms as its point of departure. At the core of this book is an emphatic argument that the category of popular punitivism or punitive populism needs to be critically deconstructed by bringing into focus how those at the receiving end of state control act upon, experience, and make use of classed coercion in their daily lives. In what follows, I will outline the ethnographic and historical arguments put forward in this book.

Ethnographic and Historical Revisions

Shifting the analytical gaze from macro-accounts of the origins and genesis of the punitive paradox to the actual experiences of citizens means to shift our focus from the 'why' to the 'how' and the 'what': from why liberal democracy has taken an illiberal turn to how it is experienced in the first place and what conditions for action and resistance this generates. Government is often produced through forceful imposition, rather than straightforward consent (Hansen and Stepputat, 2005; Kelly and Shah, 2006; Veena and Poole, 2004). As Kelly and Shah remind us, 'consent to govern is given often as much for reasons of fear as it is freely chosen' (2006: 251). Indeed, governmental attempts to produce liberal freedoms have generally faced limits to their distribution: these limits are points at which liberal freedoms interface with authoritarian forms of rule, especially regarding those deemed not to possess the capacity for self-government (Davey and Koch, 2017). Class is a central dimension of liberalism's limits (Carrier and Kalb, 2015). Examples of this abound: from Victorian ethics and reforms practised in the nineteenth-century state that enforced middle-class notions of the respectable middle-class family (Skeggs, 1997) to governance through the 'social' via agents of the welfare state that followed in the middle years of the twentieth century (Joyce, 2013) to the more recent turn to the 'iron fist of liberalism' (Graeber, 2015) and the 'law and order state' (Hyatt, 2011). Those who are precariously situated with respect to the capitalist market, have always been policed in ways not known to their middle-class counterparts.

Council estates provide a case study par excellence. They derive their name from the fact that they were built by local authorities (called councils) largely in the post-war decades as housing developments (called estates) for the working classes. The provision of council housing has often been celebrated as one of the major achievements of the post-war welfare state (see Alexander, Hojer-Bruun, and Koch, 2018): a physical statement of how aspirations for social equality and progress were written into the bricks and mortar of people's homes. In addition to political and economic rights, citizens were now to be given what T. H. Marshall referred to as 'social rights' under the new social democratic settlement reached by post-war welfare reformers between capitalism, labour, and the state. Council housing was to be a central tenet of this emerging welfare state. With the consolidation of the post-war British welfare state in the years that followed the Second World War, the provision of council housing became further repackaged as part of a generalized social contract between the worker–citizen and the state (Dench, Gavron, and Young, 2006): in return for their contributions paid in labour, taxes, and efforts in the Second World War, worker–citizens, defined in terms of the white, British, male and heterosexual worker, were entitled to benefits from the welfare state. Council housing was built across the country, and by the early 1970s a third of the British population were living in state-owned housing, a mixture of terraced houses, flats, and, later on, increasingly, tower-blocks and maisonettes.

What has often been ignored in these narratives of the post-war welfare state is that the history of council estates has also been a history of state-building and classed control. Governance through the 'social' in the post-war decades was also an intimate form of class coercion, subjecting tenants on the post-war council estates to paternalistic forms of rent and housing management that required them to live up to state-sanctioned—that is, classed—standards of 'respectability' and 'decency'. Indeed, complicating their reputation for civic inclusion, post-war policies *excluded* many from accessing council housing altogether if they were considered to fall short of the criteria that made a deserving (male, white, and heterosexual British) citizen. But it was only in the 1980s with the turn to Thatcherite policies, including the selling of council housing to private parties and shifts towards needs-based housing policies, that access to council housing turned from being an index of one's social inclusion to a token of abject exclusion and 'otherness'. In this process, many of the previous forms of state control were not only turned into more predatory and openly repressive modes of governance but also expanded to groups of people who had previously been relatively sheltered from its gaze. In this light, it becomes clear that the turn to 'law and order' on post-industrial council estates in the 2000s constitutes less an aberration of 'late modernity' than a particular stage in a much longer trajectory of class coercion and domination.

Today, council estate tenants do not form a homogenous category of people, nor are they representative of any singular notion of the 'working class'. However, an analytical focus on estate tenants does bring into focus what has not always featured within the anthropology and sociology of Britain: the role of the state in working-class people's daily lives. The classical post-war literature tended to adopt what I have called (Koch, 2013) 'a community-centred perspective': from the writings of Young and Willmott (1957) to Raymond Firth (1956) and others (cf. Bott, 1971), working-class communities tended to be portrayed as isolated, kinship-governed entities. Later work militated against romanticizing tendencies by introducing questions of identity, belonging, and meaning (Cohen, 1985; Edwards, 2000; Rapport, 2002; Strathern, 1981). It was only in response to the growing exclusion that working-class people faced from the 1980s onwards that anthropologists and sociologists began to introduce a more explicit focus on political ideology and power. Sociologists of class came to focus on inter-class tensions, often drawing on the writings of Pierre Bourdieu (Lawler, 2000; Mckenzie, 2015; Savage, 2000; Savage, Bagnall, and Longhurst, 2001; Skeggs, 1997, 2004). Anthropologists in turn tended to focus on intra-class conflicts, brought about by the decline of the post-war social settlement (Dench et al., 2006; Mollona, 2009), political disenfranchisement (Evans, 2012; Smith, 2012a), industrial decline (Degnen, 2005; Edwards, 2000), and the legacies and loss of the British Empire (Tyler, 2012).

And yet, the state has not always featured as an object of study in its own right (yet see Damer, 1989; Davey, 2016; Miller, 1988; Rogaly and Taylor, 2009). This is perhaps surprising given that working-class people, in general, and social housing tenants, in particular, encounter the authorities in a myriad of different ways, including through the penal and supposedly more 'welfarist' wings of the state. These encounters become sites where different, sometimes mutually exclusive, understandings of personhood and citizenship are enacted by citizens and officials alike. In the post-war decades, the state's own ideal of the model citizen in terms of the white, male, and British breadwinner overlapped (although it was never fully co-extensive) with council estate tenants' own aspirations for nuclear family homes. This overlap created the conditions for what I call a fragile moral union between tenants and the post-war state. By contrast, on council estates today, this moral union has been thoroughly undermined. Citizens continue to struggle to build and maintain neighbourhoods and homes, often against the odds. Informal networks of neighbour and kin relations provide them with both the economic resources for daily survival and an important source of support and self-worth in the face of persistent stigma. And yet, officials often react with suspicion to these

ties of interdependence and sometimes exercise heavy-handed intervention, thus also favouring the dominant middle class model of the self-reliant individual as the archetype of modern personhood (Skeggs, 2011). How then can we insert an ethnographic focus on state–citizen relations into this landscape of governance? The next section will introduce the book's conceptual framing in terms of how citizens 'personalize the state'.

Personalizing the State

Anthropology has moved a long way from the study of law and governance in stateless societies (Malinowski, 1926) to understanding state–citizen relations under contemporary conditions of 'advanced' liberalism. This, in turn, has also raised murky questions about domination and power: questions about how citizens often become complicit with, and even show popular support for, repressive or hostile policies and authorities. On the one hand, Foucauldian-inspired approaches have tended to foreground the operation of disciplinary logics and governmental power that are said to colonize the moralities and mind-sets of those at the margins (Ferguson, 1990; Ferguson and Gupta, 2002; Hyatt, 2011; Koster, 2014; Ong, 1996; Shore and Wright, 2011). Popular consent to being governed, often under conditions of stark inequality, occurs as a consequence of processes of internalization. On the other hand, accounts inspired by Bourdieu have focused on the ways in which the dominated come to accept the categories of perception of more dominant powers by taking on, and identifying with, their ideology (Auyero et al., 2015; Auyero and Swistun, 2009; Bourgois, 1995; Mckenzie, 2015; Skeggs, 1997; Wacquant, 2008). Rather than emphasizing the production of docile subjects through disciplinary mechanisms and governmental techniques, a Bourdieuian perspective prioritizes issues of ideology and symbolic violence. Symbolic violence is achieved when hegemonic worldviews are made to appear natural, and therefore legitimate; or rather, when their legitimacy is never raised as a problem in the first place.

These engagements with governance, power, and domination have usefully identified how institutional oppression frames the conditions of thought and action of its targets as well as its practitioners. They also reveal how responsibility for structural problems is being shifted onto the most vulnerable citizens, who are being asked to single-handedly cope with the effects of poverty and exclusion. However, if we focus on disciplinary governance or ideology alone, there is also a risk that the 'poor are [presented as] suffering from Stockholm Syndrome or some other form of false consciousness, living vicariously off the power of the very agencies that hurt and kill them' (Steinberg, 2016: 521). Indeed, anthropologists have long analysed how citizens engage more powerful authorities by challenging their claims to authority and order (Bear, 2007; Fuller and Bénéï, 2000; High, 2014; Navaro-Yashin, 2002, 2006; Reeves, 2014), whether this is by resisting (Grisaffi, 2019, 2013; Shah, 2010), incorporating (Spencer, 2007; Ferguson, 2013), or, indeed by 'personalizing the impersonality' of an abstracted Weberian legal–bureaucratic state (Alexander, 2000).

Alexander introduces her notion of 'personalization' to analyse how citizens in Turkey relate the state to persons, objects, and local ideas of patrimonialism. This book builds on Alexander's notion to analyse how citizens on a council estate appropriate officials, institutions, and the 'language of statehood' (Hansen and Stepputat, 2005) writ large where they depend upon the state for their daily struggles for security and survival, yet lack the mechanisms for advancing collective demands. On Park End, people make their efforts to be good and righteous persons as a basis for entitlement to citizenship claims: they expect local institutions to recognize them as good citizens on their own terms, they personalize the logics and rules of bureaucracy to make them fit their daily requirements and household needs, and they appropriate officials into disputes and conflicts that may have little to do with the state's own understanding of order. And yet, as they personalize the state into their daily lives, they also allow themselves to be drawn yet further into the remits of state surveillance and control. What is more, personalized uses of the state can also cement a climate of suspicion and mistrust. And when they do not have their intended effect, they can also reinforce popular disenchantment with government, encouraging widespread withdrawal from electoral processes, and anticipating the results of the EU referendum in 2016.

The point, then, is not to draw an 'either or' picture: as the ethnography revealed in this book shows, citizens are neither the victims of false ideology and disciplinary logics alone, nor are they solely agents of their own making. Indeed, it is precisely at the intersection of people's own pursuits of justice, order and righteousness, on the one hand, and the broader structural context that engulfs their lives, on the other, that productive tensions emerge. Political economy-inspired accounts have focused on how such tensions become connected with, or folded into, broader political ideologies and narratives of the moment, particularly at a time when class-based alternatives are often weak or absent (Alexander, Hojer-Bruun, and Koch, 2018). Where traditional mechanisms for 'capturing' (Nugent, 2012) ordinary citizens' demands, including through political parties, social movements, and labour unions, have been silenced by decades of neoliberal rule, popular expressions of dissatisfaction can become trapped in a language of purely moral as opposed to political and economic justice (Kalb, 2009, 2011; Narotzky, 2016; Palomera and Vetta, 2016). While Park End residents continue to express emic theories of state failure that are consonant with their political and economic lives, everyday acts of state–citizen engagement also reproduce dominant logics of accumulation and control.

This book makes a number of significant methodological and theoretical interventions. Methodologically, it advances a call for a genuinely interdisciplinary study of punishment and the state. Over recent years scholars from political sociology (Barker, 2009, 2017), political science (Miller, 2016; Skarbeck, 2014), and political economy (Gallo, 2015, 2017; Lacey, 2008, 2010; Lacey and Soskice, 2015) have contributed to debates that have historically been the preview of lawyers alone. Yet, political and legal anthropology has been relatively absent (yet see Comaroff and Comaroff, 2016; Cooper-Knock and Owen, 2015; Hornberger, 2013; Koch, 2017a; Mutsaers, 2014). More substantively, the book develops a historically grounded and ethnographically driven argument about the legacy of state coercion and class control in the lives of working-class people that centres a political theory emerging from everyday realities of citizens rather than the abstract ideals of the state. At the heart of the book is an argument about the state's inability to command popular consent for its own authority, at least in any straightforward way. To the extent that the different instances of personalization have anything in common, they do not convey a unitary desire for authoritarian governance. On the contrary, they speak of the complex ways in which citizens straddle the tension between their mistrust in, and dependence on, the authorities, and the murky, at times contradictory desires and expectations that this produces.

Doing Fieldwork in a Marginalized Place

The research upon which this book is based derives from my fieldwork on a council estate of over 13,000 residents in the south of England. My own involvement on Park End estate and two neighbouring estates in the same town began in 2009 when I spent an initial period of eighteen months conducting ethnographic fieldwork. Since then, I have returned to the estate on a regular basis, sometimes simply to visit friends and sometimes to carry out follow-up research. I lived with a number of residents: Mark and Jane, a white English couple in their thirties with four children aged between 3 months and 16 years; Sarah, a black woman in her fifties of South African descent whose grown-up children had left home; Tony (white, English) and Linda (originally from Portugal), a couple in their thirties with Linda's two daughters; and Lisa, a white English community worker with whom I was able to get access to a key workers housing scheme. I volunteered in Park End's community centre which was run informally by Tracey, a local mother in her late thirties of Afro-Caribbean descent. Lindsey, a white English mother of three, would also become a close friend. Largely through her, Tracey, and Lisa, I gained access to people and a number of local facilities. I also interviewed a range of officials, including members of the local policing team, housing officials, and locally-based politicians.

This orderly description of data collection should not be taken to mean that fieldwork was a smooth or straightforward endeavour. My own positionality framed the conditions of access and the kinds of relationships that were open to me during research. I first came to my field site in my early twenties as a German citizen, although I am of mixed German–Korean descent. Unlike many contemporary female writers and scholars of class in the United Kingdom (Hey, 2003), my interest in the research did not derive from an intimate knowledge of the lived realities of English class, but from the opposite: as a foreign national who had only been living in the United Kingdom for four years prior to the start of my fieldwork, I had little expectation of what 'fieldwork' would entail. I was wholly unprepared for the strong (if not offensive) reaction from my academic colleagues when I told them of my intention to conduct research on a council estate. University mentors and some of my fellow students warned me that I would have to be careful not to get mugged and that, if I drove to the estate, I might get my car tyres sliced or worse. One or two joked that if I wanted to 'go native' I should buy cheap shiny jewellery and stuff a cushion under my jumper to pretend that I was a single mum on benefits. A local police officer asked me if I wanted a rape alarm to carry around when I was on the estates.

Meanwhile, when I did start frequenting community centres, pubs, and other public facilities on the estate, I found that most residents were polite but extremely reserved and wary. Some were also more forthcoming and told me that they were tired of having yet another researcher come in, do their bit, and then leave again, without 'giving back'; a point that is also raised by Symons (2018). I started my research on a smaller estate, about 2 miles from Park End. There, my questions as to whether I could meet for a chat, come along to a public session, or join an activity were politely acknowledged, but rarely followed through. Eventually, Bob, the sixty-something white English manager of a community centre, agreed to introduce me to some of the residents that were frequenting his centre. Soon, I realized that Bob's willingness to admit me to his social networks had not just been altruism: the community centre was affected by a local authority-led 'regeneration' agenda, which, as part of said agenda, would be replaced by a multi-purpose building accommodating various services and residents worried that regeneration was an excuse to get rid of their communal spaces and to extend the local council's control (Chapter 6). Bob had selected me as a potential ally in the fight. In the months that followed, I helped Bob set up campaigns and public meetings about the impending regeneration plan. In turn, Bob let me into his life, introducing me to members of his family and networks of relationships. He also arranged for me to stay with his daughter, Jane and her husband, Mark, in their thirties, who would become my first host family.

However, as the months went by, it became increasingly evident that the local campaigns against the closure of the community centre would not be successful. By this point, relations between various community groups had become openly tense, as people accused each other of collaborating with the local authorities for ulterior motives. Around the same time, an anonymous letter was circulated to various community activists on the estate and on neighbouring estates, warning them of a person called 'Izzy' (the name Bob had once affectionately given to me) whose arrival in the community centre had coincided with the regeneration agenda. The letter accused me of working undercover for the local authorities, mentioning my lurking around the community centre and my eagerness to talk to so many people without any apparent reason, and questioned whether I was really a 'student' given that I never seemed to be spending any time in the library. While

I had heard people joke about the fact that they thought I was an undercover police officer, a missionary church worker, or a social worker before, this was the first time that I heard these accusations articulated in a threatening way. By the time the community centre had shut its doors about nine months after I first arrived, my relations had become so estranged that I felt forced to discontinue my work on the estate and start again in a new place.

My own inability to negotiate relations under conditions of heightened stress and suspicion had exposed the difficulties of overcoming difference: particularly in times of conflict, the foreignness associated with my appearance, accent, lack of local knowledge, and strange manners had made me an easy target and an obvious object of distrust. It had also exposed the illusion of conducting detached research: by insisting that I was a researcher, that I wanted to talk to everyone, and be friendly with all parties, I had made myself vulnerable to attacks and misapprehensions not only from people I did not know but from my closest interlocutors. And, perhaps most importantly, it had revealed to me what extractive research meant under conditions of stark inequality: a refusal to partake in the social relations that were central to people's lives. When I started again, this time on Park End, my approach to fieldwork was very different. I ensured that my first introductions happened not through a local authority *official* (as they had with Bob) but through an *unofficial* local volunteer. Tracey, who ran the community centre, invited me to volunteer alongside her at its informal 'drop-in centre'. I helped her set up community events, give ad hoc advice to residents (by mobilizing my knowledge from a prior law degree)—often to do with bureaucratic problems—and manage daily services and groups in the centre (Chapter 6). Unlike my association with Bob, however, I was willing to be taken under Tracey's wing, to be more partial and less eager to please, and to become part of Tracey's own world of friends and enemies. I became part of localized networks of 'give and take'—being called on for favours and asking for support in turn.

The conditions of access that I have encountered undoubtedly shaped the insights that I present in this book. The people who I got to know most closely are also those who are most represented in this book: the mothers who spend time at community facilities, who maintain family homes, and who are in close contact with the authorities. This includes women like Tracey, a black mother of one; Lindsey, a white mother with three children; Olifia, a mixed-race mother of five; Helen, a white mother of two; and Jane, a white mother of four. All of the women were born in England and have spent most of their lives on and around Park End. To the extent that men feature in this book, they do so either as people who are part of women's networks (not so much as breadwinners but as lovers, sons, and kin members) or because they have specific problems or roles that bring them into contact with communal institutions and facilities on the estate: this includes both those in need of help, and the brokers who step in. Most of my informants share certain characteristics: they are British-born tenants, surviving on precarious income and/or state benefits living on a council estate. Where people divert from this pattern (e.g. because they have a different nationality), I have stated this explicitly in the book. The fact that residents self-identify as having different ethnicities might also be seen as significant: the intersections between race and class in urban British communities has been the subject of trenchant analysis (Back and Ware, 2002; Gilroy, 1987; Tyler, 2012; Werbner, 2015). Throughout the book, I have noted people's ethnicities as inseparable aspects of broader processes of personhood-making. At the same time—and without wanting to contest the importance of existing analyses—I also found that as I came to know Park End people, their ethnic backgrounds proved less important as determinants of reciprocal obligations between friends, neighbours, and family, and the ways these networks interact with the state, than I had initially expected. Much of the ethnography hence focuses in on gender and class.

The Ethics of Fieldwork

In the wake of Goffman's *On the Run* (2014) and Desmond's *Evicted* (2016), ethnography of marginalized communities has come under much public scrutiny. The controversy surrounding Goffman's close entanglement in her informants' lives has generated questions about the ethics of doing fieldwork, including about the nature of informant consent, and the ethnographer's involvement in activities that are against the law (see e.g. Lubet, 2017). While these are valid concerns (that occupied me throughout my own fieldwork), they also run the risk of treating ethnography as a legalistic endeavour that judges its merits against the normative yardsticks of a positivist science. Above all, fieldwork for me was about gaining trust from people who feel threatened, and about negotiating conflicting commitments that arise when the people who one writes about have become confidants and sometimes close friends. I found that as people started trusting me and letting me into their lives, questions of informed consent became increasingly difficult to negotiate and the positivist dictate that our research informants need to be 'informed' about research was not always practical. I made a point of telling residents and officials I met that I was not simply a resident or volunteer but also a researcher interested to write a book about Park End. Yet, people also chose to forget that I was a researcher at times, and at others, were so pressed with problems that this seemed to be the least of their worries. The boundaries between researcher and trusted friend became even more blurred with people who I became close to over time.

It was through close friendships with women like Tracey and Lindsey that research became possible for me in very practical ways: people offered me a place to live, they introduced me to their friends and family, and agreed to do interviews with me. Through the relations I formed, I was able to take on a legitimate role, a role that afforded me both the protection given to fictive kin, but also the demands for loyalty that come with it. As a friend once jokingly said, 'you're only a proper person if you've got family or a dog'! Being meaningfully associated with people allowed me to make 'claims to connectedness' (Edwards, 2000) and hence to local personhood, claims that also offered me privileged access to their lives that would have otherwise not have been open to me. But it also meant that I became drawn into complicated situations including some that may be seen as 'unethical' if the point of view of a neutral and detached observer was adopted. For example, some of the women whose stories feature in this book committed 'benefit fraud' where they failed to declare personal earnings or a household income to the state. Men and women could also both become implicated in acts of informal violence that not only the state considers to be unlawful or criminal behaviour, but that might do further harm to others living in the community. But equally, state officials and those acting in a formal capacity are not immune from acting in harmful or damaging ways, and many of the incidents revealed in this book show this ugly side of governance.

Fieldwork always raises tricky questions about what observations and experiences can be turned into 'data', what even constitutes data in any meaningful sense, and who, as ethnographers, we are writing for. I worry that the stories that I wrote will end up being instrumentalized against the people who do not have any formal power to defend themselves. A perhaps early but painful reminder of this ever-present risk was when I gave a presentation about violence and crime in my fieldsite at a local university, about a year or so after I had started my fieldwork. I had not invited any of my friends from the estate to the presentation (partly because I was conscious that the presentation would not offer a representative overview of my fieldwork findings), but the presentation happened to be advertised in a local newspaper, and some residents on Park End saw it. Three residents, two of whom I knew in passing, came to my presentation. I had never spoken to any of them in depth about my research. My presentation was on structural exclusion of the estate community, on the violence that happened in people's streets, and the strained relations between police and youth. Given that the local university has historically been complicit in the structural exclusion of the town's estate residents, I found it important not to anonymize the name of the estate in my presentation. I was not prepared, however, for the reactions of Park End residents after the seminar: they wanted to know why I had focused on the 'negative stuff' on their estate. Was that all there was going on in the community? What about the 'good things' that I had been part of? They also worried that presentations like the one I had just given would only feed into negative portrayals and stigma, and further act as a justification for local authorities and other powerful bodies to cut funding and support for community projects.

The day has haunted me ever since. It has taken me years to write this book, during which time I have had some frank and difficult conversations with close friends from Park End about what doing ethnography means and what findings I consider to be important to be known. I have gone back to events or happenings that I initially recorded, and have written and rewritten them, sometimes numerous times. But I have also grown more confident in my writing, as I have found ways to address different audiences, writing at times for more policy-orientated audiences (who residents had worried need not hear more about the 'negative stuff'), and at other times for academics. I still worry though that the account I present might displease residents who have trusted me with their stories. But equally, as Bourgois (1995) has argued, to refuse to write about misery 'out of a righteous, or a "politically sensitive" fear of giving the poor a bad image' is to make oneself 'complicitous with oppression' (ibid.: 12). This does not mean that ethnography should digress into poverty porn. Nor, however, does it mean that we should romanticize marginalized citizens in the way that the 'old' school of community-studies did (Savage, 2016). Rather, I see the role of ethnography as contextualizing, and hence ultimately, humanizing the difficult choices and decisions that people have to make in circumstances that are beyond their control.

In pursuing this task, I have taken several steps to protect my informants and others whose lives resemble those of the women and the men who appear in this book. First, in writing about aspects of their lives that might be considered controversial, sensitive, or unlawful, I have decided to only write about practices that are well-known to the authorities and publicized in the public domain, largely through sensationalist media reporting (such is the case with benefit fraud). My intention is not to expose people but rather to give an insight into why people act in the way that they do against a backdrop of dominant representations that see them as 'scroungers' and as 'undeserving'. I have also taken care to anonymize the estate and its people to protect them from potential repercussions, even if this means that some of the local specificity, typical of in-depth ethnographic work, has been lost. And finally, I have attempted to present a balanced view, one which recuperates a sense of moral agency and autonomy amidst the constraints and problems that are part-and-parcel of precarious lives. While this is undoubtedly an uneasy compromise, my hope is that the account presented in this book remains close to people's own experiences without losing sight of the broader inequalities that engulf them.

Chapter Outline

My arguments about how citizens at the margins personalize the state is developed through a discussion of various aspects of state–citizen relations in the chapters that follow. However, each chapter presents a self-contained idea, so readers might wish to go straight to the chapters of interest. Chapter 1 provides a political history of the post-war British welfare state and of council estates in particular. It provides the contextual backdrop for the remainder of the book. It argues that the history of council estates can be understood as a history of state-building par excellence. Built largely in the inter- and post-war decades as homes for the working class, council estates were, from their inception, tied to projects of class segregation—by separating out working-class people from their wealthier middle-class counterparts—and class control—by subjecting council tenants to strict regimes of rent and housing management. Since the accelerated shift to neoliberal policies in the 1980s, including the privatization of council housing and the decline of the United Kingdom's manufacturing base, state control has become even more pronounced. Today, the term 'council estates' has entered the public imagination as a place of the feral 'underclass' and the poor, justifying ever-more punitive policies towards those who continue to live on them in rental housing. Judged in this light, the expansion of 'law and order' in the 2000s is only one phase in a much longer history of state domination and coercion of the working class.

Chapter 2 moves from the top-down perspective introduced in the previous chapter to a bottom-up account of council estate life. It introduces some of the central principles of sociality that guide daily life on Park End and neighbouring estates and that, taken together, constitute the building blocks of an alternative moral order. My argument is that people at the receiving end of state control have never simply accepted the state's own categories of deservingness and respectability. On the contrary, they have always embraced and developed their own understandings of the good person in interactions with and without the state, and elaborated their own concepts of the intimate relationship between the righteous person and rightful citizen (de Koning, Jaffe, and Koster, 2015). But what constitutes a good person and citizen in people's eyes has changed in accordance with prevailing economic and political conditions. In the post-war period, tenants' aspirations for nuclear family homes and neighbourhoods coincided with dominant welfare policies that were premised on the British, white, male-headed household. But as de-industrialization and welfare withdrawal solidified their dominance in the sociopolitical landscape, so more fluid and collaborative networks of support and care became ever more important sources of survival and informal support. Today, Park End residents' attempts to be good persons who remain embedded in relations of interdependence and care stand in stark contrast to dominant portrayals of them as bad citizens and subjects of lack.

The three chapters that follow integrate a perspective on both top-down control and bottom-up care in a single framing: they analyse how everyday encounters with the state are mediated through localized logics and social relations. Chapter 3 looks at how so-called 'single mothers' engage the benefit system in their daily attempts to build and maintain family homes. Homes are always potentially the site of trouble and violence, particularly for women who tend to be the main carers of families and children. To build homes that are free from violence and insecurity, women on Park End often end up relying upon the benefit system alongside their own networks of support and care. The chapter argues that the rules and logic of the benefit system come into conflict with women's own expectations of what makes a good family home. By portraying women as needy individuals defined by their lack, the means-tested nature of the benefit system also penalizes women's reliance on extended and collaborative household arrangements. While some women learn to 'play the system', their attempts to personalize the state also place them in an awkward and sometimes altogether illegal relationship with the law.

Chapter 4 shifts the focus from women's daily attempts to build homes in their interactions with the benefit system to how social housing tenants build neighbourhoods that are fit for living in their encounters with social housing providers. It suggests that social housing tenants' view of what constitutes 'neighbour trouble' is often fundamentally out of sync with the authorities' own understandings. Material neglect has deeply marked Park End neighbourhoods and streets: people's homes and sometimes entire streets have been allowed to fall into decline and disrepair through failure on the part of the local authorities to maintain them. This decline, in turn, is often the primary cause of what tenants refer to as 'trouble': badly insulated walls and ceilings, cramped living conditions, and badly maintained communal areas all give rise to tensions between neighbours who live in close proximity to one another. While some tenants learn to use the language of 'anti-social behaviour' and 'nuisance' to frame their claims, the responses that housing authorities offer fail to address the root causes of neighbour trouble. In the end, tenants' attempts to deploy housing authorities in their pursuits of neighbour relations frequently reinforce a climate of suspicion and mistrust between neighbours as well as deep-seated frustrations with the authorities.

Chapter 5 moves from the case of housing authorities and neighbour relations to that of the police in responding to the dangers of 'the streets'. The 'streets' is a term residents use to refer to the daily threats of victimization and serious crime.

As with their negotiations with the benefit system and the social housing authorities examined in Chapters 3 and 4 respectively, we find that residents' expectations for protection are at odds with official policing priorities. Residents complain that the police unduly criminalize young people and their social relations, while failing to address more serious incidents of crime. While residents sometimes personalize the police as a tool in everyday disputes with friends, kin, and neighbours, in situations of more serious threat and violence, they tend to fall back onto informal mechanisms of policing and vigilante control. This affords residents a degree of protection where the police are considered to fall short, but it also makes them vulnerable to accusations of corrupt and criminal practices. It is precisely this gap between citizens' expectations for support and the reality of police performance that comes to light when residents show support for harsher punishment in a system that is 'too liberal' in their eyes.

The aforementioned chapters have shown that everyday attempts to personalize the state rarely engender desired results: people expose themselves to yet further state control, they relinquish their autonomy to outside agents, and, as in the case of informal policing, they make themselves vulnerable to charges of vigilante and anti-democratic action. Chapter 6 examines what alternative avenues people have available to express their discontent and how these are channelled. It takes as its point of departure the landscape of partnerships and civic initiatives that aim to address local problems of disorder and crime. But official expectations for 'active citizenship' enforced in these spaces of governance do not fit with residents' own understandings. As the daily work of both community activists and locally based politicians shows, good governance from Park End residents' point of view is about bringing policies in line with their daily material struggles for security and survival. And yet, this alternative politics—that I refer to as 'bread and butter politics' (Koch, 2016)—is also vulnerable to being silenced and stigmatized by outsiders. The chapter argues that in the absence of adequate institutional and political mechanisms that can capture people's demands, bread and butter politics fails to translate into an agenda for sustainable change.

Chapter 7 asks what the implications of everyday relations between citizens and the state are for liberal democracy writ large. It takes as a point of departure an event that has been at the forefront of much public debate: the referendum on leaving the

European Union in June 2016 and the rise of what has been labelled 'popular authoritarianism'. My argument is that residents on Park End experience government, and representative democracy at large, as something that is 'not for them': negative experiences with the authorities, including, since 2010, the shift towards 'austerity' politics and public-sector cuts, translate into a deep-seated sense that politicians and politics are the antithesis of ordinary personhood and sociality. This justifies withdrawal from electoral processes, as evinced by low voter turn-out levels on Park End. However, unlike an ordinary election, the referendum on leaving the EU was not simply about choosing between competing evils: residents perceived it as an opportunity to say 'no' to a government that is failing to honour its duties of care. Judged in this light, singular explanations of 'Brexit' in terms of popular authoritarianism fail to account for the liberal state's disavowal of its moral responsibilities that is painfully felt among constituencies who voted in favour of 'leave'.

The conclusion returns to the punitive paradox with which I began this book: the paradox of how we can explain democracy's illiberal turn. It contrasts this with a different kind of paradox, an ethnographic paradox, that emerges when the focus is shifted from questions of 'why' democracy has become so punitive turn to the 'how' and the 'what': the paradox of how the expansion of state power to forcibly control its citizens is also the inverse to its powers to control the means of its own application or recruitment. The expansion of state coercion hence cements the state's crisis of authority by generating the means of its popular repurposing. The ethnographic paradox expands the debate on punishment in three ways: first, by moving beyond a focus on the criminal law to a legacy of coercion that is both of a longer duration and more encompassing; second, by demonstrating that popular punitivism and popular support for state authority are not the same; and third, by bringing into focus an emic political theory that reconnects the state's duty to provide security in its broadest political, economic, and legal sense to a moral framework of care.

1
A Political History of Council Estates: Council Estates as State-Building Projects

In March 2012, I received an invitation through a friend and community worker to attend the opening of a new local policing scheme called the 'street pastors'. The scheme, first pioneered in London in 2003 and governed by an organization called the Ascension Trust, was being launched in collaboration with local authorities and the police across the country. According to the scheme's website, street pastors are 'trained volunteers from local churches who care about their community. They patrol in teams of men and women, usually from 10 p.m. to 4 a.m. on a Friday and Saturday night, to care for, listen to and help people who are out on the streets.' Only Christians who 'have been committed to a church fellowship for more than one year' with a personal reference from a minister or church leader are admitted to the scheme, which is jointly organized by the police, local authorities, and local churches. Dressed in dark blue uniforms that give them an official look, and equipped with walkie-talkies that allow them to be in constant contact with police officers on duty, street pastors are sent out to patrol the streets after twelve days of training.

The launch of the street pastor scheme took place on a warm spring evening in a wood-panelled room in the town hall, a few miles from Park End estate. I arrived a few minutes late, by which point the small room was already full, with about thirty people in attendance, including members of local churches, uniformed law enforcement officials, local authority employees, and representatives of the Ascension Trust. The evening began with an introduction by the Detective Chief Inspector. After welcoming the people and thanking them for supporting the scheme, he relayed the good work that the initiative had done in other parts of the country.

Personalizing the State: The Anthropology of Law, Politics and Welfare at the UK's Margins. First Edition. Insa Koch. © Insa Koch 2018. Published 2018 by Oxford University Press.

Referring to the pastors as the 'lambs amongst the wolves', he described how street pastors had successfully helped to target repeat offenders, had worked in early intervention projects, and shared information about vulnerable individuals with the police, the council, the ambulance services, and the PCT Trust.[1] 'The street pastors will provide an important adjunct to what we, the police, are doing already,' he said. 'Policing by consent has now moved to policing by cooperation—and we support, endorse, and stand by the street pastor initiative!'

A few days after the launch, I ran into Kevin, a 37-year-old white resident on Park End. Kevin was working as a 'street warden', another variation of a uniformed law enforcement official employed by the local authority under the New Labour government to patrol the streets of Park End and neighbouring estates. I asked him if he had heard of the street pastor initiative. Yes, he confirmed, he had heard of it and he was very much in support of the idea of making residents more proactive about safeguarding their neighbourhoods. Schemes like this would help bring 'the man from the local fish-and-chip shop' or the 'single mother with three kids' into community policing. Indeed, Kevin himself had grown up on Park End and had done a number of different jobs in the neighbourhood before becoming a street warden a few years back when the position had been created as part of a New Labour government initiative. As a street warden, he shared his duty to keep Park End and neighbouring estates free from disorder and anti-social behaviour with other uniformed officials, including 'park rangers', also employed by the local authority to patrol the green areas of the estate, and 'police community support officers', who were employed by the police but, like park rangers and street wardens, did not have any formal powers of arrest.

Street pastors and street wardens, park rangers, and police community support officers are only a handful of the many uniformed officials that were central to the 'spectacles of police power' (Comaroff and Comaroff, 2016) in England's post-industrial neighbourhoods, when I first began my fieldwork in 2009. On Park End, they operated alongside a range of other institutions in the daily

---

[1] PCT stands for primary care trust which were part of the NHS and responsible for the commissioning of health services from providers from 2001–13. PCTs were abolished as part of the Health and Social Care Act 2012.

maintenance of public order. By day, members of the neighbourhood policing team patrolled the estate on car, bike, foot, and horse. Police helicopters regularly hovered above the estate, disturbing people's peace and quiet in their gardens. The local authorities, housing associations, and youth services also held regular public events to collect evidence and provided avenues for addressing issues of anti-social behaviour and crime. In this process, the boundaries between policing disorder and community work often became blurred. Just as civil society actors—like the churches in the street pastor scheme—were drawn into the policing of public order, so too did members of the policing team become involved in community activities. This included events like a dog chipping day, during which residents could get micro-chips put on their dogs, a football match which sported police against 'the lads', and a 'good neighbour scheme' that involved police officers recruiting volunteers to help neighbours in need with their daily chores, under their supervision.

The aim of this chapter is to situate these everyday displays of 'law and order' within a broader history of state–citizen relations in Britain. To this end, I ask: how do we make sense of initiatives like the street wardens and street pastors in places like Park End? To what extent do they reflect a continuation with, and intensification of, earlier modes of state coercion and even state control? What, in short, can we learn from a longer-term history of the post-war British state? I explore these questions through the lens of council estates: their history and their present reality. Built largely in the post-war decades to provide housing for the country's industrial working class, council estates were once owned and managed by local branches of government, so-called councils or local authorities. But from the 1980s onwards, the council housing sector was privatized, as the introduction of the 'right to buy' scheme allowed sitting tenants to buy their flats at much-discounted rates, and to sell them on at market value. Yet, government has not disappeared from council estates. Neoliberal policies have reconfigured state–citizen relations in more subtle ways, as a multiplicity of actors, including those from the private and third sectors,[2] have come to take on state-like roles as landlords and policing agents.

---

[2] '"Third sector organisations" is a term used to describe the range of organisations that are neither public sector nor private sector. It includes voluntary and community organisations (both registered charities and other organisations

Considered in this light, the expansion of 'law and order' in the twenty-first century is only one instantiation in a longer post-war history of class control.

I argue that the post-war history of council estates is best understood as a history of state-building: far from simply concerning the provision of material shelter for a working-class population, council estates have always been an arena where the state has acted out particular understandings of citizenship. Whether we speak of post-war 'social governance' (Joyce, 2013), the 'iron law of liberalism' (Graeber, 2015) that followed in the 1980s, the turn to the 'law-and-order state' (Hyatt, 2011) in the 2000s, or the most recent shift to 'austerity' politics since 2010 (Chapter 7), the state has always drawn distinctions between those it considers to be respectable, and hence deserving citizens, and those who are not. At the same time, interpretations of who constitutes a model citizen have changed in accordance with shifts in political economy over time. In the post-war decades, dominant ideals favoured the white, male, and British 'worker citizen' who had contributed to society through labour and taxes. As Britain moved towards a liberal market economy from the 1970s onwards, the boundaries of respectability were redrawn from the worker–citizen to the consumer–citizen, and in favour of the homeowner as the idealized subject of housing policy. With this shift, many residents in places like Park End came to be marked out as subjects of abject moral failure (Chapter 3). More recently, the expansion of 'law and order' shifted the boundaries once more to the idealized citizen as the victim of crime, and council estate residents could prove their worthiness through their vulnerability to others. Since 2010, with the shift to a new, Conservative-led government, the contours of citizenship have changed once more, as discourses of hyper-moralization have resurfaced (Chapter 7).

This chapter sets the historical backdrop for the remainder of the book. It does so by engaging conventional accounts of

---

such as associations, self-help groups and community groups), social enterprises, mutuals and co-operatives' (National Audit Office, https://www.nao.org.uk/successful-commissioning/introduction/what-are-civil-society-organisations-and-their-benefits-for-commissioners/). The main third sector organizations that tenants on council estates are in contact with are social housing providers, to whom the government has increasingly come to outsource the provision and management of public housing (see also Chapter 5).

post-war governance which have presented the shift to 'law and order' as an exceptional turn in the history of post-war democracy. Such a view rests upon a particular view of the post-war decades as a time when social democracy was actually achieved and fully in place. It also lends itself to a dichotomy between 'law and order' on the one hand, and welfare, on the other, which portrays the former as a locus of repressive and punitive control that has replaced the latter as a sponsor of inclusive and progressive policies. Yet, as social historians (Joyce, 2013) and ethnographers of policy have argued (Fassin, 2015; Hyatt, 2011; Morgan and Maskovsky, 2003), marginalized citizens have always been subject to various modes of state control that have included both the representatives of 'law and order' and the supposedly softer arms of the welfare state. This chapter builds on these insights to offer a revised history of state–citizen relations on British council estates. Throughout, this historical narrative will also serve as a starting point to introduce Park End estate, focusing on the period from the post-war decades to 2010, when New Labour was replaced by an incoming Conservative-led government.[3]

A note of caution is in order. By focusing on council estates as a microcosm through which to understand more general processes of state–citizen relations, I do not intend to create the impression of council estates as self-contained entities. On the contrary, many of the experiences of state control that are described here are shared by working-class people on precarious incomes and in rented housing elsewhere (Davey, 2016; Davey and Koch, 2017; Skeggs, 1997; Smith, 2017), whether they live on council estates or not. That said, the language of 'estates' was frequently used by both residents and officials (although with very different connotations, as we will see in the following chapters); 'estate' invoked at once a place and a symbolic representation of that place. It is this physical association with place-making and the various moral evaluations that come with it that make 'estates' a useful heuristic device through which to track the broader history of state control in the post-war British state.

---

[3] The period since then will be discussed in the chapters that follow as well as the conclusion to this book.

The Punitive Turn Revisited

The turn to 'law and order' at the turn of the twenty-first century has become a major point of debate. Variously interpreted as a 'culture of control' (Garland, 2001), the emergence of an 'exclusive society' (Young, 1999) intent on 'punishing the poor' (Wacquant, 2009), and a 'tectonic shift' in governance (Comaroff and Comaroff, 2016: 25), scholars have emphasized its exceptional nature. Often, the point of comparison invoked is the period that followed immediately after the Second World War: the post-war years of social democracy, during which political and societal outlooks are said to have been more rehabilitative, welfarist, and inclusive. Garland's (2001) analysis, first introduced in the Introduction, provides an excellent example of such a narrative. For him, the penal-welfare arrangements in place in the post-war decades were 'part of a wider scheme of things', one which was rooted in 'the very solidity and rootedness of the post-war welfare state and its social democratic politics' (ibid.: 28). Criminal justice professionals not only valued rehabilitative approaches to offending but also the expertise of 'social' authorities and groups, including probation officers, social workers, psychologists, educationalists, and social reformers of all kinds (ibid.: 36), who were developing into a central arm of governance in the post-war decades.

It was the uprooting of this 'social democratic politics' from the 1970s onwards that precipitated the contemporary 'culture of control', with drastic implications for those who count as its undesirable 'others'. Central to this uprooting process were a number of important changes. On the one hand, there were the changes associated with the cultural, economic, and social transformations of 'late modernity' already mentioned in the Introduction: more porous and individualized lifestyles, the decline of traditional family and household arrangements, as well as experiences of crime as a 'new social fact' all posed problems of insecurity, challenged the legitimacy of welfare institutions, and set new limits on the nation state. On the other hand, a second set of forces emerged to challenge the politics of welfarism: the 1970s saw the production of a 'dominant political bloc that defined itself in opposition to old style "welfarism" and the social and cultural ideals upon which it was based' (ibid.: 76). The correctionalist ideal of the post-war decades, alongside its focus on governance through 'social' experts and policy actors, was now 'depicted as absurdly indulgent and self-defeating' (ibid.: 77), as a new climate of more punitive and exclusive crime control started to take hold.

Garland's account rests on a contrast, then, between the post-war ideal of correctionalist justice and the contemporary moment of punitive governance. A dichotomy is invoked between what I have called elsewhere, drawing upon Comaroff and Comaroff (2006), a 'politics of welfare', defined through its inclusive tendencies and focus on social solutions, and a 'politics of lawfare' marked by an exclusionary outlook and individualizing solutions (Koch, 2018). This dichotomy has not just been invoked in commentary on the post-war British state. It also reappears in a different guise when scholars contrast punitive developments in criminal justice to their alleged counterparts in the welfare state. For example, in their excellent account of 'custodial citizenship'—the process whereby the US has turned a growing number of citizens into custodial subjects, often without the commission of any crimes—Lerman and Weaver (2014) start from the assumption that the 'relationship between the citizen and the state in criminal justice interactions is fundamentally distinct from the citizen-state relationship in social welfare programmes. Most basically, and in contrast to political experiences in other domains, contact with the carceral state is involuntary' (ibid.: 14). The assumption that interactions with the welfare state are somehow less coercive, 'voluntary', and hence more desirable also reappears in calls to move beyond a focus on the criminal law in debates of punishment to include areas of social and welfare policy-making (e.g. Miller, 2016).

As Miller (2016) rightly points out, at the very least, a broader focus on social and welfare policies is important because it helps to build an understanding not only of the symptoms, but of the root causes of violence and crime. It can also act as a critical vantage point from which to question dominant policies and imagine alternative systems of governance that are more accountable to the needs of the most marginalized citizens. But neat divisions between what Wacquant (2009), drawing on Bourdieu, called the 'right' and the 'left' hands of the state also tend to gloss over continuities both across time and different areas of policy. They run the danger of conjuring an idealized image of post-war social democracy against which the current moment appears as an aberration or misfit. Yet, as social historian Joyce argues in *The State of Freedom* (2013) 'it has to be remembered, particularly by those who wish to recall a golden age of social democracy in post-1945 Britain, that the social was necessarily a way of governing people, governance through "the social"' (ibid.: 322). Governance through the social generated its own forms of dependence and a pervasive presence of the state even during the era of welfarist reform. As Fassin remarked, 'the tension between the penal state and the welfare state is never as strong as when the population the state is dealing with is characterized by its precarity, be it economic or legal' (2015: 2).

Ethnographers of policy have started to propose readings of governance that do not start from an a priori distinction between a politics of welfare and that of lawfare, and that trace a politics of lawfare through areas of governance where they are not conventionally found (Davey, 2016; Fassin, 2015; Hyatt, 2011; Morgan and Maskovsky, 2003; Skeggs, 1997, 2004). Hyatt (2011) has offered an analysis of the contemporary 'law-and-order state' that breaks with the dichotic portrayal of a 'before' and 'after' moment that has so often been invoked in relation to the Keynesian post-war welfare state. Thus, rather than starting from the assumption that the current turn to more punitive and exclusionary criminal justice policies is wholly exceptional or new, she asks, 'what capabilities were always inherent in [post-war welfare] Keynesianism that set the stage for the eventual emergence first of neoliberalism, and later of the law and order state?' Her account proposes a periodization of the post-war state in the United States that is premised on differences as well as continuities between three periods: the post-war moment of welfare state building when the idealized citizen was the 'citizen worker'; the era of neoliberal reform from the 1980s when more consumer-oriented notions of citizenship came to the fore; and the period that followed with its focus on the 'citizen-as-crime-fighter'.

My analysis follows Hyatt's three-fold periodization of post-war policy-making but takes this to the context of British council estates. More specifically, I investigate how the punitive turn that has drawn so much attention from criminologists and criminal justice scholars is part of a longer trajectory of state control, one which is marked both by important ruptures and continuities across time and across different policy domains. I argue that the post-war history of council estates is best understood as a history of state-building: whether through paternalistic policies in the post-war decades, the expansion of bureaucratic modes of control in the 1980s, or the rolling out of criminal justice logics and tools with an incoming New Labour government in the late 1990s, people who live in rented housing in Britain's most marginalized neighbourhoods have always found themselves at the receiving end of repressive policies and moralizing discourses that have marked them out as wanting because of their position as working class citizens. They have been differently marked as subject to state intervention, predation, and aggression. This has been achieved in relation to different ideals of 'respectability' associated with prevailing political and economic conditions, defined variously in terms of the post-war citizen–worker, the citizen–consumer, or the citizen–victim. In what follows, I tell this story in three steps, beginning with the post-war decades of mass council housing; second, the turn to privatization and neoliberal housing policies in the 1980s; and third, the period of 'law and order' governance. Later chapters continue the chronology with the shift to 'the big society' (Chapter 6) and 'austerity politics' (Chapter 7) that followed with the election of Conservative leadership in government since 2010.

The Citizen–Worker and Post-War Paternalism

The history of council housing is conventionally considered as part of a broader history of the post-war British welfare state. But while this history is often couched in a narrative of social democracy and progress, or what Scott called the great utopian projects of the twentieth century (1998), these terms can also mask a more complex relationship between the state and its citizens on Britain's state-built housing developments. This becomes clear when considering the nineteenth-century precursors of council housing, when the provision of workers' housing was closely connected to the problems of overcrowding in the inner-city slums, generated by the Industrial Revolution and the influx of migrant workers it spurred in cities across the country. Social commentators, including Friedrich Engels (2009 [1887]), reported on the squalor, sickness, and inhumane conditions in which the industrial working classes lived. Such reports resonated with the broader fears of contamination and social contagion that working classes posed in Victorian discourses of the dangerous and immoral poor and popularized in the writings of authors like Charles Dickens: as Burney (1999) points out, 'the nation's health—moral as well as physical—was believed to be at stake' (ibid.: 35).

In response to this perceived sense of crisis, philanthropists began to provide tenement block housing, while some factory owners built entire villages for their workers near manufacturing bases. Following the report from a Royal Commission, the Housing of the Working Classes Act 1885 was passed; this encouraged local authorities to destroy some of the worst slums in their local areas and to improve housing for the working classes. In the first half of the twentieth century, some of the nation's major council estates built by local authorities across the country acquired fame with their utopian and modernist designs, including the 'garden cities' of the early twentieth-century period (Ravetz, 2001). Nevertheless, their residents continued to stir bourgeois anxieties. This is nowhere better illustrated than in the case of the Cutteslowe Wall in Oxford, an over 2m high wall, topped with lethal spikes, which was erected in 1934 to separate the residents of the city council's Cutteslowe council estate from private housing adjoining it (Collison, 1963). Clive Saxton of the Urban Housing Company, who had developed the private housing, was afraid that his housing would not sell if Cutteslowe tenants were going to be their neighbours, and so the wall was built to separate them. The wall only came down in 1959, and the social historian Hanley would later liken it to an act of 'class apartheid' (Hanley, 2007).

While class division and social coercion continued to afflict pre-war council housing, trade union movements had been growing since the early parts of the century and had made important inroads into labour protection (Mollona, 2009). But it was only with the emergence of the welfare state following the Second World War that social insurance became central to government policy. The emerging welfare state was premised on a new settlement between labour and capital: in contrast to the laissez-faire government of the pre-war period, capitalism's worst excesses would now be mediated by a left-leaning welfare state. Beveridge's 'five giants' of want, idleness, disease, ignorance, and squalor were to be banished through national policies that cared for citizens 'from the cradle to the grave' (Timmins, 1995: 142). Alongside the provision of a National Health System (the NHS), access to free education, the social wage, and national insurance, council housing was to be one of the pillars of this new welfare state. In response to a massive housing crisis precipitated by the destruction of housing during the war, large council estates were built across the country in the 1950s and 1960s under the auspices of local authorities. The old industrial neighbourhoods were torn down under slum clearance schemes, and workers and their families relocated to the newly built estates. The newly built homes were healthier, more spacious, and better constructed than were those in the old neighbourhoods.

The idealized citizen of the post-war welfare state was the worker–citizen, who had paid his 'debts' to society through contributions in labour and taxes, as well as military service in the Second World War. There was a sense that the social contract, following the First World War, had never been delivered and that soldiers returning from the Second World War would be entitled to have their debts repaid (Bew, 2017). Yet, as Graeber (2011) reminds us, 'there's no better way to justify relations founded on violence, to make such relations seem moral, than by reframing them in the language of debt—above all, because it immediately makes it seem like it's the victim who's doing something wrong' (ibid.: 5). Post-war policies were also premised on their own forms of hierarchy and control that excluded those unable to contribute, and hence to pay their debts, as 'undeserving' of the state's attention. The ideal favoured by the worker–citizen was the white, British, and male citizen with a nuclear household (Koch, 2015; Lewis, 2002; Patenam, 1988). Women were treated as dependants of their husbands by post-war welfare policies; their rights to most benefits, including access to council housing, were contingent upon their status as married women: the exception to this was the Family Allowance that was directly paid out to women for the birth of the second child and thereafter (Dench et al., 2006). Other social groups, including immigrants, the long-term unemployed, and the long-term ill, were often excluded from accessing the post-war social insurance scheme, and were placed at the mercy of philanthropists and means-tested social assistance that continued to exist into the post-war decades.

Within the council housing sector, these exclusionary tendencies and understandings of 'deservingness' were also applied through selective council housing policies and the daily management of council estate tenants and their homes. Just as the idealized citizen was the male worker–citizen, so the 'respectable' council home was the white, nuclear family household with a male head.

Selective housing policies enforced by local authorities excluded members of such undesirable groups as 'unwed mothers, broken families, "wandering bachelors" (and spinsters), unemployed or unemployable people, and sometimes even inter-racial marriages' (Harrell-Bond, 1967: 27).[4] But even those who had been offered council housing had to continuously prove their worth. Damer (1989) has argued that respectability and worth were defined in two ways: first, in terms of tenants' ability to keep up with rent payments; and second, in terms of more moralistic criteria of upkeep and cleanliness. The latter was specifically targeted at women who were exposed to the paternalist gaze of a range of local authority officials on the ground: rent collectors, housing officials, and health inspectors would call round to collect rent and check on the state of people's homes and gardens and the well-being of their children. The following extract, for example, from a tenants' handbook that was sent by the local authority to council tenants in Oxfordshire advises tenants of their moral obligations:

> It is a condition of your tenancy that you should look after your garden. With most tenants it is a matter of personal pride, and it is very true to say that the house inside can nearly always be judged by the garden outside ... is yours as good as it might be? ... The country still has a large number of people on its waiting list urgently in need of homes of their own. Be thankful for what you've got, therefore and make the best for it for the benefit of all—not least yourself. (cited in Ravetz, 2001: 119)

Paternalistic attitudes, fear of the 'undeserving' working classes, and selective housing policies that prioritized the nuclear family model were central to social governance in the post-war welfare state. They were also features that could be exacerbated through local histories of class segregation and control. Park End provides a good example. The town's local Labour movement had lobbied without success for better housing conditions for decades, as much of the town's working-class population was living in dilapidated and overcrowded 'slums'. The town itself is one of the wealthiest in the country with some of the largest landowners. But by the twentieth century, it had also developed into one of the country's major industrial bases due to the expansion of a local factory. Like in other parts of the country, the factory was

---

[4] The latter were left to find housing in the private sector, where rents tended to be higher and conditions poor (see Chapter 4).

attracting a labour force not only from within the region but further afield, including Northern Ireland, Scotland, and increasingly also from Britain's former colonies in the West Indies. Despite this growth, the town's local authority had been reluctant to provide any large-scale housing for its working-class population. In 1946, there were 5,000 people on the council waiting list for housing, and the need for housing was growing even further in the years to come.

Against this backdrop, the development of Park End in the 1950s was already freighted with negative associations before it was even built. The local authorities conceded to the construction of Park End but emphasized that no further housing expansion would take place thereafter, referring to it as a 'final solution' to the 'problem of an overspill population'. Park End's original location was chosen in part so as not to disrupt the architectural skyline of the old centre of the town: located at the end of a long through road, about 4 miles out of the town centre, Park End was built on open farm land. The estate was cut off from all directions: to the west there is a motorway and railway tracks (with a bridge going across them); the factory (now significantly downsized) is located to the north; and there is open countryside to the south and the east. The physical isolation of the estate is reflected in its social marginalization. From the beginning, the estate was stigmatized as a problem area by the town's establishment, including employers and the local authorities. For example, in oral history interviews, older residents recalled that they would apply for jobs giving the name of neighbouring villages as their addresses so as not to be associated with Park End and being discriminated against; a stigma that continues to persist today (Chapter 3).

Despite the local authority's original intentions to contain the growth of Park End, the estate continuously grew over the decades. In 1963, it already had a population of 7,600 residents living on the estate; today, this has grown to a population of over 13,000. The first residents were moved in 1958 on what was still an uncompleted site, and building works continued into the 1970s. In the early 1990s, a new housing development with mixed-tenures was added to the eastern part of the estate. With the growth of the estate, the ethnic and racial make-up of the estate also changed significantly over the years. In the early days of the estate, the majority of the local population were white British families. Despite growing migration into the city, particularly from the Caribbean, not many black families were offered housing on the estate. This policy changed over the years that followed and, by the 1980s, already a significant minority of black families were living on the estate. This figure has grown today. The 2011 Census recorded that 33 per cent of Park End residents were from a non-white British ethnic group, with a notably larger proportion of residents from black ethnic groups compared to other parts of the city. Many of the women of Afro-Caribbean descent I met during my research, including Tracey, were second generation residents. Relations between the white and black population ran deep, with friendship and family relations cutting across these groups.

In short, even a cursory glance at the post-war history of council housing shows the need for a revised account of the social significance of post-war British democracy generally, and its housing policies specifically. The undoubtable social and material gains that were brought about by the post-war welfare state were also mitigated by their limits. Single women, ethnic and racial minority groups, and those who did not fit the state's normative ideal of the nuclear family home were treated as a class apart. Only those who had proven their 'deservingness' through contributions paid to the system were able to gain access to some of the welfare state's most valued goods, its post-war council housing stock; and even then, this elusive worthiness was something that had to be continuously demonstrated and was measured by paternalistic systems of tenants and rent management. What, then, happened in the period that followed the post-war decades? How did the state's own projects of class control come to the fore with the ideological attack on the welfare state?

The Citizen–Consumer and the 'Iron Law of Liberalism'

The post-war social contract was premised on the idea of the worker–citizen as the model citizen of policy-making: he (he was always the male citizen) was entitled to the state's benefits and resources in return for contributions paid into society through taxes and labour. This reflected the ideological assumptions of a political economy defined through state-controlled capitalism and strong welfare policies that were able to 'capture' large sections of the wage-earning classes (Nugent, 2012). But as neoliberal policies encroached more rapidly from the 1980s onwards, Britain embraced the features of a liberal market economy, defined by deregulation, a minimal welfare state, and a mantra of labour flexibility and innovation (Lacey, 2008). The resultant ideological attack on state welfare justified what Harvey has referred to as 'accumulation by dispossession' (2003): a process whereby assets formerly regarded as off-limits to the calculus of profit-making were opened up as new fields for capital accumulation. Across much of the Euro-American world, this engendered widespread privatization of formerly state-owned or state-controlled public resources and sectors, including education, health, and housing.

In Britain, the ideological demise of the post-war welfare state was sealed with the electoral victory of Margaret Thatcher and her Conservative government in 1979, but the attitude of assent to its destruction had been in the offing for some time. As Harvey reminds us, the welfare state constructed in Britain after the Second World War was never to everyone's liking: strong currents of criticism circulated through the media which maintained the superiority of an ethic of 'individualism, freedom, and liberty' as opposed to 'the stifling bureaucratic ineptitude of the state apparatus and oppressive trade union power' ([2005] 2007: 56–7). Such aspersions, which were already widespread in the 1960s, became even more prolific in the years of economic stagnation during the 1970s, as would be what Hills (2015) has called the 'welfare myth' of 'skivers' and 'strivers', or of an 'us' and 'them'. As inflation rose and unemployment topped one million in 1975, inevitable confrontations between the state and the unions surfaced, exemplified in the prolonged 1972 miner strikes that followed wage stagnation and pit closures under the Conservative Heath government. In 1974, the government called an election seeking public support for its stand against miners. It lost, but the returning Labour government, which settled the strike on terms favourable to the miners, was unable to battle the mounting crisis of fiscal strain. The Labour government implemented draconian cutbacks in welfare state expenditures that generated further strikes.

When Thatcher was voted into power in 1979, monetarism, strict budgetary control, and privatization became the order of the day. Post-war notions of the model citizen were revised and reworked. As Hyatt puts it, 'the idealized subject of neoliberal policy [became] the citizen consumer who was "responsibilized" to make wise and prudent choices in the "free market" of utilities and services, ranging from healthcare to schooling' (2011: 107). In

Chapter 6 the implications of this strategy of 'responsibilization' (Garland, 2001) will be considered in more depth. But suffice to say that it brought long-standing projects of state control and its classed dimensions more explicitly to the fore. Under Thatcher, the consumer–citizen was coupled to an idea of the active citizen. The Thatcherite subject was a citizen required to take responsibility for him or herself, linked with Victorian values of work, family, and private charity. With their focus on individual responsibility and their moral grounding in Victorian ethics, neoliberal policies also continued to enshrine gendered inequalities (Chapter 3) and racialized practices (Chapter 5), even where they claimed to be ostensibly gender and colour-neutral. The 1980s were also a time when political opposition was violently repressed, trade union movements weakened, and class-based opposition silenced (Chapter 7).

The implications of these changes for the council housing sector cannot be overstated. Notions of respectability that had been so central to post-war ideas of eligibility to council housing were recast, away from the ideal tenant as the male breadwinner maintaining his dependent family, to that of the homeowner. The mark of respectability was equated with private ownership, and the worthy citizen defined as the person who could afford to own their own home. Already in 1977, the Housing (Homeless Persons) Act introduced a duty on local authorities to prioritize the most vulnerable applicants, including single mothers, large families, and the long-term unemployed, in the allocation of council housing. On the surface, the Act marked a much-needed expansion of the role of social housing given that in the post-war model, the prioritization of housing applicants had been on the basis of financial standing (below a certain middle-class threshold). However, the act carried a covert, and in the end, much more radical re-evaluation of the ideological meaning of claims on the state, from a confirmation of citizenship to a retraction of it: in the post-war decades, access to social housing had been a mark of inclusion, a certification precisely of a citizen's worthiness, a corroboration of merit, albeit heavily policed. By contrast, with the shift to strictly needs-based allocation, access to social housing became a mark of dismal inadequacy, a failure to meet standards of worthiness.

This restriction of access to citizenship through the paradoxical expansion of social housing to the most vulnerable categories of people was precisely what was further driven forward by the privatization of council housing that followed in the decades to come. In 1979, 42 per cent of the country's population was living in council housing: in 2012, this number had fallen to 8 per cent.[5] Thatcher won votes on the back of promising the right to sitting council tenants to buy their homes at a maximum discount of 50 per cent. Once elected into power, her government passed the Housing Act 1980 that would engender the 'selling of the welfare state' (Murie and Forrest, 1988). Local authorities were expected to use the 50 per cent of the receipts they kept from the sales to pay off debts rather than build new homes, thus further resulting in a reduction of the available council housing stock. Soon, the more desirable council estates became owner-occupied, especially inner-city estates in cities like London that have been turned into prime real estates and have been sold by their original buyers at a massive profit (Harvey, 2003). These estates are largely gentrified today. By contrast, the more undesirable council estates have retained higher numbers of rented properties where, increasingly, only the most vulnerable applicants are placed, as social housing policies prioritize the most needy applicants.

Privatization policies had an irrevocable and devastating effect on the structure of council housing and define its contemporary organization and form. Much of the remaining council housing stock is of inferior quality to the post-war builds as local authorities have replaced many of the post-war terraced builds with flats, maisonettes, and tower blocks (Chapter 4). At the same time, a range of alternative actors, including those from the private sector and the third sector, have stepped in to provide housing for the poor, often with worse standards than those on offer from the local authorities. The Social Security and Housing Benefits Act 1982 introduced housing benefit as the only form of rent subsidy. This means that tenants in receipt of benefits can also rent from private landlords, thus effectively using state subsidies as a handout to private property owners (Meek, 2014). Because there is little regulation for private landlords, many tenants on precarious incomes or on state benefits live in substandard housing conditions (Chapter 4). Finally, since the 1990s, the bulk of publicly owned housing has been increasingly provided by third-sector organizations, so-called housing associations under the name 'social

[5] https://www.theguardian.com/society/2016/jan/04/end-of-council-housing-bill-secure-tenancies-pay-to-stay.

housing'. Housing associations typically offer 'assured tenancies' rather than the 'secure tenancies' that were once given to tenants under the old council housing scheme.[6] In short, those unable to buy their own homes are spread out across a range of different landlords and forms of housing that cut across the state-owned, private, and third-sectors.

The privatization of the council housing sector has not, however, resulted in a diminution of the role of government, as might be assumed. As Graeber has pointed out, 'English liberalism ... did not lead to a reduction of state bureaucracy but its exact opposite: an endlessly ballooning array of legal clerks, registrars, inspectors, notaries, and police officials who made the liberal dream of a world of free contract between autonomous inividuals possible' (2015: 9). He has referred to this apparent paradox, where 'government policies intending to reduce government interference in the economy actually end up producing more regulations, more bureaucrats and more police' as a general 'sociological law', which he calls the 'iron law of liberalism' (ibid.). This iron law of liberalism was manifest in the lives of council estate residents. By the 1980s, post-war paternalistic welfare policies and the face-to-face system of rent and housing management had been replaced by a centralized and increasingly faceless welfare bureaucracy, as we will see in more depth in Chapter 3. Bureaucrats, for their part, came to see council estates and their tenants as 'problems' to be controlled. More than three decades ago, Francis Reynolds (1986) found that:

> The usual definition of a 'problem estate' is one which has a particlarly high incidence of social problems ... Whatever set of indices is chosen, it is clear that the objective measure of a problem area is in fact the disproportionate amount of work it causes for, and the high input of resources it demands from, various local authority or government services. Thus while the obvious implication of the term 'problem area' is that the people there *have* problems, the real meaning of the label is that they *cause* problems for the authorities. (ibid.: 24; my emphasis)

Park End is an example of a neighbourhood that features in the public imagination as a 'problem estate'. Parts of the estate count

---

[6] They have also been at the forefront of more recent shifts to promote 'affordable' housing as opposed to 'social housing' which is currently defined at up to 80 per cent of the going market rate.

among the most impoverished neighbourhoods in the country. Since the 1980s, the factory has been in steady decline, employing today only a fraction of its original labour force. In 2010, it made for 9 per cent of the local economy with a labour force of less than 3,500 workers. At the same time, the service economy has failed to offer sufficient replacement jobs for a local population that still lacks professional qualifications. According to the 2011 Census, over half of the residents had no or low qualifications, compared to the 22 per cent city average, and as we will see in Chapter 3, often work in badly paid and menial jobs; 50 per cent of households rented their home from the council or a housing association, and another third owned their home (with the remainder renting in the private sector). Nearly one in five households were headed by lone parents, over double the city average. Many adult residents with whom I spent time on Park End—in particular the women—are in close contact with a range of authority figures in their daily lives, including social workers, housing officials, benefit officers, and local authority staff. As the chapters that follow show, they spend an inordinate amount of time dealing with the authorities by chasing paper work, waiting in queues, attending assessment meetings, and filling in forms.

In interviews and informal conversations with local authority officials, it became evident that they considered Park End to be a difficult neighbourhood. Park End was known to be one of the 'worst' estates in town, a notoriety that was reinforced by its physical isolation, its size, and its high number of so-called 'vulnerable' families. The language invoked by authority figures differed depending on the context and services they were providing to residents. Similar to the talk of 'hard-to-reach' groups observed by Symons (2018), community workers and local authority officials often complained about residents being 'apathetic' and 'not interested' in their community, using low levels of civic participation in formal (and often local authority-led) activities as a sign of this apathy (Chapter 6). Benefits officers and welfare officials, who will be considered more closely in Chapter 3, spoke of problems of 'dependencies' and lack of aspiration and willingness to improve on the part of residents, including single mothers. A language of dependency was also invoked by police officers and housing authorities (Chapters 5 and 4 respectively), when they complained of Park End residents using the authorities as a 'first aid tool' for merely personal or petty problems, amounting to a waste of 'police time'. But portrayals of local residents acting in petty and infantilizing ways also existed alongside other depictions of Park End as a crime-ridden, dangerous, and violent place (Chapter 5), an image to which we will return in the next section.

In short, for large swathes of people, the neoliberal dream that created the property-owning 'consumer–citizen' as the idealized citizen remains precisely that: a dream that bears no resemblance to their daily lives. For citizens who live on precarious and often state-supported incomes in the rental housing sector, the period that was ushered in from the 1980s onwards meant a material deterioration of their homes and neighbourhoods. While this effect is due to a whole host of policy changes, not least the loss of jobs and traditional working-class livelihoods, the privatization of council housing, and its consequent reconfiguration of relations obtaining between the state, the private sector, and third sector, have been among its principal engines. Paradoxically, this reconfiguration has not resulted in a lessening of state government for those at the margins, but in a proliferation of bureaucratic and other forms of state control. From the mid-1990s, yet a further wave of policy changes was ushered in, culminating in what Hyatt has called the 'law-and-order state' (Hyatt, 2011).

The Vulnerable Citizen and the 'Law-and-Order-State'

We have already seen in the Introduction that the turn to 'law and order' first came to the fore in the mid-1990s when the Labour Party, then still in opposition, joined the Conservative government in a race to be seen to be tougher on issues of crime. In 1995, the Labour Party manifesto argued that the most pressing issues confronting the country were problems of incivilities and low-level crime affecting 'thousands of people whose lives are made a misery by the people next door, down the street or on the floor above or below' (Labour Party, 1995: 2). MPs like Jack Straw and Tony Blair drew on their own experiences of serving impoverished constituencies (including post-industrial council estates across the country) to portray images of 'neighbours from hell' who were allowed to play havoc owing to a criminal justice system that had become too lenient. Labour MPs had visited the United States in the run up to Labour's electoral campaign and been impressed with 'zero tolerance policing' strategies and their ideological grounding in 'broken windows' theory, which holds that superficial signs of disintegration are a causal factor in bringing about a deeper drift of degeneration and decline. They argued that the time had come to rebalance the rights in the criminal justice system away from those of offenders to those of victims.

The turn to 'law and order' under the New Labour government was part of a broader shift towards a centre-right or 'third way' approach that placed security issues at its heart. Across much of the world, traditionally leftist or social democratic parties were experiencing a crisis of authority following decades of industrial decline and neoliberal policy-making. In Britain, since the 1980s, with the loss of industrial neighbourhoods and Thatcher's attack on trade union movements, much of the traditional voter base of the Labour Party had been weakened or reduced. We will consider the effects of this political dispossession in more detail in Chapter 7. Some of Labour's former working-class constituencies had been absorbed into an expanding middle class (including some of those who had been able to buy their council homes under Thatcher's right to buy scheme and become part of a new class of respectable home owners); but many more had been 'uncaptured', to borrow Nugent's (2012) term, from political processes. Law and order policies, with their focus on individual responsibility and blame, became the flagship of political parties on both the left and the right. They hoped to capture a large demographic of voters, including those who had seen their livelihoods dismantled in the preceding decades by grounding the logic of consumer–citizenship within a moral language of vulnerability to threats (Ramsay, 2012; Chapter 6).

When the New Labour government was voted into power in 1997, after eighteen years out of government and four consecutive electoral defeats, it implemented its 'tough on crime' agenda with full force. Lacey (2008) drawing upon Dubber (2001), has described the policy changes implemented as an extension of policing power—a hierarchical, discretionary, and patriarchal form of power—as distinct from, within, and beyond the police force itself. Under the banner of 'community' or 'neighbourhood' policing, the police force was required to implement permanent and hierarchically organized 'neighbourhood policing teams' and to improve high visibility and community-based policing strategies. Police and policing powers were also extended into the realm of local governance itself. Local authorities set up their own units policing disorder and 'anti-social behaviour', as well as partnership agreements with other bodies, including housing associations, social services, youth services, and, as we saw in the opening vignette, even churches. Uniformed law enforcement officials, like the street wardens we encountered at the beginning of the chapter, were supplied by local authorities. Finally, police power became manifest in the law. During its nine-year tenure, the Blair government created more than 3,000 new criminal offences, one for almost every day it was in power.

Images of a public under threat from a criminal minority are, of course, not neutral. They invoke particular understandings of insider-outsider relations that conjure the existence of public enemies that need to be forcibly controlled, if not outright extinguished. As Hyatt (2011) has pointed out, if 'the idealized subject of neoliberal policy was the citizen consumer', then, 'in contrast, the idealized subject of the law-and-order state is the citizen who both polices and agrees to be policed' (ibid.: 107). The idealized citizen is the 'citizen-as-crime-fighter' who is defined through their vulnerability to disorder and crime and their concomitant vigilance against it. Ramsay has argued that the ASBO, or Anti-Social Behaviour Order, is the prime example of how 'the vulnerabilities and needs of victims [have come to] define the appropriate conditions for government intervention' (2010: 268). Implemented under the Crime and Disorder Act 1998 and superseded by the Anti-Social Behaviour, Crime and Policing Act 2014, the ASBO was a civil–criminal hybrid that allowed for the potential criminalization of behaviour deemed 'anti-social', including as we will see in Chapter 5, youth-related behaviour. Because 'anti-social behaviour' was not defined by the legislation other than through any behaviour causing 'alarm, harassment, and distress' to a member of the public not of the same household, and the evidentiary standard used was 'a balance of probabilities' rather than the more exacting criminal standard 'beyond reasonable doubt', it allowed for the vast expansion of criminal justice tools into areas hitherto left unregulated.

Social housing providers were deeply implicated as agents in the enforcement of these 'law and order' policies (Chapter 5; Chapter 6). Under the New Labour government's reign, they were given extended powers to evict tenants on accounts of 'anti-social behaviour' from their properties by serving a 'Notice Seeking Possession'. This also applies to members of the household not implicated in any action considered anti-social or illegal: for example, a mother can be served an eviction notice for her son's involvement in criminal activity if they live in the same household in a social tenancy (Chapter 6). Further, the political will to punish those in precariously situated housing has been carried over under the Tory governments, which was voted back into power in 2010. Under the Anti-Social Behaviour, Crime and Policing Act (2014), a clause now exists which gives housing providers the discretionary power to evict a tenant, or member of that household, if found guilty of an indictable offence in the context of a riot.[7] This means that a tenant, but also a family member of the tenant who resides in the same home, can face eviction from their socially rented home for becoming involved in a riot-related offence that occurs miles away from their home. These eviction powers have been likened to a 'class-based punishment' that fits into the wider agenda on public housing, including the reduction in security of social housing tenure that has been underway since the 1980s (Young, 2016).

The effect of these changes has been to discursively introduce a renewed focus on crime and its prevention centred around council estates and their tenants. Council estates are no longer only seen as 'problem estates', marked by a dependent population of welfare claimants, benefit scroungers, and apathetic tenants, but as crime-breeding grounds prone to rioting and disorder. In popular and political discourse, this has been reinforced through images of the working classes in terms of 'yobs' and 'chavs' (Jones, 2011) and talk of the 'single mother' whose fecklessness or loose morality is a burden and a drain on the public purse, but more dangerously, whose allegedly bad parenting produces children with criminal dispositions (Gillies, 2007; Chapter 3). It is also reinforced through racialized images of 'gangs' and 'gang-infested' neighbourhoods that include the country's poor council estates (Chapter 5). But while the focus on criminality and disorder has further reinforced long-standing stigma and negative labelling, it has also expanded the categories of 'respectability' in perhaps unexpected ways. As we saw earlier, in justifying its turn to 'law and order', the New Labour government drew precisely on the

---

[7] The Act was passed following a few days of 'rioting' in English towns in 2011 when youths, mostly from post-industrial neighbourhoods and estates, took to the streets following the killing of a young mixed-race man from Tottenham (Chapter 8).

experiences of disaffected tenants in post-industrial neighbourhoods. On council estates, those who are unable to define their worth through their market independence (by buying their homes and hence purchasing privacy from state intrusions) can do so by becoming agents of the 'law-and-order state'.

The point is perhaps best illustrated when turning more closely to how neighbourhood policing was rolled out under New Labour. On Park End, the distinction between a 'law-abiding, respectable' group of tenants, and those who constitute dangerous and criminal threats from within, was activated and defined through daily activities and partnership initiatives that required citizens to become 'active' participants in their own governance (Chapter 6). On the one hand, citizens were encouraged to think of themselves as potential victims and fighters of crime; public events that drew residents into conversations with law enforcement officials frequently took place. For example, every month, the neighbourhood policing team chaired an inter-agency meeting called the 'neighbourhood action group' in community centres, attended by statutory providers and non-statutory bodies, including housing associations, youth services, social services, and invited community activists. As explained in Chapter 6, during this meeting, information about locally occurring incidents of disorder and anti-social behaviour was collated. Members of the neighbourhood policing team regularly held so-called 'surgeries' outside schools and in the community and handed out their business cards to residents on the streets. The police also recruited residents to work as 'civilian officers' alongside police on duty, and they collaborated with civic initiatives and volunteers like in the 'street pastor' scheme, with which I started this chapter.

On the other hand, a tough approach was adopted towards those who were deemed to be outliers: the authorities installed CCTV and 'mosquitos' (technical devices that emit a high-pitched sound, audible only to children and young people, for the purposes of dispersing them) outside commercial areas to prevent 'unruly' youths from loitering. Random stop-and-searches were carried out on young men, and occasionally even armed raids of people's homes and public facilities are conducted (Chapter 5). Helicopters patrolled at night, while the police were present on horses, bikes, car, and by foot during the day. Information about local offenders or sought-after criminals was widely publicized and disseminated, including through text, emails, and pictures on the police website and social media; I started receiving emails from the police while I lived on Park End without having ever formally subscribed to their mailing list. The same type of broadcasting applied to convictions and court orders, however minor or insignificant they might be, including court actions over dog-fouling incidents, or against young men wearing their hoods up over their faces and playing football in public areas. These imagined distinctions between a community of victims and crime fighters on the one hand, and external threats on the other, came through in an extract from a letter that was delivered by the local neighbourhood policing team to my home in Park End in 2009:

> Together, we the police, the wider partnership, and you, the public, need to work on reducing ... levels of crime and disorder ... [T]o enable us to act on your behalf and to tackle these issues, we need you to tell us what is happening. The issues are occurring in your neighbourhood, affecting you and your neighbours and most likely, caused by those who live in the neighbourhood or by visitors.

In this letter, the police conjured a community of allies, defined as the 'wider partnership' and the public, against which images of the enemy from within were constructed. In short, we can see how the 'law-and-order state' that was legislatively ushered into existence from the late 1990s onwards was enacted on England's council estates: through a rhetoric of vulnerability and threat of crime that discursively projected a distinction between a law-abiding, respectable public of suffering citizens, and a criminal underclass. How does the vulnerable citizen imagined by the policy-makers of this punitive turn sit with the consumer–citizen of neoliberal policy-making? And what can the history provided in this chapter tell us about projects of state-building on council estates more broadly? The conclusion will turn to these questions.

Conclusion

Dominant narratives and analysis have seen the turn to 'law and order' as exceptional and new. The present moment, marked by its turn towards more exclusive modes of governance, is constructed not only as an aberration from an earlier period of post-war democracy, but also as displaying an unwelcome leaning towards what I call a politics of lawfare instead of that of welfare. This chapter has offered a different starting point, one which acknowledges both differences as well as continuities across time and across social and penal policy-making. In order to do so, it has asked what happens when the turn to 'law and order' is placed within a longer trajectory of state governance. Council estates provide an excellent case study: built largely in the postwar decades, the state has never receded but always loomed large in the everyday lives of working class tenants. Neoliberalism has not resulted in a withdrawal of the authorities. Whether the state's presence is defined in terms of the agents of post-war paternalistic welfare, the bureaucratic agents of the neoliberal state, or from the late 1990s onwards, the representatives of 'law and order', people on council estates have always been monitored and policed through a variety of agents that cut across welfare and criminal justice.

My argument has been that council estates have never simply been places of dwelling for the working classes: rather, they are also sites where the state, via its local authorities and those that state-like responsibilities have been outsourced to, has enacted projects of statecraft through the construction of 'respectable' citizens. But what constitutes a 'respectable' citizen has changed with prevailing political and economic conditions over time. In the post-war decades, when Britain's welfare state was being consolidated and built, paternalistic policies were geared towards the creation of the nuclear family home. The 'respectable' citizen as council estate tenant was the male breadwinner with his dependent wife and children. With the shift to neoliberal policies in the 1980s, the status and form of council housing changed. Once a marker of social inclusion, a certification of a citizen's worthiness, albeit heavily policed, access to council housing became a mark of inadequacy and failure to meet worthiness. The boundaries of citizenship became redrawn to define anybody who was unable to buy into the dream of private ownership as a threat to respectability. Under the New Labour government's reign, the discourse shifted again, as the idealized citizen of policy-making was reconstructed as the crime fighter and the victim of crime. Respectability became collapsed with vulnerability to threats (Ramsay, 2012). In Comaroff and Comaroff's words, a 'metaphysics of disorder, of transgression and malfeasance' became central to political discourse which allowed politicians to craft a narrative of 'what and who they are, and where, in the process of becoming, their history has taken them' (2016: 69).

For citizens who live on council estates, the turn to 'law and order' under New Labour meant a perhaps paradoxical expansion of the categories of entitlement and citizenship. Those who were unable to live up to the consumerist dream of private ownership could now make claims to recognition based on their inherent vulnerability to others. However, this expansion should not be seen as constituting a radical break with the past, still less as an emancipation from more exclusionary models of citizenship. As Ramsay has argued, the assumptions about vulnerable citizenship present in the criminal justice system under New Labour were already an axiomatic proposition of political theories in the 1980s and 1990s that have enjoyed influence 'precisely because that axiom offers a normative basis for the duties of citizenship in circumstances in which others have failed' (2012: 112; Chapter 6). This chapter has traced the sociological logic behind this claim: just as neoliberal policy-making in the 1980s effected the expansion of welfare benefits to those previously excluded by certifying their worthlessness as economic agents, so the 'law-and-order' state incorporated working-class citizens as subjects in need of heightened policing and protection. In both cases, Park End residents became identified through their alleged inadequacies, even failures. But this meta-narrative was never fully accepted by those at the margins. The next chapter will introduce a story parallel to the historical narrative provided thus far: how citizens on council estates have always brought their own understandings of morality and personhood to the table, thus challenging the state's claim to be the arbiter of rightful citizenship. This chapter will set the backdrop against which the subsequent chapters develop the notion a different kind of failure to that of the failing citizen assumed by the state: the failures of government to be accountable to citizens on their own terms.

2

The Good Person and the Bad Citizen: History, Class, and Sociality

On a summer's day in 2009, during my time as a volunteer in the local community centre on Park End, Tracey decided to help residents with curriculum vitae (CV) writing. CVs were required when applying for jobs, but, equally important, they were required as part of welfare claimants' regular benefit assessments. In order to receive continued benefit payments, welfare recipients typically had to prove that they were actively looking for work—and the proof they were expected to produce was a CV to show to a work adviser at one of their regular consultations at the jobcentre, the agency administering their benefit payments. Many local residents did not have the skills or, indeed, a computer at home, which they could use to meet this requirement; they would come to the centre, looking distressed about the task they had been set. 'I don't have anything to put on it', women sometimes complained. Tracey challenged them: had they not successfully raised kids? Did they not look after their grandchildren? Did they do any voluntary work in the local community? She made clear that when she got her job in the local community centre (a position that was funded by the local council), she had put on top of her CV that she was proud to have raised her teenage son and manage a household while studying and working part-time: 'It's the most important thing I've achieved in my life, and I'm bloody proud of it', she once said.

When Tracey helped residents, their faces would light up. Vicky, a white English woman in her forties, was one of them. She was going through a particularly difficult time when she came to inquire about Tracey's CV clinic: her partner was in prison, her son had been expelled from school, and social services were threatening to take her grandchildren into care. Her youngest son was about to turn six, and according to the rules of the benefit

Personalizing the State: The Anthropology of Law, Politics and Welfare at the UK's Margins. First Edition. Insa Koch. © Insa Koch 2018. Published 2018 by Oxford University Press.

system[1], she now risked the loss of her benefit payments if she could not prove that she was actively seeking work. Tracey sat down with Vicky, using her own CV as a template; about half an hour later, Tracey had finished Vicky's CV and printed it on an A4 page. The top line stated that Vicky was a mother of two and a grandmother of three and was skilled at managing her large family and household. It said that Vicky enjoyed volunteering for the local community and followed this introduction with a brief résumé of the school Vicky had attended and various low-paid jobs she had in the past. Vicky had tears in her eyes, when Tracey handed her the CV, and she thanked Tracey profusely. As she left the centre, said: 'I feel like I'm a proper person now—thank you!'

In Chapter 1, I asked what a historical and ethnographic focus on state–citizen relations can reveal about the legacy of state coercion in the history of the post-war British state. Here, I once more take state–citizen relations as my point of departure, but examine them from the reverse perspective: how those at the receiving end of state control have acted upon their own distinct desires to create family homes and neighbourhoods, drawn their own boundaries of inclusion and exclusion, and articulated expectations of the state in the process. I ask: how do dominant categories of respectability and decency feature in people's daily lives on Park End and what alternative values do they ascribe to personhood? How do Park End residents construct themselves as subjects of value in the face of persistent stigma and negative labelling? And, finally, what implications does this have for the way they engage with the authorities? My focus is on the Park End mothers with whom I lived and who I encountered in my research in the community centre. I do not claim that their views exhaust the experiences of all residents on Park End. However, their their daily care work is exemplary of the broader dilemmas that residents experience between their own attempts to be good persons and their engagements with outsiders, including state and state-like agents, such as the jobcentre in the example outlined above.[2]

My argument is that as subjects of state coercion, residents of Park End have never simply accepted the state's own criteria of

---

[1] The rules changed again with the welfare reforms introduced under the Conservative-led government that was voted into power in 2010.

[2] It is for this reason that I also speak of 'residents' in general rather than just about women.

deservingness and the categories of legal and moral inclusion implied by them. On the contrary, they produce their own counterpoint understandings of what it means to be a good person that is embedded in their daily pursuits for homes and neighbourhoods. What is more, there is an intimate relationship between the 'proper person' (someone who behaves appropriately) and the 'proper citizen' (someone deserving of the full array of appropriate claims on the state): from the point of view of my informants at least, it is precisely through their particularistic and localized commitments of care that deservingness to the state's benefits is also asserted. Yet, citizens' ability to bring their own understandings of personhood and citizenship in line with those of the state have differed over time. In the post-war decades, paternalistic policies on council estates that merged with tenants' own aspirations for nuclear family homes ensured a fragile moral union between citizens and the state. It was only in the decades that followed, as the state's language of undeservingness was extended to entire estates and their residents, that the fragile moral union between citizens and the state was explicitly brought under attack. Today, Park End residents find that their own understandings of what makes a good person, and by extension a good citizen are ignored by, and in some cases directly feed, into the same processes that also mark them out as potentially 'bad' citizens in the eyes of the state.

Sociological work on class and care and ethnographies in the anthropology of post-industrial life have moved away from the pathologizing narratives of working-class people in the media and certain strands of academic scholarship by drawing attention to alternative 'political ontologies of the self' (Koch, 2017c; Skeggs, 2011; Skeggs and Loveday, 2012). I build on calls to attend to more diverse 'political ontologies of the self' by drawing attention to an aspect that has hitherto received little attention: how, on a council estate in England, local understandings of what makes a good person bear on the kinds of claims people make—as citizens—on the state. This allows me to correct two prevailing assumptions of citizen–state relations: first, that it is the state which is the sole arbiter of the form and content of citizenship (de Koning, Jaffe, and Koster, 2015); and second, that liberal democracies are defined by a uniform acceptance of this state-sponsored imagination. On the contrary, it is by virtue of the divergence between state moral person and local moral person, that local claims to personhood exceed the state's political theory of citizenship: of what citizenship *is* and of the state's own priority of citizenship over personhood. If the bestowal or withholding of citizenship is the weapon of the state, then citizens' reserve of citizenship on condition of moral personhood, and on *local* moral personhood, constitutes a different kind of weapon: an oppositional fight against the state's legitimacy.

History, Class, and Alternative Personhood Values

The reasons why women like Tracey or Vicky find it imperative to construct their own identities as mothers and residents that diverge from dominant social models of 'deservingness' on the one hand, and 'scrounging' on the other, should not come as a surprise: as we will see again and again in the course of this book, working-class people in general, and women in particular, live their daily lives in the shadow of others who judge them harshly. In much of the media, and in certain strands of academic writing, working-class people are attacked with images of their own imagined lack: their status and identity as a class is defined by their failure to live up to middle-class identities—that is to say, the standards of virtue and respectability enforced by the middle classes (Jones, 2011; Lawler, 2000; Skeggs and Loveday, 2012; I. Tyler, 2015; K. Tyler, 2015). Narratives of this fundamental lack are invoked in different ways. In much of the media, they are 'visualized through clothing, location and bodily appearances of working class people that are all designed to indicate a deeper underlying pathology' (Lawler, 2005: 432), and they resurface in images of particular places, spaces, and neighbourhoods as sites of pathos and decline (Hanley, 2007; Rogaly and Taylor, 2009). We saw in the previous chapter, for example, that politicians frequently depict council estates as 'ghettoes', inhabited by 'chavs' or 'chav mums' (Tyler, 2008), terms used to describe the white working class and that stand for, among other things, 'council house and violent' (K. Tyler, 2015). Black urban youth, by contrast, are commonly conflated with images of gangs and violence in dominant media representations (Malik and Nwonka, 2017).

The axiomatic moral denigration of working-class people, and council estate inhabitants in particular, has also been reproduced in some of the sociological scholarship of working-class community life, albeit in different ways. The early generation of 'community studies' scholars couched the relocation of working-class people from the old urban industrial neighbourhoods to the postwar council estates in narratives of decline: the relocation was said to entail a shift from a 'neighbourhood centred' lifestyle to a 'family centred' one (Kuper, 1953; Mogey, 1956; Young and Willmott, 1957). Neighbourhood life, once marked by dense networks of matrifocal support and care, was said to have given way to a more private existence, damaging working-class values in the process. Three decades later, similar discourses of moral deterioration and crisis resurfaced. As Lawler (2005) points out, sociologists came to link the collapse of industries and their associated livelihoods to an alleged loss in the worth of the working class—a troubling association that loops together the decline in workers' value production with a diminishing value of working-class people themselves. As the earlier generation of sociologists had analysed a shift from the neighbourhood to the nuclear family, so these authors identified the demise of the nuclear family in favour of the disembedded individual (Charlesworth, 2000) and the rise of an 'underclass' (Dahrendorf, 1989; Murray, 1996).

Despite important differences between (and within) the two bodies of sociological work that are separated by a generation, they share important overlaps. Like the state-centric accounts of the punitive turn the last chapter describes, they have tended to rest on a linear narrative of decay, one which locates a romanticized working class in the distant past, alleging the moral collapse of the contemporary working class whose defining characteristic is its fall from some earlier state of grace. They suggest timeless working-class kinship and social patterns (Mollona, 2009: 70) which inculcate virtue and 'authentic' values, and, as Savage points out (2016: 62), their inability to live up to these ideals in the present is taken as proof of a contemporary degeneracy. To the extent that they conjure a static, ahistorical image of working-class social relations (whether these are identified as matrifocal networks or nuclear household relations) that have been abandoned, each body of writing therefore tends to gloss over the fact that social relations do not operate outside particular economic and political structures, or indeed, the specific forms of domination those structures engender. If at various moments patterns of working-class sociality resemble each other, this is due not to relative degrees of fidelity to an 'authentic' model of working-class relationships, but should be understood rather in connection with

History, Class, and Alternative Personhood Values 63

the broader social and political landscapes in which they are embedded and to which they relate. The predominance of a romantic narrative of an 'authentic working-class' should come as no surprise. As Kalb points out (2015), it might well be down to the historical association of class with the largely white and male Fordist industrial class: hence, 'when industry began to fade from view, commentators often concluded that class itself was finally, and fortunately, disappearing' (2015: 3; see also Carbonella and Kasmir, 2015). And yet, the 'death of the idea of class in the West', reinforced through the rise of neoliberalism that placed the economic individual at the centre of focus, is contradicted by 'really existing world history' (ibid.), including the proletarization of large populations on a global scale and the concomitant rise in inequality and its related problems (Friedman, 2003; Kalb, 2011; Narotksy, 2016). In Britain itself, more recent sociological engagements have also re-introduced a focus on history, power, and domination. Correcting a sense that class and classed identities have receded in relevance as lenses of sociological analysis, this literature has looked at how class continues to exist in hidden ways, drawing on Pierre Bourdieu's work on misrecognition and the 'naturalization' of power through symbolic violence (Lawler, 2000; Mckenzie, 2015; Reay and Lucey, 2000; Skeggs, 1997). Indeed, the very recession of class in general, and the working class in particular, as explicit discursive categories is analysed as a symptom of their ongoing force. Here, the absence of class as a form of positive identity reflects processes of misidentification, whereby those at the margins learn to adopt a particular world view that is legitimized by the dominant middle classes: as Skeggs (1997) showed forcefully in her study of a group of working class mothers, class was something that the women tried to distance themselves from, a presence in the negative.[3]

---

[3] Similarly, for Savage, Bourdieu's concept of misrecognition resolves what he has termed the 'paradox of class'; that is, how an increase in social inequality has been accompanied by a decrease in people's subjective class membership (2016: 67). Among a group of northern middle-class people, Savage found that categories of class were generally eschewed when talking about their own lives in favour of more complex narratives of social mobility and achievement (Savage, Bagnall, and Longhurst, 2001).

But at the same time as working-class people (and their middle-class counterparts) are caught up in processes of dis-identification and misrecognition, their repertoire of experiences is never exhausted by dominant categories alone. Working-class people also draw upon alternative sources of value in the face of stigma imposed on them by outsiders (Gillies, 2007; Lawler, 2000; Mckenzie, 2015; Reay and Lucey, 2000). Skeggs has argued for a recognition of personhood values that provides a different 'political ontology of the self' to that projected by individualism. This is not a matter of reviving ahistorical or static notions of working-class patterns but rather of recognizing that interdependence and mutual relations of care constitute crucial strategies of survival for working-class people today. 'Living with precarity produces different orientations towards others', she writes; 'keeping an eye out for others has sound economic reasons where insecurity is on the horizon, pre-disposing [people] to different forms of sociality than individualism' (2011: 507). Meanwhile, anthropologists of Britain have scrutinized how extensive kinship networks and localized forms of belonging continue to persist in the face of struggle (Degnen, 2012; Evans, 2006; Smith, 2017b; K. Tyler, 2012; 2015). Edwards (2000) has demonstrated that residents in the northern town of Bacup continue to make connections not only between people but between people and places, including houses, factories, pubs, and streets through particular claims of knowing, while Mollona (2009) has looked at the fluid practices of cohabitation and sharing central to some of his informants' lives in Sheffield.

In this chapter, I analyse how residents on council estates have formed social relations inside and outside the home over time; the moral values these relations engender and embody; and the points of their convergence and divergence with dominant assumptions made by policy-makers and local authorities. By identifying the points of connection and disconnection between local personhood and local citizenship, as well as between local personhood and official citizenship across different periods of time, this chapter extends the ethnographic endeavour so poignantly summarized by Danny Miller (1988) as studying the 'state on the council estate'. To parallel the chronology already introduced in the last chapter, I turn first to life in the council estates of the post-war decades, when differences between the state's and tenants' own aspiration were obscured, perhaps even minimized, by paternalistic and patriarchal values embodied in welfare policies that prioritized the British, white, male-headed household as the unit and emblem of respectability. I refer to this as a fragile, intensely gendered and racialized, moral union between citizens and the state. Second, I examine the decline of the nuclear family household, both as a policy ideal and as a lived experience. An analysis of this historical trajectory with attention to the experiences of citizens rather than the policies of the state reveals a fracturing of the moral union in the decades that followed, as policies came to present council estate tenants, and their living arrangements, as evidence of failure and lack. The final part illustrates how local conceptions of personhood that are radically out of sync with those drawn up by official policies continue to persist.

A Fragile Moral Union Between Citizens and the State

In the 1950s and 1960s, as the 'classical' industrial neighbourhoods were torn down under slum clearance schemes and many council estates erected, analysts portrayed the relocation of workers and their families to the newly built estates as marking a shift from a 'neighbourhood-centred' ideal to a 'family-centred one' (Harrell-Bond, 1967; Kuper, 1953; Mogey, 1956; Young and Willmott, 1957). In the old neighbourhoods, sociologists had reported the importance of extended matrifocal networks of support and care that created close ties between neighbours and kin; by contrast, as the workers and their families were moved to the newly built estates, they were also said to retreat from the structures of sociability that had been so central to the earlier industrial working class. Young and Willmott, in their study of relocated workers from London's former East End, recorded residents complaining that there was no 'neighbourliness' in the new surroundings: 'You seem to centre yourself more on the home', one person reported. 'Everybody lives in a little world of their own' (1957: 119). Similarly, Mogey quoted a resident who had been rehoused from the old industrial neighbourhood of St Ebbes' to the council estate of Barton in Oxford: 'In Barton, everything is new and there is no neighbourlihood' (1956: 85).

Mogey's 1956 account of the Oxford estate testifies to the prevalence of this newer, more private, 'home-oriented working class culture' (Ravetz, 2001), defined in large part through a gendered division of labour. Residents were repeatedly reported saying that they 'keep themselves to themselves' and do not 'mix with others' (Harrell-Bond, 1967: 293; Mogey, 1956: 83), and they took pride in pursuing this style of domestic life. According to Mogey, the long list of household and family attributes deemed to be 'respectable' included: to have a wife who is a good cook or a husband who brings home a steady wage; for the house to be tidy; to have a one-child family; to keep the children inside the house and garden; to dress neatly; to be clean in person; to have no debts; to keep one's affairs to oneself; to have a well-kept garden; to value privacy; and to have a lawn with flowers in the front of the house and vegetables at the back (Mogey, 1956: 144–5). The ideal of home-centred living was, moreover, becoming enmeshed with a new culture of consumerism afforded by a rise in living standards and higher wages. Residents strove to acquire items for their homes, including a television, a 'wireless' (radio), new kitchen appliances, carpets in the house, and fancy clothes, as well as objects of value, including porcelain dolls (Harrell-Bond, 1967: 293; Kuper, 1953: 71; Mogey, 1956: 144). Sought-after ornaments were placed in full view of the neighbours; Kuper noted in 1953 porcelain figurines arranged on the windowsill, with their 'hindquarters turned to the family and the glittering front to the window' (1953: 71).

The residents on the post-war council estates, with their strongly gendered practices of home-centred living, were examples of what Goldthorpe et al. famously referred to as the 'affluent worker' (1968) who benefited from a political economy of state-controlled capitalism, including high wages, full employment, and a post-war welfare state. This is perhaps best illustrated in post-war practices of conspicuous consumption, in the ways consumer items mediated relations between people as indices of respectability whose subtlety and potency demanded careful attention and vigilance. Indeed, it was the 'conspicuousness' itself that assumed as much importance as the increased scale of 'consumption': the necessity of displaying consumer articles such that their full significance could be perceived and deciphered. In her study of the Blackbird Leys estate in Oxford, Barbara Harrell-Bond reported that women were fearful of the 'gossiping', 'preying', and the 'watchful eyes' of their close neighbours. They were 'copying' one another in putting up clean clothes on the washing line (1967: 293), in 'providing as much pocket money, toys etc. for your children as [were] given to those next door' (ibid.), and in polishing 'front door, knocker, keyhole, front doorstep, and grate' (Mogey, 1956: 143). She observed that 'Neighbours were accused of being jealous of cars, clean houses, fancy underwear hanging on the clothes line, neat gardens, new appliances for the house, children's toys, and carpets on the floor' (Harrell-Bond, 1967: 293).

However, it is a mistake to conclude that desires for material improvement and the associated quest for middle-class standards of living on the post-war estates reflect a complete break with earlier patterns of community, let alone the absence of sociability itself. As Strathern (1992) has argued, respectability is a means by which morality is rendered public, and hence the object of communal judgement. While the early generation of sociologists had been quick to read the importance of home-centred practices as evidence of community and neighbourhood decline, privacy was not necessarily opposed to sociability. For example, Mogey likened the allotment that husbands on the Barton estate used to work on during weekends to 'something much more than just a place to grow vegetables, [...] it is in a sense a married men's club' (1956: 30). Harrell-Bond wrote of informal group savings schemes for clothing and household goods, and of women leaving their weekly rent payments with their neighbours to pass on to the rent collector. In oral history interviews, it was precisely the collective spirit of communal celebrations, such as bonfire nights, fancy dress parties, street parties on Coronation day, and day trips to the beach, that were most fondly remembered. A white English mother and daughter who were among the first residents to move to Park End in the late 1950s told me:

Daughter: Everybody in the street used to meet up at the top of the street, everybody would take fireworks along, and the older boys used to build massive bonfires on the street. You used to know everybody, it was sort of like a party really, wasn't it? And then right at the very end of the road, there used to be like a track. And it used to be cycle races and they used to come from all over the place for it ...

Mother: Yes, that's right, and did you know about the wooden huts? It used to be a community centre. In them days, we enjoyed it. In the evenings, all the young teenagers used to come with their records, and then mothers and fathers mostly around here used to be what they call 'the committee' and we all took turns in doing things, like going behind the bar to serve cold drinks and tea, and they used to be good nights, didn't they?

The women capture here the social character of neighbour relations commonly reported in the 'classical' industrial neighbourhoods that was replicated rather than eradicated between tenants on the post-war estates.

But the tendency towards nostalgia for social relations as an object for mourning stands to be corrected on yet other grounds. Not only did relations endure rather than vanish, but they were neither free of tensions, nor inherently benevolent. Social divisions could cut deep as tenants expressed punitive sentiments towards those who had fallen short of expected standards of respectability: 'problem families' where the male heads were unemployed or in prison, and had fallen into rent arrears, neighbours who were said to be making excessive noise, and families with unruly children (Harrell-Bond, 1967; Taylor and Rogaly, 2007). These complaints about neighbours who fell short of expected standards were often sharply racialized. Harrell-Bond's study of the Blackbird Leys estate in Oxford reports how racial prejudices informed neighbour relations on the post-war estates, resulting in the exclusion of families of Afro-Caribbean descent from the usual neighbourhood sociality: 'the expressions of antagonism towards the increasing numbers of coloured immigrants being housed on the estate, the number of parents who expressed ambivalence towards the idea of their children playing with coloured children, and the general condemnation of the several racially-mixed marriages which occur in the population' all suggested that 'this cleavage based on racial background profoundly influences neighbourhood relations' (1967: 273).

Harrell-Bond's examples illustrate how post-war tenants policed moral boundaries in their neighbourhoods through the pursuit of gendered practices of care and consumption, as well as through ostracizing and excluding from localized networks of sociability those who did not 'belong', both between and within different ethnic groups. Importantly, these endeavours did not operate in isolation from the state. As we saw in the last chapter, tenants were acting within a dominant political climate that prioritized the nuclear, white working-class family and that facilitated the process of enlisting the post-war welfare state in their daily endeavours to create neighbourhoods and homes they considered to be 'nice' for living. Far from seeing the state as an alien entity that was governing them from afar, residents integrated their own moral assumptions of what made a good neighbour and family—the necessary boundaries of inclusion and exclusion—into their demands and expectations of the post-war state. In oral history interviews, older white English residents recalled with appreciation figures of paternalistic care who came to their homes to check if 'anything needed doing' and to carry out any outstanding repair and maintenance work: the rent collector, the housing inspector, and other local authority officials that were identified in the last chapter as mechanisms of state control. Similarly, in the post-war literature, residents were quoted showing their satisfaction with the selective housing policies that were in operation: 'There's nobody in these houses who isn't nice', one woman told Mogey, 'If somebody who wasn't—well, you know—and they had to be given a house, they wouldn't put them around here: they'd give them a house in another part of the estate' (1956: 23).

Expectations for state support and care also translated into demands for policing and punitive attitudes towards those who were seen as a threat to common standards of decency. Rogaly and Taylor (2009) have observed how 'thrust into a world of mass council housing, working class tenants expanded their existing support networks to include officials in their range of strategies for accessing the services of the welfare state and for managing neighbour problems' (2009: 120). Harrell-Bond's study of Blackbird Leys gives an insight into what this meant: residents pressured the council to agree to a housing exchange 'when some unpleasant incident ... occurred which made relationships in the neighbourhood more difficult. In one case the husband had just returned from serving a jail sentence and in another case the husband committed adultery with a next-door neighbour' (1967: 32). In Mogey's study of the post-war Barton estate in Oxford, a female resident also expressed concern that the neighbourhood was overrun by disreputable characters. This resident made clear that it would be the role of the local authorities to ensure that these people would be carefully supervised and managed so as to ensure that his neighbourhood would not be dragged down yet further:

You ought to walk round here in the daylight and see the place, it's overrun by dogs, cats, everything except pigs and horses are allowed to wander at large. I know people keep dogs in upstairs flats to the great inconvenience of the people underneath and against the council rules. There's a lot of rough customers in this area. Mind you, I think that mixing the people of all types is a very good idea. People who have known nothing better must be given a chance to improve themselves. But it is therefore up to the council to supervise these people very carefully otherwise they will drag decent people down their level. (1956: 85)

Enlisting the post-war paternalistic structures into the maintenance of moral neighbourhoods and their boundaries was not an unequivocal endeavour. Power relations continued to run strong, as illustrated in the cases where residents felt unable to appropriate the state's own structures and mechanisms of enforcing 'respectability'. For instance, Rogaly and Taylor's analysis of a council estate in Norwich shows that residents who had been labelled 'problem families' by social services often expressed bitterness and anger about the onerous regime of surveillance that was imposed upon them (2009: 120 ff.). Similarly, Harrell-Bond (1967) notices that some of the young mothers mistrusted the health officials who would call around to houses with newborn babies. One woman told Harrell-Bond that, in matters relating to her child's welfare, she would seek help from her own mother rather than a health official. And Mogey mentions the case of an elderly woman who refused to open the door when a researcher from his team arrived to conduct an interview: the woman feared that the researcher would turn out to be from the church or a public authority official (1956: 23).

Mollona argues that 'the history of working-class families is strictly interrelated with the trajectories of state capitalism: welfare capitalism standardized factory production, nationalized the economy, targeted nuclear family households as recipients of public entitlement and put the family at the centre of working-class respectability' (2009: 69). On the post-war council estates, this intimacy between political economy and the family, mediated by particular codes of 'respectability', gave rise to a constellation between citizens and the state that we can call a fragile moral union, one that reflected a mutual embrace of the dominant post-war values of the white, male-headed, wage-earning nuclear household. As housing inspectors and rent officials engaged in paternalistic forms of housing management in the newly built and often generously sized council houses, so tenants were engaging in a quest for respectable living that was driven by a climate of full employment, consumption, and general affluence; as selective housing policies excluded anybody the authorities considered to fall short of their own standards of respectability, tenants policed their neighbourhood relations through gossiping, prying, and ostracizing. These shared moral endeavours also meant that the highly uneven power relations between tenants and the post-war authorities were masked or hidden, although by no means in all situations.

What is more, as the next section will show, the fragile moral union came under attack in the decades that followed, as Britain moved towards financialization, industrial decline, and welfare retraction. With shifts in the political economy, classed relations between citizens and the authorities were reinforced and brought more explicitly to the fore, with dramatic consequences for those living on council estates.

A Moral Union Under Attack

Across the country, sociologists and journalists of the 1980s and 1990s began to depict the working class in states of crisis, and white working-class people came to be presented increasingly in terms of images of a pathological 'underclass' devoid of the old relations of family and kinship life that had once been central to the industrial neighbourhoods. Some focused on the decline of the nuclear family household (Campbell, 1993; Dench, Gavron, and Young, 2006; Dennis and Erdos, 1999). Others identified the figure of the single mother as an indicator of a rising underclass (Dahrendorf, 1989; Murray, 1996). Yet others identified intergenerational conflicts as the source of a putative breakdown of family values (Campbell, 1993; Charlesworth, 2000). As the post-war literature of community studies had done, this second generation of scholars presented a working class that was unable to adapt to change, invoking and reproducing the image of a vanishing 'authentic' working class that was increasingly located in the distant past, and a present state of stunted sociality. What was shared across these narratives of decline and working-class decay was a tendency to locate the failures within the working class itself and its self-abandonment. Even those who saw these changes as a consequence of broader structural changes following Thatcherite economics still located the rise of a pathological culture within the working class once said to be more 'respectable' and intact.

But the reality of moral lives and social bonds was more complex. Residents on the increasingly post-industrial estates were trying to come to terms with the impact of unemployment, increasing welfare dependence, and material hardship that had been largely absent from the post-war decades. Take the example of Reynolds' (1986) account of Omega estate, the estate in the Midlands originally built for the workers of a local car factory. By the early 1980s, the decline in industrial manufacturing had started to affect factory production, driving up unemployment to almost 20 per cent among the male working population and exposing the resident population to new experiences of hardship and poverty. Residents told the researcher that they could no longer cope without the help of welfare institutions. Even with the financial support of the benefit system, people struggled to make ends meet. One family with four children and an unemployed male head was quoted as saying: 'We can't afford to go out. We spend £18 on rent (of which £2.40 was arrears), £13 on the electricity meter, £10 on the buses to town, a bit on the gas, and that doesn't leave enough to live on when you've bought food and you can't have the children going without' (1986: 43). Another male resident said:

> It's this government, soon there'll be nothing, a man out of work, how will he start again after two or three years on the dole? It's worse for those trying to be good and respectable. When unemployment is bad, people get money trouble and go out and steal. You want to be seen that you can provide for your family. (1986: 45)

The material assault of people's livelihoods on the once relatively homogenous well-off working-class estate had intimate effects on people's lives: it was experienced as a moral affront to people's sense of value and self-worth, 'worse for those trying to be good and respectable' as Reynold's source put it. Shame and loss of self-respect—the pain of being in financial distress—was also reported by other residents Reynolds interviewed. One woman admitted that a neighbour called her unemployed husband a 'scrounger', with the result that he now avoided going out socially: '[H]e's never got over that. He had an accident and every now and again his back goes. He's a really hard worker and he was very upset so he never bothered with anyone after that' (1986: 44). Others tried to set themselves apart from those they considered to be less deserving. Residents invoked images of disreputable 'others' who were dragging down their neighbourhood, including the unemployed, 'single mothers', and teenagers who were 'allowed to run wild'. 'I don't like the type of family living here', one man told the researcher. 'The children are picking up bad language from the other children' (ibid.: 62). Others mentioned not feeling safe on the estate, that they avoided going out at night, and wanted more police presence (ibid.: 77–94).

Narratives of moral crisis and blame were not restricted to council estate tenants in the 1980s. On Park End today, older, predominantly British and white residents often recalled the period in the 1980s as the time when the community changed and when their estate began to be transformed. What stood out in these narratives is that, very much like the residents that Reynolds interviewed thirty years ago, change was inextricably associated with the figure of the 'other'—with outsiders who were set apart from oneself, including 'single mothers,' large families, and the homeless. 'The estate changed when they built the other part of the estate [containing large blocks of flats]', Dorothy, a white elderly resident, recalled. 'There was people who moved there and they didn't work. And they couldn't care less about their houses and their kids. They would let them run riot and stuff.' Others invoked the 'single mother' as a trope of decline: 'Over where they built the flats', Molly, another white resident, said, 'they are quite, I shouldn't say it, but they are quite rough. There's girls there with one, two, three babies, no husbands, just a boyfriend comes in. It's that type of girl that lives around there. That's where a lot of trouble is. We're lucky down here.' Still other residents complained about homeless people being placed on Park End at a time when the addition of maisonettes and flats meant that many single people were moved to the estate to occupy its smaller properties.

By placing blame with 'others', whom they located outside the symbolic boundaries of their community, residents like Dorothy and Molly were deflecting the stigma that was directed towards people precisely like them. In the same conversation I had with Dorothy, it emerged that her own daughter had split up from the partner of her children and was living in a street nearby. Dorothy was looking after the grandchildren several times a week, while her daughter went out to work as a cleaner in a nearby Science Park. Molly told me later on in the interview that her husband, a Polish man, had been made redundant when the factory downsized its work force in the 1980s, leaving the family 'hard up' as he struggled to find work. Yet, for her, her husband's unemployment was different from that of other people on the estate whom she blamed for their unwillingness to work. Howe (1990) made a similar observation about the co-existence of apparently mutually exclusive discourses among unemployed male workers in Northern Ireland. He writes: 'one of the most interesting features of their derogatory statements about other unemployed is that these are nearly always linked, directly or indirectly, to much more positive descriptions of themselves, particularly their own strong desire for work' (ibid.: 2). Strathern outlined the dynamics of this complicated ascription of blame and sympathy, remarking that in the working-class village of Elmdon 'at one level meanings may be shared—as to what the implications of being an insider or outsider are—while at another—to what category this label applies—they may not' (1992: 46).

For Skeggs (1997), these examples of moral distancing are indicative of a process whereby the targets of class stigma and labelling accept the categories of the dominant powers and become complicit in processes of symbolic violence associated with it. We saw in the last chapter that the 1980s were the decade when stigma and labelling of council estates and their inhabitants became more explicitly pronounced. I argued there that this shift was due to the moral reconceptualization of council housing (and the 'respectable' working classes for whose purpose it had been built), from something that had denoted inclusion (although heavily policed), to one of exclusion, as council tenancy became synonymous with undeservingness and lack. Council estate tenants were regularly presented in the media and public policy discourses as citizens whose claims as citizens were contemptuously dismissed: they were persons whose insufficient economic value as a producer, consumer, and property-owner defined their insignificant moral and civic value. The last chapter also showed that the changes that took place in the 1990s and 2000s as policy shifted towards the 'law-and-order state' failed to redress these processes of stigma; if anything, the moral stakes damning council house tenancy climbed even higher, as council tenants became habitually associated not only with their vulnerability but also with crime, disorder, and violent breakdown.

Park End residents today have grown up with these negative associations. Very early on in my fieldwork, I came to realize how strongly the stigma was felt by the mothers with whom I spent much of my time. One day, a few months after I had arrived in Park End, I was sitting around the large table in the community centre with Tracey, and her friend Irie, a local mother of three young boys, of mixed-race white and Afro-Caribbean descent. We had been having a cup of tea, and Irie had been telling us with pride that she was studying towards a college certificate in youth work and only had a few more assignments to go before she would be able to graduate. Impressed by what she had managed to do while raising her children on her own, Tracey and I were asking Irie questions about her studies when three young women walked in. They were undergraduate architecture students from the local university, who had been instructed by their tutor to do a field project on 'urban decline and regeneration' on Park End. This was not unusual: students would sometimes be sent to the estate for field projects, causing resentment among residents who complained that they were sick of being used as 'guinea pigs' for 'experiments'.

Nonetheless, Tracey made an effort with them. The conversation was flowing reasonably well until the point when one of the women asked Tracey about how she felt about the bad reputation of the estate. At this point Irie, who until now had been silent, suddenly spoke up. Her face was tense but her voice firm when she launched into an agitated speech: 'on the estate there is fences everywhere, there is brick walls, rubbish, and places that are not really looked after. The postcode has a bad stigma: people don't wanna give their postcodes away because they know they won't get a job if they do.' She had been trying for years, she continued, to get a housing exchange for her socially rented property, but to no avail: other people on the housing swap list would see where her house was and refuse to move there because they were afraid of the estate. In schools, children from the estate were treated differently to people from other parts of the city. She had three sons (and was pregnant with her fourth child) and hated to think that this was the feeling they were growing up with. 'People are told here that they are not worth anything, that their lives don't matter. How are people ever meant to change and get out? It's a disempowering experience.' 'Wow Irie, you're making me cry', Tracey said into the silence that fell in the room when Irie had finished.

Journalist and social historian Hanley (2007) describes in her autobiographical narrative of council estate life that estate residents have 'walls in their head' (ibid.). The walls in people's heads mirror the physical barriers which they encounter in their daily lives as residents of stigmatized places and represent the profound division between their own lives and the actions of those with power over them. Irie's spontaneous speech captured the visceral consequences of being from a place that was considered a 'problem estate': the inability to get a housing swap, to find a job, to thrive in school because of prejudice from fellow students and teachers. And it spoke of how this social failure filtered into an acute sense of state failure and betrayal that will be further unpacked in the chapters that follow. We saw above that in the post-war decades, there was a moral overlap between a political ideology that saw eligibility to council housing as a confirmation of people's inclusion in hierarchically racialized and gendered citizenship, and citizens' own aspirations for decent homes. In the intervening decades this consensus was thoroughly dismantled—not by the extension of the fruits of citizenship to racial and sexual 'others' who had been placed outside the bounds of respectability, but by the very expansion of the grounds of 'otherness' and exclusion. However, as state control became ever-more present (and intimately felt), citizens also continued to draw on alternative moral tropes. The next section shows how these social relations provide an alternative basis for claims to moral personhood and civic value.

Alternative Processes of Value Accrual

Mollona (2009) has argued that while industrialization and the consolidation of the post-war welfare state nuclearized working-class families, de-industrialization and welfare deregulation have disposed working-class families towards more 'hybrid networks of friends, kin and parents fluidly moving between the spaces of "home" and the spaces of the "neighbourhood"' (ibid.: 77). These networks are neither static nor should they be idealized. The chapters that follow will show how neighbour relations continued to be fraught with tensions, and people often drew on the received tropes of upkeep, maintenance, and cleanliness to refer to others they consider to be falling short of communal standards. For example, my first host family consisted of a young white couple called Jane and Mark with four children (aged between six months and sixteen), both parents were working full time, Jane as a shop assistant in a large supermarket chain off the estate, and Mark as a lorry driver for a local building society. Mark often complained to me about neighbours who failed to look after their council house in the same manner as he and Jane did, despite the fact that they had full-time jobs and child care duties. 'They shouldn't be given council housing', was his opinion, 'if they don't look after it.' When walking with him across the estate, he would point at houses where the grass in the front garden was not cut, where there was rubbish lying around, or curtains missing in the front windows.

Mark made clear that to show care for one's home and by extension neighbourhood was a matter of maintaining homes, gardens, or apartment blocks. But it was also more than that: it required investment into people and social relations. 'People think it's a shithole', Mark once said, 'and yeah, it's true, it's not great here, is it? But then again, I wouldn't wanna live anywhere else, this is home for me.' Mark had grown up on an estate nearby but he and Jane had moved to their current house after their first son was born. They now had family living on the same street, the children had attended the local primary school, and Jane was sitting on the board of the community centre. She, the children, and Jane's mother also attended the local bingo night in the hall once a week and the children made use of the youth club and the IT hub on site. For other residents, 'home' also meant the intense familiarity of a neighbourhood that one had lived in for a long time and established multiple connections with. 'I like it because you always have someone to talk to, there's always someone around. I know everyone up here', Tracey once said. As we have already seen, Tracey was a local woman who was running a popular drop-in centre at the community centre. The practical implications of Tracey's claim were made clear to me when being out together: what should otherwise be a ten-minute walk from my house to the 'top shops' (the shops in the centre of the estate where many residents do their daily shopping) could easily turn into a half-hour stroll as Tracey would stop to greet passing residents, chat to neighbours, and inquire about the whereabouts and health of family and friends.

Tracey would tell me about how she knew the different people that she was greeting on the streets: through school, work, volunteering, and having family or friends in common. Tracey was proud of her Jamaican heritage (her parents had emigrated to England in the early 1960s), but her friendship and social circles were spread across racial divides, including her own family, friends, and godmother to her son, demonstrating the 'multi-cultural' realities of estate life (McKenzie, 2016). These connections not only linked Tracey to the individual biographies and relationships of other people but also demonstrated the importance of particular sites where she had spent time with them. They emphasized the importance of 'knowing' as a phrase and as a practice of asserting belonging, a point made in the ethnographic literature on Britain (Degnen, 2005, 2013; Edwards, 2000). Individual connections between people could also be scaled into a more general sense of belonging to the neighbourhood or what residents referred to as 'the estate'. People sometimes joked that their life on Park End was like in *EastEnders*,[4] referring to Park End people as 'ParkEnders'. Here, the reference to the TV show was meant to indicate both the closeness and intimacy of people who had a strong connection to a place and via a place to the people and 'drama' that came with it. 'It's a bit like a village up here', Tracey said to me on another occasion, 'there's always some gossip and sometimes it gets too much, but it never gets boring.'

Particularly for the mothers with whom I spent much of my time, fluid networks of care and support were integral to their attempts to build family homes, thus disavowing the normative assumptions of the white, male-headed household that had organized and regulated 'acceptable' sociality in the post-war decades. For Jane, for example, 'friends are the family you choose'. Her close friend Kate came by every day after work and stayed over some nights. Friends were people one called on for practically any favours. Tracey, for example, who was living with her 17-year-old son, would regularly threaten to kick him out of the house when he was misbehaving. While I had initially been shocked by what seemed like heartless acts, I soon realized that Tracey fully expected Mandy, her son's godmother and a local white woman, or her own mother, to put him up in their respective homes. Tracey, in turn, went to live with a friend in 2012, when she had fallen into rent arrears and needed to leave her house. Years later in 2016, she would take in her six-month-old grandchild, along with the mother of the child with whom her son had broken up and

---

[4] *EastEnders* is a TV soap opera that broadcasts the daily life of working-class people in London's East End. It was a popular show that many of my interlocutors watched. In my first host family, for example, *EastEnders* was the focal point for organizing social time and meals as the family would get together to watch the most recent episodes over a shared meal.

who was unwilling to take on caring duties. She also extended parenting support to include the moral education of her 17-year-old godson, Luke who was Mandy's mixed-race son. One evening, Luke had hit his mother in the face in the midst of an argument. Tracey ordered Luke to meet her in the pub the same night. She told me the next day:

> I got really shitty with him, I was so angry. I asked him: 'Have you ever thought about the consequences? Your mum could have died.' And [I told him] 'If you get pissed up [drunk] and that, then you have to deal with the consequences of it, it's no excuse whatsoever to say that you was pissed and that's why you did what you did!' [...] And his eyes started welling up. And then there was a bloke sat next to the table and he come over and he was like, it wasn't any of his business but like he'd overheard what we was saying, and he goes to Luke: 'I am 40 years old now, and I am sofa-dropping because I've lost everything, my wife, kids, house ... and the reason why I've lost everything is 'cos I never thought about my actions before I done them. If I can give you one bit of advice, then always think about the consequences of what you're doing first.'

Over half a century ago, Young and Willmott (1957) argued in their sociological study of the 'old' East End (the classical industrial neighbourhoods of London's working-class bastions) that 'the extended family was [...] the woman's trade union, the source of informal mutual aid for women and children, and for men too when they were in need of support' (ibid.: xiv). The examples of Tracey and Jane show that this was still very much the case on Park End today.

Connectedness was then a way of demonstrating personhood, and hence value. As such, it also provided the means by which people drew moral distinctions between insiders and outsiders, or, in the local vernacular, between an 'us' and 'them'. Commitments and moral obligations that connected people to one another and to a place provided the basis to advance claims for moral recognition on Park End. When Tracey helped Park End residents write their CV for employers and, more commonly, the benefit agency, they constructed narratives of personhood that revolved around residents' daily commitments of support and care: a person's status as a mother, a community volunteer, or a friend were precisely what made them stand out as what Vicky had referred to as a 'proper person' to themselves and others. Conversely, those who failed to display the requisite requirements that made a morally good neighbour, kin member, or tenant, were often harshly judged and seen as undeserving of all sorts of entitlement, including those sponsored by the state. We have already seen how Mark set himself apart from neighbours who he criticized for not looking after their houses adequately and who he considered to be undeserving of their homes. But accusations of undeservingness could also be directed towards family and friends where expectations for loyalty and care had been betrayed.

The following example illustrates the point that where moral personhood was in doubt, claims to citizenship—entitlements to benefits and protection from legal jeopardy—were equally uncertain. I had been staying with Jane and her family for two months, and Jane had slowly started integrating me into her social life, inviting me along to her weekly bingo games in the community centre and introducing me to her friends. One night, we had gone to bingo together with Jane's children. I noticed that Jane did not greet her neighbour and close friend, Tina, a white resident in her late thirties, upon arrival, nor did she pay any attention to Tina's four children. This was highly unusual: Tina's children were frequently playing in Jane's house and Jane's own children often went over to Tina's in turn. Tina would frequently come by Jane's house before bingo night and the two women would walk together to the community centre, catching up on the week's news and happenings in the neighbourhood, and talking about their children and mutual friends. That night, however, the atmosphere was frosty between the two women. Throughout the evening, Jane made rude comments to me and her mother about Tina's children: their clothes were dirty, they smelled, and their behaviour was unruly. She instructed her own 6-year-old daughter not to play with them. At the end of the evening, Jane walked past Tina and hissed 'selfish cow'.

On the way home, I learned why Jane had been so angry: Tina had taken her ex-boyfriend, Darren, back into her house, even though her friends and family had persistently warned her not to. Darren had a history of violent behaviour towards her and her children, and at that time was on police bail, which banned him from going anywhere near Tina's home. Jane refused to speak to her friend until there was a fresh twist: a few weeks after the bingo incident, Tina came by Jane's house and demanded to speak to Jane. She told us that Darren had been arrested and taken away by the police earlier that day. Her 16-year-old daughter, Chloe, had reported Darren to the police, following an argument with

Tina. Tina had suspected Chloe of hiding an unwanted pregnancy and had threatened to kick her out of the house; in retaliation, Chloe had called the police about Darren's presence. Daily practices of calling the police into intimate disputes of the kind illustrated here will be further analysed in Chapter 5. What is of interest here is that Jane, who had been listening to Tina's account with a dispassionate face, told me later that she had been happy to hear about these developments. In fact, in the weeks leading up to this incident Jane had told me repeatedly that someone should 'grass up' Darren. She had told me that this would 'teach Tina a lesson' and make her think twice in the future.

At one level, the story demonstrates that intimacy was not only the place of unequivocal care and selfless love (cf. Geschiere, 2013) but a site of conflict and tensions, and that expectations to care engendered the gravest feelings of betrayal where these remain unmet. As Thiranagama and Kelly (2009) remark, '[a]ntagonism is produced not only between the citizen and the one who appears to be the different but among those who seem to be the same, those who, at first glance, seem to share the most intense sense of solidarity. Intimacy is not the antithesis of fear but can be at its core' (ibid.: 2). In this case, by placing her relationship with a man who was known to be violent above the safety and well-being of her children and ignoring the warnings of her friends, Tina had failed to honour her commitments towards those who mattered to her the most: her friends, her own children, and family. But there was more to Jane's falling-out with Tina: her failure to be a 'good' person in the eyes of her family members, neighbours, and friends had also disqualified Tina from being the rightful recipient of public benefits. Jane had made repeatedly clear in the aftermath that not only was Tina a 'scrounger' who was abusing the benefits system, but she was also someone who deserved to bear the brunt of the criminal law. Jane did not normally criticize people for being on welfare benefits, nor was she interested in upholding the law in the abstract: many of Jane's friends and family members were surviving on welfare benefits as we will see in Chapter 3 and, as we will see in Chapter 5, her own teenage son was routinely victimized by the police. Rather, her judgement of Tina as someone who was undeserving of support was contingent on her prior failure to act as a good person.

In short, everyday processes of labelling and stigma on Park End did not, then, exhaust the moral categories that residents themselves drew upon to establish themselves as persons of value. The mothers with whom I spent much of my time foregrounded their loyalties and commitments towards those who were closest to them to make claims to personhood and to set themselves apart from others who they considered to have failed. What are the broader implications of the ethnography presented in this section? How does it challenge the state's own priority of citizenship over personhood?

Conclusion

In the last chapter, I countered dominant narratives that see the shift to 'law and order' as an exceptional turn in the post-war history of state–citizen relations, arguing instead that council estates have always been places of state-building and control. In this chapter, I have provided a crucial supplement by analysing how those at the receiving end of this state control have acted upon their own desires to create family homes and neighbourhoods. Across much of the ethnographic scholarship on class and post-industrial life in Britain, sociologists (Gillies, 2007; Lawler, 2000; Mckenzie, 2015; Reay and Lucey, 2000; Skeggs, 2011) and anthropologists (Degnen, 2013; Edwards, 2000; Evans, 2006; Smith, 2017b; K. Tyler, 2015) have identified how people who are regularly victimized and policed by agents more powerful than themselves draw on alternative understandings of personhood and social relations to create 'value' for themselves. This scholarship has provided important correctives to received portrayals of working-class people in terms of images of pathos, pathology, and moral decline. In this chapter, I have joined these critical voices by drawing attention to an aspect that has hitherto received little attention: how on a council estate in England, local understandings of what makes a good person have a bearing on the kinds of claims that people make as citizens on the state.

My argument has been that people over whom the state attempts to exert control have never been simply passive recipients of the state's own categories of deservingness and respectability. On the contrary, even where on the face of it, they seem to be compliant with state discourses and moralities, they have always brought their own understandings of personhood to the table. But what constitutes a good person and citizen in peoples' eyes has changed in accordance with prevailing economic and political

Conclusion

conditions over time. On the post-war council estates, tenants' aspirations for nuclear family homes and neighbourhoods coincided with dominant welfare policies that were premised on the Fordist white, male-headed household, giving rise to a fragile gendered and racialized moral union between citizens and the state. Tenants tended to exclude those unwilling or unable to live up to such ideals from localized relations on the estate and expected the local authorities to do the same. This changed in the decades that followed, when the political–economy of the post-war years was dismantled in favour of rampant privatization and neoliberal policy-making. As council housing was recast from a marker of social inclusion, reinforced by its racialized and gendered scaffolding, to one of exclusion and lack, so the people in precarious conditions who continued to inhabit estates found that their lived realities were radically out of sync with those projected by the state.

Anthropologists of citizenship have argued that official policies and state constructions that see people as abstracted and individualized actors often do not sit well with the more relational, affective, and embedded understandings that people bring to the picture. This is not to conjure a dichotic picture between the 'individual' and the 'relational' or the 'collective' but rather to acknowledge the complicated ways in which social relations continue to frame a person's understanding of self and value (Comaroff and Comaroff, 2004; Lazar, 2008, 2017; Merry, 2009; Strathern, 2004; Von Benda-Beckmann, 2015). On Park End, this point can be pushed even further. The importance of alternative 'political ontologies of the self' (Skeggs, 2011) also reveals a reversal of the assumptions governing orthodox liberalism. Affective relations embody the fundamental dependence of the status of the 'good citizen' (someone deserving of rights and claims to the obligations of the state) on the *primary* status of being a 'good person' (someone who appropriately honours their obligations to others). The inextricably bound nature of local moral personhood and local citizenship practices is most forcefully illustrated in intimate relations between family members and friends. As the densest site for the emergence of personhood and its betrayal—the site where the obligations that compose persons are forged, and where good or bad personhood is measured by the degree to which those obligations are honoured—intimacy constitutes a crucible for citizenship and making demands on the state.

If, as per Max Weber, the state was that which commands a monopoly over legitimate violence, then this chapter adds to this another dimension: the state is that which commands a monopoly on legitimate personhood and the social interactions that come with it. And the liberal democratic state which has marginalized its population has forfeited its power through that process of marginalization, by forcing people to adopt and enforce their own rubric of personhood. In the chapters that follow, then, I further unpack how localized expectations and social relations come into contact, and often violently clash, with official policies and the law, generating emic accounts of state failure that contrast with the state's own ideas of failing citizens. In Chapter 3, we will see that working-class mothers' attempts to build family homes are destabilized in their interactions with benefit policies that force them to choose between their commitments towards their homes and their individual needs for material security. Chapter 4 explores similar inadequacies as housing tenants find that social landlords respond to their requests for more noise insulation and better protection by shifting the blame onto them. And in Chapter 5, residents find that, in facing serious violence and threat, the police's unresponsiveness pushes them into vigilante action and therefore implicates them in crime. In each of these cases, I will focus on how residents respond to the inadequacies of the system they face by withdrawing, bypassing as well as personalizing authorities, institutions, and state powers into their daily life, often with unanticipated or undesired outcomes. The next chapter will turn to the case of the benefit system.

3
Precarious Homes: Encounters with the Benefit System

One warm evening in July 2010, Emma and I sat drinking tea in the cramped kitchen of her two-bedroom house that she shared with her then 17-year-old son. Emma, a mixed-race woman in her late thirties, had raised her teenage son by herself, and worked as an administrative support for a business in town. However, because her income was not high enough, she was also in receipt of 'top-up' housing benefits to help her cover her monthly rent and council tax payments. A news item came on the radio about impending welfare cuts. The government, a coalition between the Conservatives and the Liberal Democrats, had been in power for two months, and it had announced a host of so-called welfare reforms—a term given to the biggest cuts to the post-war welfare state undertaken in its history. That evening, we were getting a flavour of the policies to come as the voice on the radio announced a 'clamp down' on 'benefits scroungers' who had been 'getting something for nothing' for too long. Emma took a sip from her mug and, turning to me, said, 'I hate being on benefits, I really hate it'. She continued, 'I tell you why I hate it so much. It's like the state has just replaced the man. But at least when it was a man you didn't have to fill in them forms every year; you could rent out your room to somebody else to make a bit of money ... But if the state pays: it is the state's and nobody [else]'s rights.'

Emma's observation that 'the state has replaced the man' lingered with me long after that evening. I had begun my fieldwork with an intention to focus on how punitive policies, like the expansion of the criminal justice system, were affecting daily relations on Park End; but as my residence and connections there developed, I realized that citizen–state relations were ineluctably gendered even where policies claimed to be gender-neutral. Hence, to concentrate on the state was unavoidably to examine how it

Personalizing the State: The Anthropology of Law, Politics and Welfare at the UK's Margins. First Edition. Insa Koch. © Insa Koch 2018. Published 2018 by Oxford University Press.

was mediated by the gendered patterns of life. Most of my close contacts and friends on the estates were mothers who took on primary caring roles for their children. Many of them had struggled to build stable homes for themselves and their children. Men often featured in their lives not as sources of support and help but as threats to their homes and their children. But it was not only men who could threaten to undermine women's homes. Mothers were also the primary point of contact for various authorities whose presence they often experienced as intrusive and controlling. As Hoggart already pointed out more than half a century ago, 'it will be the mother, who has the long waits in public places, at the doctor's "for a bottle", at the clinic with a child who has eye-trouble, at the municipal office to see about the instalment on the electricity bill' (1957: 28).

This chapter focuses on one particular aspect of women's encounters with the state: their daily engagements with the benefits system. By benefits system, I refer to the various forms of benefits that welfare recipients can claim, including housing benefit that helps them with rent payments in both the social and private rental sector, council tax benefit that covers monthly council tax payments, and income support or jobseeker's allowance that covers personal benefits.[1] I ask: what are the difficulties that women like Emma confront in their daily attempts to build and maintain family homes? How do they experience their engagements with the welfare state and, more specifically, the benefits system? And what does Emma mean when she says that the state has replaced the man? In policy terms and popular language, women like Emma are classed as 'single mothers' because they raise their children without the long-term support of male breadwinners, partners, and the fathers of their children. According to the 2011 Census figures, they make up one-fifth of all households on the estate. 'Single mother' is a stigmatized term: public discourse constructs them not only as anti-mothers but as anti-citizens par excellence, who bear children in order to acquire access to public

---

[1] The different forms of benefits are administered by different agents and institutions to which the government has outsourced its services. Much of this ecology of assistance changed since 2011 when the coalition government implemented its welfare reforms, including the so-called 'universal credit' which streamlines all benefits into a single form of public welfare and which started being rolled out in the town from 2017 onwards.

resources and services (Gillies, 2007), thereby corrupting both the immaculate trust of a mother to her child and the civic trust of a citizen to the public.

The aim of this chapter is to provide an alternative account of 'single mothers', one which takes as its point of departure women's own daily pursuits of family homes and the social relations that matter to them, as well as how these relations come into conflict with the rules and logics of the benefit systems. I use the term 'single mothers' in quotation marks throughout, because it is precisely the normative and historical assumptions embedded in the term that this chapter rejects. To use the word 'single' is to start from the nuclear family model's dubious assumption that mothers require the presence of a husband to make them complete, to give them, as it were, integrity. By contrast, I argue that the rules and logic of public welfare are radically at odds with women's own expectations of what makes a good family home. The means-tested nature of the benefit system not only portrays them as needy individuals defined by their lack, drawing on broader misogynistic tropes, but also penalizes what they value the most: their reliance on extended and collaborative household arrangements that frequently cut across generations, kin, and friends. While some women personalize the system by 'playing its rules'—creatively manoeuvring its stipulations in order to reconcile them with their own systems of social and intimate obligations—this also places them in an awkward, and sometimes illegal, relationship with the law, as they find that they make themselves vulnerable to charges of benefit fraud.

Ethnographic insights on policy and law have shown that liberal democracy has always regulated the working-class family, in general, and the working-class mother, in particular, even where it enforces formal equality or claims to be acting in women's best interests (Lawler, 2000; Mollona, 2009; Skeggs, 2004; Walkerdine and Lucey, 1989). But vectors of misogyny and the means of enforcing it have taken on different forms at different moments in time. In the post-war decades, a welfare system intent on enforcing the white, male worker-citizen as the idealized welfare recipient excluded women and racialized others from accessing many benefits altogether (Chapter 1). This changed in the decades that followed as policies shifted towards more gender-neutral categories. Yet, at the same time as social citizenship was extended to those who had previously been excluded from its scope, public and policy discourses also came to present women as making claims to freedom that place their needs above those of children and husbands. In other words, the gendered assumptions that governed the inequitable distribution of post-war comprehensive social insurance did not dissipate with that institution's systematic undoing, but rather persisted in the era of stigmatized means-tested assistance. This chapter examines how the pattern of their effects has shifted in the new operation of state-administered class control, and the complex, sometimes contradictory, responses that this has generated from below.

Women, the Benefit System, and the Citizen–Consumer Revisited

To understand how the current benefits system affects women's daily lives on the estate, it is necessary to briefly review the major tenets and developments of benefit policies. The UK benefit system was largely consolidated in the post-war years, although the origins of a wider commitment to social provision can be traced to a much earlier period, notably the idea of the worker's compensation in the late nineteenth century (Lacey, 1998: 50). Prior to the emergence of the post-war welfare state, social security had been administered through a range of disparate and often ad hoc measures, including the old 'Poor Law'—a locally administered and highly stigmatizing form of means-tested assistance for the poor—philanthropic institutions, and limited forms of social insurance sponsored by the state, trade unions, and friendly societies (Alcock, 1999: 200–2). Whereas limited forms of social provision thus existed prior to the rise of the welfare state, it was only in the post-war years that a comprehensive social security system was established that reflected the settlement between labour, capital, and the state detailed in Chapter 1. Social security was to be a central tenet of a paternalistic welfare state: that is, worker–citizens were to pay contributions to a national insurance fund in return for which they would receive benefits. The expectation of the post-war reformers was that this would provide a comprehensive cover by paying benefits to those categories of people—the unemployed, the sick, and the retired—most at risk in the capitalist economy.

Contrary to the expectations of the post-war reformers, however, the national insurance scheme failed to become the dominant model of social security cover in the long term. The old system of Poor Law provisions was never fully abolished by the post-war reformers; on the contrary, a system of means-tested benefits, labelled national assistance, continued to operate alongside social insurance for those unable to pay into the national insurance fund. Over the following decades, as Britain's economy was deregulated and unemployment rose, the number of claimants depending on national assistance grew steadily. This trend was further exacerbated by the development of new means-tested benefits, including housing benefit and council tax benefits for the poor (Alcock, 1999: 208). As the dominant model of citizenship shifted away from that of the productive citizen to that of the consumer as discussed in Chapter 1, welfare dependence became understood as an obstacle to progress. Further policies were introduced that reduced benefit levels and entitlement criteria to national insurance protection, with the effect that ever-greater numbers of people became dependent on means-tested assistance. The New Labour government introduced important tax credits as part of its 'new deal' (Lewis, 2002) as well as parents' support through its 'sure start' policies, but it also left the system of means-tested social assistance in place. This has been further tightened under the turn to 'austerity politics', to which I will return in Chapter 7.

The logic of means-tested assistance is one that makes entitlement to benefits contingent on proof of need: while in receipt of most benefits, claimants have to show, on an ongoing basis, that they do not have the means to support themselves. They have to declare any additional income—including gift payments, savings, and wages from jobs—and they see their benefit payments reduced in accordance with the amount earned. Moreover, in assessing income, the state 'encourages "independence" and the centrifugal dispersion of the members of the family' (Mollona, 2009: 68): it is the needy individual, rather than the working household unit, who is imagined to be the proper object of its welfare. Welfare claimants must declare any additional person who is living in their household, and their financial situation will be taken into account when assessing the amount of benefits to which claimants are entitled. For instance, claimants have their benefits reduced if they live with a non-dependent person who has employment—including their own grown-up children, partners, or lodgers. Where a person is in a cohabiting relationship with a partner whose income is deemed high enough, their entitlement to benefits can be cut altogether, thus also effectively giving the earner the power to withhold or supply support. As a general rule, Mollona (2009) has shown that single people receive more benefits than couples, and children aged between sixteen and eighteen who live with their parents receive less benefit money than if they claim as independent persons.

The shift away from social insurance towards means-tested assistance has had important implications for women's access to the benefit system. As analysts of social policy have argued (Lewis, 1992, 2002; Orloff, 1993), the post-war system treated access to social citizenship as a male prerogative. This is because the Beveridge welfare system was set up on the basis of the male worker–citizen; most benefits were claimed by men, and women were treated as dependants of their husbands. By contrast, under the system of means-tested assistance, entitlement to the vast majority of benefits depends on proof of need alone. But this move towards formal gendered and racialized equity has not been an unqualified blessing; indeed, it has perhaps had the effect of *cementing* the domination of gendered and raced 'others' by embedding this domination more firmly within a violent logic of class. As Chapter 1 argued, at the exact moment that policy-makers expanded categories of inclusion for those dependent on welfare, they also branded those who were now included within its remits as undeserving. This shift in the disposition of policy was not engineered in isolation from broader ideological shifts. Thus, the 1980s were also a time when discourses of 'hypermoralization' (Muehlebach, 2016) that had 'already [been] apparent at capitalism's inception, where the figure of the civilized, austere and temperate market actor relied on that of excess' (ibid.: 363), were once more revived.

The proliferation of figures of 'excess' is perhaps best illustrated in the figure of the 'single mother' (Gillies, 2007) or her US counterpart, the 'welfare queen' (Morgan and Maskovsky, 2003). As Gillies has argued, policy-makers and academics on the 'new right' came to see women's liberation and welfare benefits as undermining men's incentive to work and provide for their families. They became 'portrayed as increasingly placing their own needs above those of their children and their husbands, facilitated by the availability of welfare support enabling them to live independently' (2007: 5). The 'single mother' emerged as the woman who bears children in order to acquire access to council housing and other forms of state welfare. Her excesses are multiple: she is marked by an excess of fecundity because she bears children not to raise a family but for her own pleasure; by an excess of rights because she claims state support without having contributed financially to the system; and by an excess of benefits evinced in the putatively too-abundant, too-generous availability of council housing and other forms of benefits. In short, the single mother is not only the anti-mother for her manifest failure to display maternal love but also the anti-citizen who betrays the social contract by accessing public resources for her personal benefit; corrupt in herself, corrosive of the public good, and a leech on the public purse.

Social theorists (Brown, 1995; Lacey, 1998; MacKinnon, 1989) and anthropologists (Collier, Maurer, and Suarez-Navaz, 1995; Lazarus-Black, 2001; Merry, 1996) have called for closer attention to the ways in which seemingly neutral policies produce gendered inequalities; formal equality often masks—both disguises and shields—substantive inequalities that continue to operate outside of the law. In this respect, the 'single mother' trope discursively fosters continued ideologies of patriarchal power that circulate and flourish within and outside the law. But more than that, the intersection of gender and class inequalities establishes gender itself as an instrument of class coercion that operates in ways on working-class people that do not apply in the same way for middle-class people. As Skeggs has argued, 'at the core of all articulations of the working class was the discursive construct of the modern, that is middle class family, in which the behaviour of women was interpreted in relation to their role as wives and mothers' (1997: 5). In *Democracy in the Kitchen* (1989) Walkerdine and Lucey showed that 'bourgeois' liberal democracy depended precisely on the production of the pathological working-class family as the antithesis of freedom, noting that 'liberalism and libertarianism [also] got hopelessly mixed up and in the process working class families were watched and monitored as never before' (ibid.: 30).

In this chapter, I take these insights as my point of departure to analyse the lives and reflections of 'single mothers' on Park End. Women who seek and receive social benefits also engage with the realities of punitive policies on their own terms. And when they do so, they cite their own understandings of moral personhood that are not exhausted by a focus on official ideologies alone. My aim is to investigate how the incorporation of working-class mothers into the means-tested benefit system has acted as a site for both the challenge and the fortification of gendered class-coercion and control. Mothers on Park End personalize their dependence upon the welfare state by learning to 'play the system': they try to bring the benefit system more in line with their own requirements for family homes by cleverly engaging with its injunctions, and sometimes performing explicitly for the 'law'. However, these daily acts of personalization also make women more vulnerable to yet further state supervision and control, and cement a climate of suspicion and mistrust. In what follows, I develop these points first by introducing the mothers of Park End in more depth, drawing out the context of their lived experiences with men—the details of which are far removed, if not occluded altogether, in the policy and social discourse outside the estate. Second, I turn to their specific experiences of the benefit system; and third, I examine the techniques they use to personalize the state—to interpolate its effects on personhood in a complicated interplay of resistance and reproduction.

Precarious Homes

'People judge me because they think I'm a single mum. I feel the pressure all the time that I'm sort of a "scum of the earth single parent" that got pregnant to get a council flat and things like that, and I really hate that feeling', Helen said. Helen was white, 31 years old, and she had grown up on Park End. She was a mother of two children: Charlotte, a 6-year-old girl who was living with her, and Isobel, a 16-year-old who was currently living with her father. Helen had spent almost her entire adult life getting by on benefits that helped her cover her daily expenses, rent, and council tax payments. When I interviewed her, Helen had just been offered a two-bedroom house by one of the social housing associations on the newer part of the estate. The process of getting a social housing tenancy had been expedited after a support worker had helped her get on the list for emergency housing: Helen's house was infested by mice; the back door was broken; and the boiler was permanently out of use (Chapter 4). Helen had not told anybody about the broken back door but Matt, her ex-partner knew: he had come in one night through the back and vandalized the home while she was asleep, taking her hair dryer and straightener, TV, and X-Box with him.

Like the women and residents introduced in Chapter 2, Helen was acutely aware that others judged her for who she was: hence, her first words to me that she hated how she was made to feel that people thought she was 'scum of the earth', exploiting, if not endangering, her family in order to secure access to benefits. But the story she relayed in the interview provided an insight into a very different life to that ascribed to her. Helen had met the father of her first daughter when she was fifteen: 'I had this dream', she said, 'I suppose from not really having a good family home and that, that I would meet this partner, and have a family and that he would be the magic answer to everything, it was very much a Cinderella story.' She fell pregnant a few months after they started dating, moving in with Dave and his mother. Shortly before she gave birth, she dropped out of school at the age of fifteen. But soon after their daughter was born, her relationship with Dave deteriorated. Dave would stay out late at night, coming home drunk, and he spent the money that was meant for the household. He also became physically violent towards her, especially when he was drunk. One night he came home and beat her 'black and blue'. For Helen, the final straw came when he recklessly endangered their daughter Isobel while intoxicated. She recalled:

I got a phone call one day from a bloke on the estate, and he said: 'Tell Dave that he's lucky. The only reason why we're not going to get him is because of you.' And I'm like, I said to him: 'What the hell is going on, what's that phone call all about?' And, um, no one had told me nothing. [What happened was that Dave had] developed a drinking problem: where he worked [in a local pub] he was allowed to drink, and it was like 80p a pint for staff sort of thing—his dad had allowed him, he worked with his dad, he had allowed him to drink at work. So that night, he'd come home, pissed up, him and his mates, picks up Isobel from his mum's house, *pissed*, got in the car, with Isobel, and flipped it! […] One of his mates brought Isobel out the car, yea. And no one told me in three days, Izzy, I couldn't believe it when I got the phone call. And all [Dave's] mum could say was 'Oh well, if he killed her, he'd have to live with it!'

Eventually, Helen managed to make a break, and moved back in with her parents who took care of her and her baby daughter. These were the best years of her life: her parents helped with child care, she found a job working for a fast food chain in town, and for the first time in her life she had a small amount of leisure time and disposable income. When she met Matt a few years later in her early twenties, she felt stronger. Matt was handsome, and also from the estate; he was popular, and they had friends in common. Soon Helen went to stay with him, taking Isobel with her, and she fell pregnant again, giving birth to a second girl, Charlotte. She quit her job and started receiving benefits. 'I thought it was like a Cinderella dream come true. And then it happened again', Helen recalled. One night when Matt had gone out, she heard a bang on the door: the police were looking for Matt, having received information about stolen goods on the premises. The police did not find anything that night, but they left the door broken; it remained damaged for some time, leaving her home vulnerable. After that incident, their relationship began to fracture. Helen became suspicious of Matt; while he denied that he was involved in anything illegal, she worried that he was lying. One day, she found a stash of cocaine under a lose tile in the bathroom floor of the flat. She feared that social services may come and remove her children if she stayed with him.

Helen left Matt after a few years, and with the help of a support worker she met through a local charity, was able to secure a tenancy in a privately rented home. She stayed there for nearly two years, but the house was mouse-infested and the heating almost permanently broken. She moved when she was offered a two-bedroom social tenancy through the emergency housing list. Helen was determined to look forward: 'All I want is for my daughters to have a better life, to go to college, get a job, and have the opportunity to go on holiday.' And yet, she also seemed resigned to the possibility of its contrary: 'but then again, it's not my life, is it?', she said. Helen's story—the aspirations and desires for herself and her family, for their well-being, safety, and emotional health—was not a narrative that I heard from women. What stood out in each of the stories I heard were the dogged ways in which women tried to build homes for themselves and their children in circumstances that militated, repeatedly and in virtually every respect, against their efforts to secure the well-being of their families and loved ones: violent or absent fathers, precarious labour market conditions, and insufficient housing. Consider the lines drawn in the history of Helen's homes, in both the relational and material senses of 'home' (Alexander, Hojer-Bruun, and Koch, 2018): from not having had 'a good home and that' in childhood to dodging and defending against threats to herself and her daughters from within—violent or reckless partners, infestations of disease vectors—and without—after the police visit, escaping a literally broken home, a home exposed and vulnerable.

For many women I met, being involved with a man meant putting one's family home and obligations to children at risk. And this translated into a strong sense that one might be 'better off' without a man. Sometimes, the women I got to know could be extremely judgemental of others who they considered to be gullible and to make themselves too dependent on a man. Tracey, who was introduced in an earlier chapter as running the front desk of the community centre, once told me that she would 'never accept a drink from a man'. While this was an exaggeration, Tracey often commented on women who were too quick to accept money from men: 'if you accept a drink from a man', she once told me, 'they think they own your body and you owe them something'. In judging other women for accepting drinks from men in the pub, Tracey was making a point about her own sense of self and outlook on life: she considered herself an independent woman who did not want to 'owe' anything to men, that is to say, to be in any relation of reciprocal obligations with a man that she also maintained a romantic relationship with. And more than that, she showed contempt for any woman who did. When, for instance, a news story in the papers reported that the Manchester United football player Wayne Rooney had had several affairs with prostitutes behind the back of his wife, Tracey placed blame with the women, both with the prostitute and the foodballer's wife:

> If there weren't women like her around, then these men would have to stick their jollies, I don't know, through a hole or something, d'you know what I mean. But these girls are going out deliberately to shag a footballer. And what makes me laugh, all these women, they kind of think the only way they're gonna make it in life is to become a footballer's wife … why?! Go and earn your own fricking money!

But it was not just the lives of stars that Tracey judged from afar. She sometimes gossiped about women like Helen who she saw as depending unduly on men who she got nothing from, 'not even good sex'. Her view of men as selfish, irresponsible, and utterly incapable was held by other women I met. 'Men think they can have families without having a wife or a household!', Stacey, a white local woman said: 'When they break up with a woman, they just find another one and think it's quite alright to have kids with her!' I met Stacey when she dropped into the community centre, looking pale and obviously distressed. She told me and Tracey that, having been with her partner for fourteen years, he had split up with her when she had told him that she was pregnant by him. He had simply walked out of the house, leaving her by herself, at the age of thirty-six and with two more teenage sons. 'He just said, he didn't want any more kids!' she explained with a very matter-of-fact voice. Tracey looked at her. After a moment's silence, she just went: 'Men, ey?' before moving on to another topic. Like the women who cultivate indifference as a response to the structural suffering and high rates of child death in Scheper-Hughes' (1992) study of a favela in the northeast of Brazil, Tracey was also normalizing the trauma that Stacey was experiencing by reacting with an apparent lack of interest.

Indifference towards men, and women's independence from them, was also normalized in other ways. I soon learnt that it was inappropriate to ask about the father of people's children, not because it might suggest promiscuity but because men were often sources of threat. One of my most painfully embarrassing moments was when I met the baby son of Serena, a mixed-race youth worker, who was well respected among residents for what she had achieved. When Serena brought her baby son, then aged just over a year, into the community centre one day, I commented on how beautiful he looked and asked her who the father was. Serena looked at me blankly and made clear that the father was out of the picture. Later, I heard that Serena had split up with the father of her baby boy, after the latter had gone to prison for an armed robbery attack and Serena had decided that she did not want anything to do with him. I learnt from this experience not to ask about children's fathers unless they were clearly present in people's lives. Tracey, for example, never told her own son who his father was, even though he was a local man living in the same town. She was distraught when she found out one day that her teenage son had sought out the identity of his father without her knowledge and had tried to contact him. As with all social prescriptions and proscriptions, norms of courtesy and respect are braided with the fabric of affective bonds and kinship relations.

Gillies notes that for many working-class mothers that she worked with, parenting with a supportive man was 'simply not an option, given their need to deal constructively with violent, undermining or absent fathers' (2007: 47). The stories of women like Helen, Serena, and Stacey push the point. Even just a cursory glance at their life histories refutes some of the cruder, crueller narratives of 'single mothers' that circulate in society outside social housing and the benefit systems, and makes better sense of the struggles that Park End mothers encounter in their daily attempts to care for their children: for them, being 'single mothers' was not an active choice, much less a position envisaged when they were younger, or desired for purposes of material acquisition and ease. While they normalized their situation by judging others who they considered to be too reliable on men, their own words also spoke of the pain they felt. What role did the benefit system play, then, in their lives? What relations existed between the benefit system and the men they encountered?

'The State has Replaced the Man'

For many women, even with the support that they received from their kin and family members, setting up an independent household was often not a realistic option by virtue of the near impossibility of juggling child-care responsibilities with paid employment. Many women had their mothers, kin, or friends stepping in to assist with these responsibilities. And still, finding a job that would pay enough for them to survive without the support of state welfare was often impracticable. Mandy, for example, a single mother with a teenage son, was working three jobs to pay her bills and rent: she started her first cleaning job at 5 a.m., then went to work in a school canteen at 11 a.m., and finished the day with a second cleaning job. Maria, a woman originally from Poland, and a mother of two, who was married to an English man, was working as a carer for the disabled son, a 10-year-old child, of a wealthy family who was living in an expensive neighbourhood on the other side of town. While she cared deeply about the child, the unsociable working hours (she had to work thirteen hours shifts from 6 p.m. to 7 a.m. the next morning) meant that she was away from her own children several nights every week. Maria's husband as well as Maria's neighbours would look after the children, get them dressed in the morning and take them to school while Maria was travelling home from work.

The long working hours in the menial service sector that interrupted rest or family life were not, however, the most insurmountable obstacles employment posed. Even more crushing on women's lives and livelihoods was the irregularity of waged labour that they faced. This was particularly pronounced in the case of so-called zero-hour contracts—a form of contract where an employer is not obliged to provide minimum working hours. Take the example of Olifia, a British born Muslim mother of five who was working as a part-time youth worker for a local authority-run youth club. Her employer would often set the hours with only a week's notice. In addition to creating child-care problems, the fluctuations in her wages did not allow her to predict how much money she would have and whether she would be able to pay her rent and bills for the coming month. And even more critically, when she turned to the authorities to get help with 'top up benefits',[2] her application would take several weeks to process, during which time she was forced to borrow money from family and friends. To put it another way, the solution offered by the state for the instability of her waged labour—itself the consequence of an employment law construct that the government had contended was essential to the health of Britain's economy—compounded the precise condition it was intended to remedy. And even further, it placed additional stress on the very social and kinship relations that were required to support her employment, and for which her employment was undertaken to sustain in the first place.

Given the difficulties that women encountered in finding employment that was not only compatible with their family obligations but also allowed them to plan ahead, it comes as no surprise that many had, at least at some point in their lives, been surviving 'on the social'. Many women expressed feeling profound relief when they received their first benefit payments. They spoke of how grateful they were for 'the social' and did not know how to cope without it. Lindsey, a white mother of three children, introduced in an earlier chapter, recalled the moment when she held her first benefit payment in her hand, sometime in the late 1980s:

> I never understood about benefits, I never really knew what they were and when [her support worker] took me to the benefits office, I didn't actually believe they were gonna give me any money. [When] I first got my Giro[3] I went running down the road with the Giro in my hand, shouting

---

[2] Benefits that cover the shortfall between the minimum amount that a welfare recipient is entitled to from the state and any wages that they are receiving.

[3] Name given to a paper slip addressed to a bank branch instructing it to credit a specified sum of money to a named account at that branch.

'Good ol' Margaret Thatcher!' [*we laughed*]—I got money without doing anything, I couldn't believe that, fifteen pounds a week! And I had to pay for my tobacco, my food and everything, I just can't believe how happy I was about that stupid little bit of money that I got!

But when digging deeper into women's stories and experiences, a more complicated picture of the benefit system's functioning emerged. Claiming benefits took up an inordinate amount of time as women confronted a bureaucracy that was Kafkaesque for its arcane features, and even where it wasn't Kafkaesque, it was Orwellian, exposing women's private lives to the state's minute scrutiny. To prove their 'need' to the agents of the state, women had to engage in everyday 'performances of being poor' (Smith, 2017b) including going to regular assessments, filling in forms, continuously proving their efforts to find a job, getting requisite medical evidence where they were claiming disability benefits, and, above all, also patiently waiting for bureaucrats to process their claims and requests, learning to be what Auyero (2012) has called 'patients of the state'. Conversely, as claimants, they had to report any change in personal circumstances immediately: who stayed and left their homes, where and when they were travelling, when their children reached a certain age or left education, and what sources of income they had. 'They want to know everything, down to what toilet paper you are using', Rose, a white woman in her late fifties whose story will be elaborated in Chapter 7, said. She continued:

It's hard enough for me, I freak out every time I see any of their forms. I hate them. I mean they are so complicated, and so comprehensive, as I say, they wanted to know what brand of toilet paper you use, almost, the kind of information they are asking. And part of me thinks, well, more than part of me thinks that they are deliberately made complicated, you know the form is big and there is lots of silly questions and you have to think back for dates, and ... it takes a long time ... I freak out, I keep procrastinating, I eventually tackle them at the last moment because I hate them so much. I don't like the feelings that arise in me when I look at them. Whenever a letter comes through the door and it's a brown envelope with you know, department of work and pensions, my heart sinks: oh, what next?

Navaro-Yashin (2006) describes the power of bureaucratic documentation to incite intimate effects, thus also challenging the idea that governmental practices produce rational and compliant subjects. A similar sense was captured by Rose when she spoke of how seemingly neutral bureaucratic forms and letters incited strong anxiety and panic in her.

But even worse than the endless form-filling, of having to prove one's need, and of enduring the humiliating treatment of unresponsive and sometimes outright hostile officials was the fact of having to live by rules that prioritized individual claimants over shared households. As we have seen, the benefit system allows people to claim more benefits as individuals rather than as members of households and that penalize their lodgings with a married partner, grown-up children, or lodgers—literally assigning more value to the individual than the system of mutual care, support, obligation, and responsibility central to women's lives. The idea of having to claim as an individual claimant was recognized as an affront to women's moral understandings of what they should be doing as 'good' mothers. We saw this in the last chapter: that women's sense of self-worth was precisely contingent upon being a good person, defined through an ability to show care and commitment towards those close to them. Women sometimes spoke of how they had been told by a benefit officer to 'kick their children out of the house' once they turned eighteen (or sixteen if they had left education) and were no longer classed as dependants in the eyes of the law. This was Lindsey's retort, for example, as she recounted how one of her friends had recently been put in this situation while undergoing a benefit assessment: 'But what mother would do that to their own child?' she said in outrage. 'It makes you feel like you are a bad parent!'

In the face of punitive means-tested benefits, welfare recipients often ended up hiding, withdrawing from, and disengaging from those they did not trust. In his account of tenants on a post-industrial housing estate, Davey (2016) observes how welfare recipients 'fortify' their homes from the potential intrusion of outside officials: they refuse to open the door, they unplug their phones, and they do not open official letters in an attempt to shelter themselves from unwanted messages that implicate them in yet further state control. 'Burying your head in the sand', as some welfare advisers referred to this behaviour, was also a common strategy for dealing with punitive benefit rules on Park End. But this practice could also precipitate dramatic repercussions on women's lives. Emma, for example, was in receipt of top-up housing benefit payments because her work as an administrative support did not pay enough to cover her monthly rent payments; but her housing benefits were reduced when her son left education at the age of seventeen and was no longer legally classified as a 'dependant'. Emma did not discover the reduction in her benefit payments until months later, quite possibly because she did not open the letters that were sent out in advance. By the time she realized, however, she had already fallen into rent arrears. Emma could not afford to pay the balance and decided to 'go on the run' from the bailiffs before she could receive a formal eviction order: one early morning in April 2011, almost a year after we had been sat in her kitchen, drinking tea and listening to the radio programme, she packed her belongings and left the house for good.

Emma had been able to arrange alternative accommodation for herself at Helen's house (although in doing so she put Helen in jeopardy with the law as Helen was claiming benefits as a single welfare claimant). But not everyone was as fortunate as Emma. Some people only discovered that they had fallen foul of the benefit system when the bailiffs were at their door. I heard one vivid story several times during my time on Park End, as women would talk about it as a traumatic moment in the life of the neighbourhood, and it was reiterated to me in an email from Lindsey which I reproduce almost verbatim below. It involved a local woman of Afro-Caribbean descent called Debbie, who was living in a socially rented house with her son, who was over the age of sixteen and had left education. What happened to Debbie was similar to Emma's experience: Debbie's son was no longer classed as a dependant and Debbie lost a portion of her housing benefit payments. Unaware of this, she had gone on holiday and left her son at home. Lindsey wrote to me:

So what had happened is that housing benefit stopped when her son left college some time before and rent arrears started to build up. Debbie thought that it was a housing benefit problem that would get sorted out in the end and buried her head in the sand about it and ignored the letters that kept coming through the door. I can understand this because they send out letters automatically and so it can all seem like another piece of bullshit comes through the door.

Months must have gone by and she went on holiday for a week—while she was away [the housing association] evicted her with her son aged 19 [who was] the only one home and he was terrified—it was so bad, I got involved through Malcolm [a mutual friend] who was supporting the young man—we moved their stuff—their whole life into the community centre—what was funny was that the goings on in the community centre just carried on around all this stuff you know sofa's clothes, a whole life of stuff for a family and the kids were like doing youth club around that we just carried on!!!

So when [Debbie] returned from her holiday her and her family were homeless—council said that it was intentional homelessness as she was evicted for not paying her rent—it's a heartbreaking story it really is.

The 'heartbreak' in this story is a constellation of care and cruelty with state–citizen relations at its core. It contrasts the local authority's refusal to accept any responsibility for housing Debbie and her son by calling her case 'intentional homelessness' with the support that residents showed through the community centre as they moved Debbie's furniture and belongings into the midst of youth club activities. The state perceived Debbie as being in financial and moral dereliction—reckless, feckless, and possibly duplicitous—and presumably itself as legally and ethically justified in the seizure of the property. By contrast, Park End residents condemned the state's shameful neglect of its duty of care to Debbie and her son to ensure their safety, housing, and dignity: a moral imperative they displayed and assumed themselves. As the community continued to maintain and fulfil its obligations to its residents, Debbie's family's effects were literally absorbed into its heart.

In sum, for many single mothers on Park End, the benefit system was an indispensable resource for survival. And yet, in making themselves dependent on its financial support, women also exposed themselves to forms of control and intervention that they neither expect nor condone: not only did they have to live their lives in accordance with a complex, seemingly arbitrary, often demeaning system, but they also learned that their intimate relations with family members, friends, and kin were policed and punished in ways that they had not anticipated. A parallel hence arises with the way women experienced their dependence upon violent, erratic, and absent men and the agents of the benefit system: both were defined by their inability to be trusted, and more so, by their ability to take away, upset, and disrupt the kinds of relations and social practices that were central to the social reproduction of their homes. It is precisely in this sense, then, that we can understand Emma's statement at the beginning of this chapter that 'the state has replaced the man'. Against this backdrop, how did women personalize their dependence on a hostile and repressive system? And to what extent did their own practices challenge but also reproduce the power inequalities that they face?

Personalizing the Benefit System

By the summer of 2014, I had been living away from Park End for a couple of years, although I had come back for occasional visits. That summer, I had decided to return to do research on how social housing tenants had been affected by the government's turn to 'austerity' and so-called 'welfare reforms' introduced by a Conservative-led coalition government that was elected into power in 2010 (see Chapter 7). I was looking to interview social housing tenants who had been affected by the so-called 'bedroom tax', a name colloquially given to a policy that imposes penalties on social housing tenants occupying properties that are deemed to be too large for their needs. Lindsey agreed to introduce me to her neighbour Anne, a white mother of two, because 'she would have an interesting story to tell'. Anne's adult children had left home and Anne had been signed off work due to health reasons and was claiming benefits to support herself. One evening, we walked across to Anne's house, a few houses down from Lindsey's, where Anne was standing outside smoking a cigarette, her dog Fiji, an old black Staffordshire bull terrier, lying next to her on the steps. She greeted Lindsey warmly. Lindsey confirmed that Anne would be happy to 'have a chat with us', adding that she would 'bring the fags'. Anne agreed and we arranged a date two weeks ahead when we would meet again at her house.

On the day of our arranged meeting, Lindsey called me and asked to come to her house instead. She had cooked an elaborate meal, and even bought some beers for us to share. Eventually, having eaten the pasta she'd cooked, she broke the news: 'I think it's best if we leave it', she said. Since she had spoken to Anne about the interview, Anne had started coming around to her house, asking her for favours and wanting to speak to her all the time. Lindsey felt that the favours were getting too much; a point whose significance will be explored in the next chapter. I was surprised that a simple introduction and request for an interview should have had such dramatic consequences on neighbour relations between the two women (such that they even rippled into my own participation in the women's relationship, the meal and the beers that Lindsey prepared offered perhaps as compensation for the loss of my interview). But I had failed to appreciate what was at stake for Anne in talking to me, a stranger and a researcher, and the reciprocal obligation Lindsey was expected to discharge: as Lindsey explained in the course of the evening, Anne had a lodger living with her, a local man from the estate who was renting the spare bedroom in the house that had once been occupied by her children. She had not declared his presence to the authorities so as not to have her benefit payments reduced. The arrangement worked both ways: her lodger got a good deal because the rent was below market value and Anne, in turn, was able to make a bit of extra cash.

As I came to pay more attention to women's stories about the benefit system, I realized just how widespread, and how wide-ranging, these daily practices of 'playing the system' were. The phrase 'playing the system' was often used by residents on Park End, usually to describe 'others' who were savvy at dodging the official rules. Playing the system could mean different things in different situations: it could mean, as in Anne's case, taking a lodger into one's home and making a bit of extra cash to pay for things that one could otherwise not afford—Christmas presents for children and grandchildren, household goods, or a drink once in a while. Or it could mean having a job on the side that was paid for 'cash-in-hand', and that was not declared. In other cases, people claimed benefits under a false address. Sharon, for example, had a council flat that she had registered as her living address for herself and her three young children. In practice, however, she spent most of her time at her sister's residence, who had her own children. The two sisters shared child-care duties and organized most of their daily activities together. Others allowed lovers or friends to stay in their house without declaring their presence to the authorities; we saw above, for example, that Helen accommodated Emma when Emma lost her house. Emma arranged informally with Helen that she would pay her £50 a month in rent for offering her a room, money that Helen did not declare.

In pursuing these practices of personalization, women were responding to economic pressures: as Mollona (2009) found, benefit payments are so low that families have to rely on collaborative living arrangements to get by; that is, as a simple practical effect, the comparative financial disadvantage of extended social and kin households demands the deepening and broadening of precisely those relationships that the state penalizes. But these strategies also had a moral quality that has been widely overlooked. Thus, by pretending to meet the state's own requirements of vulnerability and need, women were also carving out a space that allowed them to be exactly the opposite: mothers, lovers, and kin members that defied any image of them as 'single' mothers. Remember the moral outrage which Lindsey had expressed when telling me the story of her friend who had been told by a housing officer to throw her adult child out of the house to avoid having her benefits reduced. For women like this mother, 'playing the system' could be the only option they had to keep their families together without incurring economic penalties that might push them beyond the brink of survival. Engaging in these practices was at once a practical course of action and a moral dictate—something that one did to protect one's family, to put up one's friends, to supplement an income to pay for Christmas or birthday gifts for children and grandchildren, or perhaps simply to cover necessary daily costs.

Women like Anne were right to be cautious about sharing details about their living arrangements with outsiders: I was a stranger after all, and the authorities were well aware of women's practices and intended to police them as evidence of benefit fraud. Penalties included loss of benefit payments, fines, and even the threat of jail, on top of the stresses associated with lengthy investigations. During these periods, benefit payments would be stopped and the reinstatement process could take months. The state's position on benefit fraud as a shameful offence was also widely advertised in the form of posters and leaflets that were put through the door and hung in public spaces asking residents to step forward and report any knowledge they had of fraud; I once received a leaflet through the post that warned me that benefit fraud was happening in my neighbourhood. The letter invited me to step forward to report cases of fraud in return for a financial award (the sum of which was not specified). Benefit officers would listen closely for any inconsistencies or lies in women's narratives during benefit assessments at the Jobcentre. Women also spoke of how they feared surprise visits by housing officers and other welfare officials who checked if there were any signs of undeclared persons living in women's households. While I never saw this happen in practice, the fear that it might created a background expectation in which mutual suspicion and mistrust were sowed.

But it was not only the actions of outsiders—like the anthropologist–researcher—that caused women worry or alarm: threats came from within as women feared that those with intimate knowledge of their lives could use it against them. In the last chapter, we already saw how residents sometimes enlisted the police in the pursuit of disputes with neighbours. Similarly, with respect to the benefit system, women expressed anxieties that those in close proximity to their lives, including next-door neighbours, boyfriends, or jealous friends, might 'grass them up'. More typically, men also exploited their knowledge of women subverting the benefit system by weaponizing or acting in the shadow of the law, to put pressure on women to act in ways that further relieved or prevented them from assuming their potential responsibilities. This is what happened to Helen, after she split up with her first boyfriend Dave—while the two were together, Dave had moved in, and Helen continued to receive benefits as a 'single mother', covering all of the rent and council tax payments with her benefit money; Dave contributed household goods and leisure items with his income. When their relationship ended, Dave insisted on taking the TV and DVD player, amongst other goods with him; Helen explained: 'He said to me that he had paid with his money, which is true, of course, but at the same time, I had been paying rent and bills and that. And he said to me: "No, you ain't paying rent! It's just benefits money!" But I'm saying: "It's still rent!"'

Dave's refusal to accept Helen's benefit payment as a valid form of contribution to the household mirrored a broader attitude on the part of other men I met, who subscribed to and echoed typical motifs of the 'single mother' as feckless and undeserving. Sometimes, these were men who were happy to rely on benefits and the support of women in their own lives, but who repeated mainstream society's misogyny, and exploited the very discourse of the state to encourage—and then condemn—women's contravention of the state's commands, often on their behalf. Take the example of Calvin, a resident of Afro-Caribbean descent in his forties. He was single and living with his mother in the council house where he had been raised. While he never disclosed this to me personally, I heard from mutual friends that Calvin had at some point been in receipt of jobseeker's allowance. Nonetheless, during a recorded interview, he told me:

I know a lot of single parents and all the rest that kind of stuff, but what I'm saying is … their visions is [to have] five kids, have a shag every other night, it's the reptilian part of the brain, you know... and they talk amongst each other about, 'did you know that there is this benefit you can get, and that benefit you can get, and this?' They educate each other on stuff, their social network with their own personal twitter which is gabby, gabby, gabby on how to diddle this, how to diddle that, how to get that benefit, how to get that clothes allowance, how to get that housing allowance, how to get those, you know, furniture allowance ... I'm not saying we should do with them what Hitler did [to Jews], but you know ... The nanny state wipes their arse. We got a bunch of pussies now!

Calvin's comments brutally reflect pernicious accounts of women's motives in securing social assistance; but they also draw attention to suspicions about the collaborative nature of women's relationships in the face of the state, highlighting them as a source of singular corruption and perversion: the practices of 'educating each other on stuff ... gabby, gabby, gabby'. It was this fear of judgement, as well as the risk of 'being caught out', that could also militate against women taking a collective stance against the struggles that they were facing. I became aware of this when in the summer of 2010, shortly after the new Conservative-led government had been voted into power, a BBC team came to the community centre in Park End. They were looking to interview 'single mothers' about the impending changes to the benefit system. While I knew from informal conversations with women like Tracey or Emma how afraid women were of the announced welfare reforms, nobody wanted to come forward to speak on camera. In the end, a local mother of three called Caroline agreed to do the interview, provided her name remained anonymous. Tracey judged her harshly. Tracey would have never wanted to speak on camera because 'they' were bound to misrepresent her views in order to give her and the estate a 'bad name'. But more than that, Caroline had been 'naïve' to speak up. Tracey was outraged because Caroline had a man living with her whose presence in her household she had not declared to the authorities. Even if Caroline's name would remain anonymous in the TV programme, she had made herself vulnerable by drawing attention to herself.

Conclusion

MacKinnon wrote that 'the state is male in the feminist sense: the law sees and treats women the way men see and treat women. The liberal state coercively and authoritatively constitutes the social order in the interest of men as a gender through its legitimating norms, forms, relations to society and substantive policies' (1989: 161–2). But if the state assumed the role of the 'husband' even after the *collapse* of the mid-century male breadwinner model it championed, it behoves us to probe the ways in which it assumed that institution's familiar patriarchal effects. This chapter has explored how liberal policies that ostensibly place the sexless individual at their core can reproduce gendered inequalities by shrouding forms and practices of misogyny on working-class women. Contemporary benefit policies are framed in a gender-neutral language: they take the vulnerable individual as their point of departure. And yet, for Park End mothers, the state—in the form of the benefit system—comes to occupy a role not all that different from that of absent, unreliable, or violent men, and indeed the men who weaponize the state's own dicta against them. Contrary to women's expectations for support and help, the means-tested nature of the current benefit system portrays them as needy individuals defined by their lack, encouriging narratives about them that are defined by their unmistakeable misogyny: condemning women who access benefits for their immorality, their loose sexuality, and their scheming, duplicitous behaviour, and affording them assistance only insofar as they are able to demonstrate and bare their abject victimhood.

And yet, we find again and again, dominant ideologies and policy enforcement do not exhaust women's experiences of the welfare state. I have argued that women bring their own moral frameworks to their engagements with the benefit system that are based on the relationships that matter to them the most as mothers, lovers, kin members, and friends. What is more, it is precisely by recalling their obligations to their family homes that women justify situational forms of disobedience towards official rules. When 'cheating' the benefit system by hiding loved ones in their homes, having cash-in-hand jobs, or claiming welfare under false addresses, women defy the state's logic of individualized assistance and act on their own ideas of what it takes to protect their family homes. In doing so, they personalize the welfare state: they appropriate the existing system by making it work in ways that are compatible with the moral dictates of their daily lives, revealing social logics that are radically incommensurable with those assumed by official policies alone. And yet, their attempts to personalize the state can also backfire as they make women vulnerable to allegations of benefit fraud and, equally seriously, sow a seed of suspicion and mistrust. In the end, everyday acts of 'playing the system' also end up drawing women more closely into the remit and logic of state control and fray informal relationships that are necessary to provide material and affective relief where the state will not, or where it impedes, such self-support.

Everyday acts of cheating, avoiding, and performing for 'the law' are not the only responses that people display in the face of punitive welfare systems. They exist alongside more proactive, collectivist, and cross-community calls for redistribution and the recognition of an alternative 'ethics of care' (Gutierrez-Garza, n.d.; James and Koch, n.d.; Skeggs, 2011; Wilde, n.d.). For example, Wilde (n.d.) has analysed how London-based activist networks enact a 'militant ethics of care' by mobilizing collective protests against punitive housing policies that present those at the bottom of the market as undeserving of public housing and welfare resources. Similarly, the activists and claimants in Spain who affiliate with the movement La PAH (plataforme de Afectados por la Hipetoca) studied by Gutierrez-Garza (n.d.) call for a redistribution of public resources in the face of austerity and a dismantling welfare state. On Park End, the logic of mutual support and care is only too well-known to the women who depend upon informal networks in their daily struggles for survival. But these rarely develop into support movements that take on a political momentum. For the mothers with whom I spent my time, the responses they cultivated—including withdrawal and selective personalization of welfare agents and policies—are often the only available way to mitigate a benefit system at once intrusive and punitive. The next chapter demonstrates how similar constraints play out in social housing tenants' attempts to ask their landlords and local authorities for help in negotiating badly built and maintained buildings, such as apartment blocks, rows of houses, and flats.

4

Troubled Neighbourhoods: Encounters with Housing Authorities

In 2010, Val, a white, fifty-something-year-old housing official who had had a life-long career in social housing, made an exception to the rules by allowing me to rent a social tenancy in a close for keyworkers.[1] Some of the houses had remained empty for weeks because no keyworkers could be found who were willing to move there, and so Val had decided to loosen the criteria for eligibility. I moved into a two-bedroom house, together with Lisa, a friend and community worker. In the spring of 2011, the housing association sent me a letter. Bearing the headline 'Anti-Social Behaviour Consultation' and addressing me as 'Dear Resident', it stated, 'some time ago you mentioned an interest in being consulted on your views about Anti-Social Behaviour. We are currently reviewing how we deal with these issues and would like to invite you to come along to a meeting.' When I duly arrived at the hall, housed in a community centre and sponsored by the same housing association, four housing officials, including two from offices working in nearby towns, were seated around a large table stacked with tea and biscuits. No other tenants had yet turned up, and when Val asked, 'do you have your researcher's or your tenant's hat on?' I confirmed that I had come as a researcher. No tenants would attend, she predicted, because many were 'apathetic'. 'And', she added, 'when they come they are only interested to talk about their personal problems.'

---

[1] Keyworkers are public sector employees who provide services to the public, including police officers, nurses, and teachers. The housing association that I rented with have since abandoned their keyworkers' tenancies.

Personalizing the State: The Anthropology of Law, Politics and Welfare at the UK's Margins. First Edition. Insa Koch. © Insa Koch 2018. Published 2018 by Oxford University Press.

Val's concerns about tenants' attendance turned out to be well-founded. The letter I had received had been sent out to more than seventy households across the town, and free transport had been offered to anyone who wanted to attend. But only one tenant showed up and he was half an hour late. Nasiru, a man of Nigerian origin who had lived in his one-bedroom socially rented apartment in a 1990s built four-storey building for nearly seven years, was visibly tense and angry when he arrived. He introduced himself by saying that he was one of many tenants who were suffering in silence because nobody wanted to help them. He told the officers present that he had been ringing them for months, trying to make an appointment to get someone to visit his flat and take note of the state of it, and of the apartment block it was in, but to no avail. Nasiru was getting more agitated as he spoke, and exclaimed at one point, 'Are they meant to be houses to live happy lives [in], or are they just meant to provide housing?' Val replied that, of course, the housing provider meant to provide 'good quality housing' but that Nasiru was 'going off on a tangent' by speaking about a 'one-person problem'. Nasiru tried again: 'But we need real life experience! It's the real experiences that matter!'

In the last chapter, we looked at how Park End mothers experience their daily interactions with the benefit system. We saw that in their attempts to build family homes, women find that they are 'damned if they do and damned if they don't': they are damned if they stay on the right side of the law (because the benefit system fails to accommodate their living arrangements, so central to their aspirations for family homes) and they are damned if they subvert the system to suit their own needs (because they make themselves vulnerable to charges of fraud). In this chapter, I shift the focus from welfare claimants' attempts to maintain their family homes to social housing tenants' daily 'trouble' with neighbours who live on the same street, apartment block, or row of houses. I ask: how do social housing tenants—both men and women—experience neighbour 'trouble'? What expectations do they have of the authorities in helping them deal with their problems? And what do tenants like Nasiru mean when they say that the authorities are not interested in 'real life experiences'? This chapter's focus on social housing tenants, who make up about 50 per cent of tenancies on Park End, highlights, once more, the classed nature of state control. Social landlords, including local authorities and so-called housing associations (that the local authorities have outsourced traditional social housing duties to), have extended powers to deal with 'nuisance' and 'anti-social behaviour' problems. Unlike people who live in homes that they own, social housing tenants can be evicted from their properties for acting in what the authorities consider to be socially inappropriate ways.

The aim of this chapter is to move beyond the categories of 'nuisance' and 'anti-social behaviour', so frequently invoked by the authorities, to what social housing tenants themselves sometimes describe as neighbour 'trouble'. Like in the case of 'single mothers' we looked at in the last chapter, I argue that tenants' expectations of what their social landlords should provide are radically out of sync with the reality of contemporary housing policies. This is well illustrated in the case of 'neighbour trouble', a term that residents use to refer to anything that impedes on their ability to maintain neighbourhoods they consider to be adequate and fit for living. Recent policy has framed problems that arise from poorly maintained and managed social housing in terms of 'anti-social behaviour' and neighbour nuisance: blame is shifted from the landlords' responsibility to provide adequate and well-insulated housing onto individual tenants for their failure to act in a socially appropriate manner. Tenants who turn to the authorities for help in dealing with 'trouble' find that their calls for help are frequently dismissed and side-lined as not serious enough. Perhaps even worse, their attempts to appropriate the official language of 'anti-social behaviour' to make themselves heard can end up taking them yet further away from tackling the structural problems with inadequate housing that gave rise to many of the disputes in the first place, while at the same time reinforcing a climate of suspicion and mistrust between neighbours.

Anthropologists of housing, social historians, and socio-legal scholars have argued that the built environment is a place where relations of class and domination are written into bricks and mortar (Alexander, Hojer-Bruun, and Koch, 2018; Bijsterfeld, 2008; Fennell, 2015; Hanley, 2007; Mulcahy, 2001). The built environment speaks of how a society values particular kinds of people, or rather, fails to value them, in the case of social housing tenants today. The materiality of social housing illustrates this point. As we saw in Chapter 1, the provision of public housing, including the council housing sector in Britain, had never been free of processes of 'othering' and exclusion. Yet, it was only with the gradual decline of building standards and changes in management policies (Alexander et al., 2009; Hyatt, 1997) that the classed dimensions of social housing have become the basis for, and mechanism of, coercive policies that police so-called 'anti-social' and nuisance-related behaviour. This chapter examines how tenants' engagement with the built environment simultaneously challenges and reproduces their own classed position as low-income tenants in cheap social housing, as contemporary housing policies are radically at odds with tenants' expectations of what their social landlords should provide. If the last chapter interrogated the trope of the 'single mother', this chapter's guiding motifs are noise, nuisance, and, above all 'anti-social behaviour', each of which have invoked classed connotations of disorder and pathos in policy-making and discourses.

Material Homes, Nuisance Disputes, and the Vulnerable Citizen

In *Baxter v Camden LBC (No 2)* ([2001] QB 1, CA), the Court of Appeal was confronted with the question of whether a local authority, in its capacity as social landlord for tenants in low-income housing, was liable where one tenant's use and enjoyment of their flat is interfered with by noise from another tenant. The complainant in question was Yvonne Baxter, a young 'single mother', who occupied the middle flat in a Victorian building, with tenants living in both the flats above and below her, separated by plasterboard ceilings and wooden floors that were in poor condition. As a result, Ms Baxter could hear all the everyday domestic activities of the other occupants. The evidence included the noise of electrical switches, people defecating in their toilets, and radios playing. The court found that the local housing authority was not liable for Baxter's exposure to constant noise. In reaching the decision, Lord Justice Tuckey stated that the court had 'to consider the locality, age and physical characteristics of the premises in question. Occupiers of low cost, high density housing must be expected to tolerate higher levels of noise from their neighbours than others in more substantial and spacious premises'.

The decision reached in the case might have confirmed to Ms Baxter what she knew already: that as a poor tenant of socially rented housing, the state had little interest in her and that she was expected to resign herself to low quality housing because of the rental class to which she belonged. Social housing tenants have not always been treated as second-tier citizens in this respect. Indeed, we saw in Chapter 1 that council housing was once set up as a central tenet of the post-war welfare state demarcating the rights of citizens, alongside other provisions such as social insurance described in Chapter 3. It was in the post-war decades when 'politics merged with concrete, the proletarian building material par excellence, to manifest [a] new social settlement' between citizens and the state. Housing complexes fashioned models of the 'respectable' family as 'nuclear family units with indoor sanitation, heating, hot and cold water were set within larger spaces that included shops, basic health and child care, green areas and playgrounds' (Alexander, Hojer-Bruun, and Koch, 2018: 125). While we saw in Chapter 1 that this settlement was premised on its own forms of gendered and racialized exclusion, those who were offered council housing were also considered to be part of a 'respectable' class deserving of more spacious and of higher quality housing than its equivalent provided in the private rental sector. In 1961, so-called Parker Morris standards were implemented which established mandatory standards in public housing, including a minimum size for new council homes.

Yet, as policies shifted away from the worker–citizen to that of the consumer–citizen, these changes became embodied in the new materiality of council housing. The Local Government, Planning and Land Act 1980 ended the Parker Morris standards, resulting in a rapid deterioration of building quality and size in the council housing sector. It also introduced the 'right to buy' for council tenants (see Chapter 1), and relaxed long-standing restrictions on mortgage lending and landlords. When new public housing was built, it tended to be of lower quality than its inter- and post-war counterparts, and from the 1990s onwards, increasingly outsourced to non-state bodies, the social housing associations. Moreover, everyday wear and tear meant that by the 1980s much of the inter- and post-war housing stock had begun to fall into disrepair. On a Midlands council estate, Reynolds (1986: 33) reported widespread complaints among residents about faulty drains, creeping damp, leaks, and an almost complete lack of noise insulation between the maisonettes. Two decades later, Alexander et al. (2009: 3) echoed these concerns on an inner-city housing estate in London, including broken cupboards for storing waste, communal areas and corridors being used as shelters by homeless individuals, blocked chutes, and endemic fly-tipping. And Mulcahy found that community mediators in a south London centre saw 'noise' as the most frequent cause of conflict between tenants. This was caused 'by more general problems with the quality of housing provision in the borough', including 'poor insulation; high-density living; poorly converted Victorian houses not designed for multiple occupancy; and the scarcity of safe outdoor areas for children to congregate and play' (2001: 518; Mulcahy and Summerfield, 2001).

The material decline of council housing provoked an important shift in the management of tenants and their homes: 'governance through the social' gave way to a rhetoric of individual responsibility and blame. From the 1980s onwards, the post-war system of local authority run housing management was abandoned and tenants themselves increasingly held responsible for the decline of their neighbourhoods. As Hyatt argues, Thatcherite policies constructed tenants as 'the agents best qualified to rescue their communities from an accelerated spiral of deterioration and decline which, by the mid-1980s, was widely recognized to have rendered most British public-sector housing estates virtually unliveable' (1997: 166). In tune with the general shift towards individual responsibility, initiatives like Tenant Management Organizations (TMOs) encouraged tenants to take responsibility for functions once carried out by their councils, including collecting rent, organizing repairs and maintenance work, and ensuring that buildings were kept clean and tidy (1997: 166–7). But it was only in 1997 with the election of the New Labour government that tenants were turned into explicit agents of policing: under the expansive 'anti-social behaviour' legislation and tools discussed in Chapter 1 and 5, social landlords were given extended powers to evict families from social housing tenancies for accusations of 'anti-social behaviour', whose legal outlines and principles were hazily defined. As the vulnerable citizen, or the citizen-as-crime fighter became the model citizen (Ramsay, 2010), so social housing tenants found themselves policed in heightened ways.

According to Burney (2009: 168), 'long past are the days when housing law was just about land and property rights'. While we can question whether housing law was ever 'just' about that, the quote betrays a central point: the growing burden of enforcing good behaviour that is carried by local authorities and social landlords in the regulation of tenants. The possession of a social tenancy today 'is treated as a privilege to be earned, conditional on the good behaviour of the tenant, his or her family and visitors' (2009: 168; see also Chapter 5) and 'anti-social behaviour' constitutes a legitimate ground for evicting a social housing tenant from their property. As we already saw in Chapter 1, under the legal definition of 'anti-social behaviour', as adopted under the Crime and Disorder Act 1998, any behaviour that causes 'alarm, harassment and distress to a member of the public' other than from within the same household could be subject to official interventions. This constituted a significant expansion from the term's original usage in policy documents and the New Labour government's thinking (Chapter 5). The term 'anti-social behaviour' morphed from being originally used in New Labour discourse and policy documents to describe aggressive and criminal behaviour of a few select individuals to incorporating a 'diverse mix of environmental and human incivilities that affect neighbourhoods in a more impersonal and generalised way' (Burney, 2009: 168).

Anthropologists, social historians, and socio-legal scholars have documented how inequality, class, and state power are ineradicably built into the material environment of neighbourhoods, homes, and work places (Alexander, Hojer-Bruun, and Koch, 2018; Bijsterfeld, 2008; Fennell, 2015; Hyatt, 1997), giving rise to environmental suffering (Auyero and Swistun, 2009). Environmental suffering is also experienced by social housing tenants, for whom life in crowded and badly insulated buildings can be an intimate violation of their homes, and 'noise' a generalized, ambient sensory assault registered in the body. What is more, contemporary state policy which addresses nuisance complaints not as problems of structural fault with building quality and maintenance but as questions of individual policing legitimizes this environmental suffering as an inevitable fact of urban life. Policies that construct the social fact of noise as 'natural'—neutral and implacable— depoliticize the foundations of nuisance at 'a moment when the right to create noise made noise problems between neighbours increasingly likely' (Bijsterfeld, 2008: 191) and illustrate a central premise of 'advanced liberalism' (Rose 1996): the idea that social housing tenants should not just be passive recipients or 'objects of policy', as was the case under the post-war system of social governance, but active 'practitioners' of policy (Hyatt, 1997; see also Chapter 6).

In the last chapter, we saw that while the reproduction of classed and gendered inequalities through the workings of social policy has been well established in the literature, less explored have been the lives and reflections of those at the receiving end. This chapter takes this focus on the actual recipients of welfare to the case of tenants who turn to their social landlords to help them deal with a variety of often disparate problems that result from, or are exacerbated by, material neglect. Material neglect has deeply marked Park End: people's homes and even entire streets have been allowed to fall into decline and disrepair through failure on the part of the local authorities to maintain them. This architectural decay, in turn, is often the cause of what tenants refer to as 'trouble': poorly insulated walls and ceilings, cramped living conditions, and badly maintained communal areas generate tensions between people who live in close vicinity to one another. While tenants learn to use the language of 'anti-social behaviour' and 'nuisance' to make their claims for help heard, these framing exercises also make them vulnerable to being called 'petty' and 'infantile', and serve as a justification for the authorities to yet further discharge their responsibility. In what follows, I will turn first to a closer analysis of neighbour 'trouble'; second, to an examination of the material neglect of people's neighbourhoods; and third, I will analyse how tenants appropriate the state's official resources to make themselves heard.

Troubled Neighbourhoods

'When I moved into the house, it was a dream come true. My grandmother gave me the bed, sort of insinuating that everything would be all right now.' These were Brian's words to me, when I met him for an interview at his mother's house in 2010. Brian was a white, single man in his late forties. When I met him, he was living on disability benefits due to severe back problems he had been experiencing for years. Brian had been in a variety of mostly low-paid jobs, including community-level work, before he became too sick to work. He had also engaged in criminal activity as a young man; Brian described himself as a 'Robin hood character' who used to take 'from the rich' in the nearby situated, mostly privately owned neighbourhoods but was 'too clever to ever get caught'. Now, however, he lived in a two-bedroom house in a row of six identical houses that he and their other occupants had built ten years prior as part of a 'self-builders' scheme run by a local housing association. This had given tenants a secure tenancy and an equitable share of 25 per cent in return for the labour they put into constructing their houses. For Brian, the self-building scheme had been a once-in-a-life time opportunity: it was the first time that he had been given his own house, something in which he could invest and call his own.[2]

When he moved into his new self-built home, it marked a new beginning. However, shortly after the move, things started to go awry. The problem, Brian said, was Jay, a man of Afro-Caribbean descent, who was slightly younger than him. Jay had been on the same self-builder scheme, but unlike the other members, he had been difficult from the very beginning: he would rarely turn up for work, and when he did, he would be aggressive and intimidate the other self-builders. Then, Jay was given the house next to Brian's. From the beginning, relationships were strained. Jay had a very different rhythm to Brian, playing loud music at all times of day and receiving visitors late at night. Jay could not care less about his home: he would leave his back-garden looking like 'World War III', dumping his rubbish and old furniture there, and sometimes even throwing rubbish over the fence into Brian's own back garden. But perhaps worst of all was the lingering feeling that Jay was 'up to no good', that there was drug-dealing going on next door with 'shifty characters' coming in and out of the house. One night the police, in full riot gear, raided Jay's house, destroying the front door in the process. Jay was arrested but allowed to return a few days later. The door remained damaged for several months; Brian was concerned that people visiting the street would think that the houses in the row had been abandoned because of the sorry state of the house.

Brian's story might appear extreme. But unwanted exposure to neighbours was a source of frequent conflict in Park End, as it is elsewhere in working-class neighbourhoods (Bottoms, 2006; Reynolds, 1986) and can be in rural communities where people live in close proximity to one another (Peay, 1999). Park End tenants sometimes used the word 'trouble' to describe these

---

[2] As a single man with no dependent family members, his chances of being offered a social housing property were otherwise virtually zero, given the shortage of available social housing tenancies. Nor would he have been in a position to buy his own home.

situations: the word included anything from mundane tensions that resulted from forced exposure to the smell, sight, and especially sounds of those living in close proximity, to more serious disputes that involved criminal and seriously threatening behaviour. This is not to say that all 'trouble' was irresolvable. Indeed, most 'trouble' resolved itself over time. Violet, for instance, was an older woman in her seventies living in a small house by herself. She was a Park End resident of long standing, having come to the United Kingdom from Jamaica with her parents when she was less than 10 years old. A few years ago, she had problems with teenagers using her porch as a hang-out spot. Violet felt intimidated by them because they were smoking marijuana and staring at her when she left the house. One day, she found one of the teenagers there on his own, obviously upset. It turned out that he had problems at home and Violet took him into her house and offered him a cup of tea. After this, the dynamics were turned around: the teenagers started greeting her, stopped smoking weed outside the house, and even dropped by her home once in a while to say hello. In this instance, then, a chance happening had created the occasion for an adjustment in intimacy and a different pattern of sociability to emerge between residents.

But as we saw in the example of Brian and Jay above, not all 'trouble' resolved itself. And when it failed to do so, its occurrence could be experienced as completely debilitating. As one resident said angrily to me when I asked her why 'trouble' was experienced as such a grave problem: 'you can just get up and leave, Izzy, but we can't!' What this meant in practice was illustrated to me when I met Tanya, a white woman who was renting a two-bedroom social housing property in a cul-de-sac on the new part of the estate. Tanya was living in the house by herself with her teenage daughter. 'He just opens his curtains and watches me through the window', Tanya pointed out of her kitchen window in the direction of Simon, her next-door neighbour's house, the day she invited me over to her house. Tanya was nervous that he might hear us through the thin walls of the living room, and so we sat crowded around a small table in her tiny kitchen. During the course of the conversation, it became clear that Tanya felt her own home had been besieged by the constant threat of Simon: he was everywhere; he could watch her through his bedroom windows; he could hear her through the walls; and his behaviour had become increasingly threatening. One day, when she left the house, he followed her around; another evening, he sneaked into her back garden to look into her bedroom at night; and yet another time, he put up a CCTV camera pointing towards her house. The worst was that he was spreading rumours between neighbours that Tanya was going out at night and leaving her child on her own at home, thus making Tanya fearful that social services might get involved.

When asked how she dealt with the situation, Tanya told me that she was trying 'to keep her head low'. In the last chapter, we saw that some women cultivate an attitude of indifference to, and independence from, ex partners and the fathers of their children who they cannot trust. A parallel can be drawn with how social housing tenants—both men and women—approached neighbours who they consider to be threatening: the general mantra was to 'keep oneself to oneself', to 'keep your head down', and to 'not go out looking for trouble'. Take the example of Tracey's move into a new home. In early 2010, Tracey was offered a two-bedroom house on my street. While Tracey's part-time position in the community centre did not technically qualify her for the status of a 'keyworker', the houses in the row had been empty for months and the housing association was desperate to fill its 'hard to let' properties on Park End. For Tracey, the move into her new home was a step up, something that afforded her more space from the cramped flat she had rented in the private sector before. She celebrated the move into her new home: like Brian above, she invested in a new bed, bedding, and cushions, and bought a brand-new flat-screen TV on a loan scheme that she would pay back over the year to come. Her efforts to build a pleasant home extended to the outside of the house. Almost immediately after moving in, she paid a friend to cut the grass in the front yard, and she kept the windows and doors spotlessly clean. At Christmas, a large Christmas tree was placed in the front window, with the best decorations facing the cul-de-sac.

But Tracey's attempts to be outwardly orderly and respectable also came at the exclusion of neighbours whose presence she did not consider to be welcome. Tracey often compared herself to neighbours in the close, and she would comment on others' behaviour, particularly when she considered it to fall short of 'expected standards'. The 'African family,' who lived two houses down, were 'taking the piss' by leaving their children's toys lying around on the parking space outside the house; the Chinese family next door cooked 'smelly food' that seeped through the thin walls; and the family opposite her house, a white, English family, were acting 'out of order' by drinking beer in the front yard instead of in their back garden. Tracey also complained about her neighbours being 'nosy' and wanting 'to know too much': every time, she walked past their houses, she felt that they were looking at her 'from behind their net-curtains' or coming out to 'have a look'. Indeed, the first thing she did on the day she moved into the house was to cover the windows with newspaper to stop neighbours from prying (the paper was soon replaced by net-curtains). Implicit in this act was a moral evaluation of what counted as respectable neighbourly behaviour, of what counted as acting in appropriate ways. And those who failed to live up to these standards could be harshly judged. Priya, for example, a nurse of Indian origin from Trinidad in her thirties, had suffered from problems with her next-door neighbour who she considered to be acting in inconsiderate ways. During a recorded interview, she said:

It hurts me what they're doing because I'm a keyworker [a nurse], I'm paying a lot of money for this flat, and I worked bloody hard for it. And [then] we are having people here who don't pay that kind of money that we are paying and they are enjoying a lifestyle that is even better than ours. I don't have anything against them, but they are deteriorating the environment, they are smoking, they are breaking things, they just have no value for the environment. And you know, it bothers me, it hurts me, because I worked for my flat and I am so proud of it. It hurts, it really does hurt.

While the emphasis on distance and appropriate manners here contrasts with the openness and density of social relations between kin and friends that we encountered in the last chapter, on a deeper level, relations between neighbours and those between household members shared some central features: the importance of demonstrating care. Here, Priya was contrasting her own efforts to care and to be a good tenant—someone who had 'worked' for her flat, who was proud of it, and who was looking after it—to her neighbour's failure to do the same.

In short, the danger to domestic life that intimate partners presented to the mothers in Chapter 3 is repeated more broadly in the figure of menacing neighbours, where daily efforts to maintain 'decent' neighbourhoods fit for living were threatened by the ever-present possibility of intrusion, even invasion. Social housing tenants found that the source of 'trouble' came from those living in close proximity: their next-door neighbours in a block of flats, street, or (perhaps tellingly) close. 'Trouble' was extremely upsetting for the women I met, but it could also affect men, as the case of Brian and Nasiru shows. But before we delve into the particulars of neighbour disputes and tenants' means of resolution, we must ask what general role the authorities play in maintaining adequate neighbourhoods and homes that are sufficiently comfortable for living. What is the tenor of their approach to matters of upkeep and building maintenance? And how do tenants like Tracey or Brian experience the authorities' presence in their daily lives?

'They Become Part of the Problem'

In the last chapter, we saw that contact with the benefit system often occurred at a point of crisis: women found that their dependence on the benefit system was initiated by a relationship breakdown, a loss of job, sickness, or some other difficulty that exposed them to financial hardship. In these initial moments, they had turned to the welfare state as a source of support, with the hope that it would help them maintain the family homes they aspired to and cherished. We can draw a parallel with the way Park End residents spoke about the prospect of a council house (a word that was commonly used to include also socially rented tenancies that had been outsourced to third sector social housing associations) as something they aspired to obtain. Many residents had been on the waiting list for social housing properties for years (Tracey, for example, had been waiting for over ten years when I met her), as demand for social housing by far exceeded its supply. Park End residents considered living in socially owned housing to be preferable to renting in the private market: tenancies in the private sector were less secure, with some landlords not even giving their tenants contracts; the rent in the private sector was often higher than in the socially rented sector due to a lack of rent controls; and there was a perception that private landlords could 'get away with anything' in a way that social housing providers could not. Some private landlords were also reluctant to take on welfare claimants as their tenants for fear of tenants falling behind on rent arrears.

The potential predations tenants faced while renting in the private sector are illustrated in the case of Helen, who was introduced in the last chapter as a so-called 'single mother'. After splitting up with the father of her younger daughter, Helen moved into a privately rented two-bedroom house on Park End. She knew that the house was not perfect, but she struggled to find anything else nearby. In any case, she felt she was lucky to get this place because many private landlords rejected applicants who were on housing benefits. From the outside, the house was one of the better, postwar builds. However, on the inside, the house was, in her words, 'a mess'. It was chilly and damp, with mould growing on the walls. The heaters in most rooms had long since stopped working and the windows were leaking, letting in rain and the cold, and making the house freezing on the inside in the winter months. The boiler kept turning off because the relight switch was broken; it had to be lit manually with a match. The railing on the staircase was missing. Her younger daughter had fallen down the stairs on several occasions. In parts of the living room, the carpet had been ripped up by a previous tenant, exposing sharp nails in the wooden flooring. Mice were coming into the house from underneath the floorboards. But perhaps worst of all, the back door to the garden was broken, leaving Helen and her children dangerously vulnerable. One day, her ex-partner had let himself into the house through the back-door when Helen was sleeping, taking her hair dryer and straightener, TV, and X-Box with him.

Helen had asked her landlord to fix various things in the house, including the broken back door, the boiler, and the rotten window frames. Having received no response, she decided that the situation was intolerable and resolved to move. She found a flat in the private rental market she liked on a neighbouring estate in town, informed her landlord that she was moving, and asked to be returned the deposit of £900 she had paid when first moving in, in order to pay the deposit on the new flat; and this is when 'the nightmare' started. Helen and I met with her landlord in her home at the same time when he was showing around a new potential tenant, another woman in her thirties who had come on her own. Helen's landlord was a stocky Asian man in his late forties, with short hair and a menacing attitude, and in the course of the meeting he accused Helen of being 'filthy' and 'dirty', and of having let the house 'fall to bits'. No inventory had been made when Helen first moved into the house, so it was difficult for her to prove that she was not responsible for most of the damage and dilapidation in the house. At one point, when Helen tried to defend herself, he said that it was no surprise she had treated the house so badly being 'a single mum on benefits', thus echoing the gendered tropes of undeservingness that were considered in Chapter 3. Fighting back her tears, Helen went silent, turning her head away from the woman who her landlord had brought along for a viewing.

While her landlord eventually agreed to pay her £300 of the initial £900, it took him weeks to process the payment. In the meantime, Helen lost the new flat because she could not transfer the deposit in time and faced imminent homelessness. Luckily, with the help of a support worker, Helen was moved onto the council's emergency housing list, and was shortly after able to move into a socially rented house on Park End. For Helen, the offer of this house had meant that she was able to escape a rogue landlord who was taking advantage of her vulnerable position as a single tenant. It also meant that she was given a clean house with two bedrooms, a house that she considered to be 'beautiful' and that came with a more secure tenancy that the one she had had in the private rental market. But for many other tenants, living in a socially rented property was far from ideal. Their stories revealed that they experienced social housing authorities as behaving in ways that were not too dissimilar from private landlords, as they allowed properties to fall into disrepair or failed to keep up with maintenance work. Mark and Jane, introduced in Chapter 2, were living in a three-bedroom 1990s terraced house; Mark often complained about the 'shit' condition of the house—the walls were 'paper thin' so he could hear all of the domestic activities of his next-door neighbours, the floor of the one of the bedrooms sloped, and the boiler regularly broke down. The back garden was waterlogged, and as a result, the wooden fencing was rotten.

People living in apartments and towerblocks, most of which had been built from the 1970s onwards, reported additional problems. They objected to the authorities' failure to maintain communal areas, including the hallways, corridors, lifts, courtyards, and even the walls of their own homes. Common complaints included broken lifts, litter that was left lying around in the hallways, post boxes and door bells that were left out of order for long periods of time, as well as lights that were broken in the communal corridors. In one case, Priya, who was introduced above and who was living in the same low-rise 1990s apartment block as Nasiru, had made repeated complaints to her landlord to fix the broken lights in her hallway. When she came home from an evening shift in the local hospital, she had to find her way through the dark to her flat which was at the end of the corridor. One night she tripped over the body of a man; it turned out to be a homeless person who had let himself in through the front door because the main gate had not been properly shut. Priya complained bitterly that it took her housing association weeks to sort out the lighting problem; in the meantime, however, the homeless person had come back almost every night, frightening her every time she walked past him.

Compounding the shoddy building quality, insufficient repair work, and failure to maintain communal areas were the cramped and poky conditions in the more recently built social housing tenancies. This applied particularly to the new housing development on Park End, built in the early 1990s and managed by a consortium of housing associations on a mixed-tenure basis.[3] The houses and apartment blocks were arranged in a series of cul-de-sacs, connected through an elaborate maze of one-way roads. Residents told me that the one-way road system had been planned and implemented as an act of deliberate policing: shortly before the new housing development was built, young people from the estate had engaged in a summer of 'joy riding' when they displayed and raced stolen cars along the main road of the estate. Some local people were of the opinion that the 'joy riding' had been hyped-up by the media: journalists were said to have come to the estate and encouraged young men to engage in illegal joy-riding in order to create sensational stories. The one-way road system on the new housing estate made joy riding and police chases practically impossible. People who had lived on the new estate for years told me that they still got lost in their neighbourhood because the lay-out was so confusing. But it was the cramped conditions in the cul-de-sac that most distressed residents; they felt like they were living 'on top of each other', constantly exposed to the sight, noises, and sometimes the smell of those living next door, across from, above,

---

[3] Some of it was socially rented, some of it was part-owned, and some of it, like the close where Tracey and I lived, was rented out on keyworkers' schemes.

and below. Brian held the building quality of his home responsible for the constant exposure to Jay:

> These houses are shit; they look nice but I can hear people move around two doors down. It was only when it all [his next-door neighbour] kicked off that I realised how shit the insulation is. He started taking the piss out of the heating system, he was mimicking the noises [of the heating system] and that's when I realized he can hear me ... It's torture. It's basically like sharing a house with somebody else, that's what it feels like, it feels like Big Brother, you know. You live in a Big Brother house but you are actually sharing it with a next-door neighbour.

Brian's language of 'torture', and of 'living in a big brother house' with a next-door neighbour, also reflected a more intimate offence that he felt at the hands of material neglect: the authorities' failure to provide and to maintain his house directly negated the moral basis of his home. Similar to the women in the last chapter who likened the welfare state to men, so an analogy was established between the way social housing tenants spoke of next-door neighbours who failed to abide by dominant codes of 'care' and the authorities who failed to condone, and even directly contributed, to such behaviour. What should have been a safe and 'nice' home—something that Brian himself had attended to and invested in by acquiring furniture, planting flowers, painting the walls, as well as receiving help with from his grandmother—was being directly undermined by the poor building quality of the walls of the house. 'I have always done my bit', Brian said to me on another occasion, referring to the fact that he had looked after his home, paid his bills on time, and contributed to the 'local community' by being active in a claimants' union that was advocating for welfare rights. Similar then to the women in the last chapter who experienced the benefit system as a direct affront to their daily struggles to maintain family homes, we can see, once more, how the workings of housing policies had an impact on tenants' homes that went far beyond the material neglect itself.

In the last chapter, we saw that dealing with a byzantine bureaucratic system induced practices of withdrawal, as residents ended up barricading their homes from the unwanted intrusion of benefit officials, whether that link be severed by refusing to answer phone calls, to respond to a knock on the front door, or to open a letter with an official heading. Similarly, social housing tenants frequently withdrew from housing officials and authorities that they did not consider to be responsive to their needs. Let us come back to the public meeting described at the beginning of the chapter, during which Nasiru—the only tenant to attend—had asked the housing officer if the houses were meant to be 'houses to live happy lives [in]' or just meant 'to provide housing'. After the meeting (which quickly ended after Nasiru was silenced), he and I got talking. I was surprised that only he had come to the meeting, given that the kinds of problems Nasiru was experiencing were common to social housing tenants. 'What do you expect?' he said, 'It's this whole thing that you have to be there when it suits them, but they never listen to you!' Nasiru subsequently decided to withhold his monthly service charge payments.[4] This constituted a breach of his contractual obligations under his social tenancy (and could potentially lead to an eviction if arrears were accrued), but he felt that the authorities had, in turn, breached *their* duties to maintain and look after the building.

In short, badly maintained houses and streets, the neglect of communal areas, and thoughtless planning and urban design were part and parcel of daily neighbourhood life on Park End. As the women we encountered in the last chapter experienced the benefit system as inhumane, obstructive, and directly contrary to their own efforts to build and maintain family homes, social housing tenants experienced the authorities' indifference and material neglect of their neighbourhood as a direct affront to their own efforts to have neighbourhoods fit for living. It comes perhaps as no surprise then that social housing tenants sometimes invoked a homology between the 'trouble' that they were exposed to at the hands of neighbours and the attitudes and policies of housing authorities and officials. The latter were congruous with, and sometimes even directly facilitated or enabled, the activities of the former. Brian expressed this sense very strongly when he complained that 'they [the housing authorities] are on his [Jay's] side' and that 'they' [the housing authorities] are part of the problem'. But how does the government's shifts to 'anti-social behaviour' feature in this story? And what opportunities did these policies give tenants like Priya or Brian to personalize the state?

---

[4] Services charges are levied by landlords to recover the costs they incur in providing services to a building. The landlord provides the service, while the leaseholder pays for them.

Personalizing 'Anti-Social Behaviour'

As we saw in the opening vignette to this chapter, the authorities' unresponsiveness in maintaining homes and neighbourhoods contrasted with their manifest presence in matters of public order maintenance and the policing of tenants' behaviour in their homes. The authorities spoke of this in terms of a language of 'nuisance' and 'anti-social behaviour' that mirrored the New Labour government's policies outlined in Chapter 1. Tenants were constantly reminded in writing correspondence and during meetings, such as the one described in the opening of the chapter, that they should report any incidents of 'anti-social behaviour' that were occurring in their neighbourhood. Posters were hung up on notice boards in public facilities featuring slogans that invited tenants to step forward and report any problems they were experiencing: 'Fed up with nuisance problems? Call CanAct—your Crime and Action Nuisance Team'; 'Vandalism! Getting a visa to travel won't be easy if you're a convicted vandal!'; 'Problems with neighbours? Fed up with complaints? MEDIATION! Solving problems in the community. Call our number'. A range of institutions were trained to respond to nuisance problems, including social housing authorities, the local authority's crime and nuisance action unit, and the environmental health unit, and, as we will see in Chapter 6, private–public partnerships set up to address these issues.

All tenants I spoke to who reported 'trouble' with their neighbours were aware of the 'anti-social behaviour' policies put in place for dealing with problem tenants. Many had at some point during their tenancy tried to pursue claims for help through these official mechanisms. In fact, it was not unusual in daily conversations for Park End residents to exchange information about the various institutions and bodies, even if help was rarely forthcoming. For example, Pete, an older white resident who was living on his own and who had become prey to vicious behaviour from his neighbours came into the community centre to get advice. Pete's tormentors had harassed him in a number of ways, including making threatening remarks on the streets, uprooting the flowers he had planted in his front yard, poisoning his hedge with bleach, and they had most recently left a mug outside his front door with 'twat' written in large letters across it. Tracey advised that he get in touch with his social housing association. She told him to report his neighbours for 'anti-social behaviour', using a language that was not commonly used by tenants in their daily lives. Like the working-class citizens studied by Engle Merry (1990) who learn to express their grievances in terms of a language of enforceable rights and obligations that those in power can understand, Park End tenants learnt to frame their demands in terms of the state's own masked moral lexicon of blame, offence, breach of obligations, and the proof of wrongdoing that went along with it.

Learning to frame problems of 'trouble' in terms of a language of legal rather than social or moral obligations, however, was not always easily done. It required that social housing tenants make a leap of faith as they had to set aside their own more nuanced, complicated, and multi-faceted understandings of 'trouble' in favour of a more simplistic, legalistic, and black-and-white picture. For example, Brian was aggrieved when he first turned to his social housing provider to speak to him about his trouble with Jay. While he blamed Jay for his unreasonable and increasingly violent behaviour, we also saw that he felt that the authorities were to blame for the low building standards that had contributed to noise problems in the first place. Likewise, Nasiru's complaints about his neighbours' behaviour were also interwoven with his frustrations about the housing authorities' failures to maintain communal areas in his block of flats. However, with the procedures that were being put in place by the social housing associations and local authorities, these more complex stories, from Brian's distributed attribution of fault to Nasiru's enumeration of the range of delinquencies of housing authorities, could simply not be heard. For Nasiru, this unresponsiveness was evidence that the authorities were not interested in creating houses that would be 'happy homes' for the tenants who had to live in them. Their indifference, their deafness, that contrasted so dramatically with tenants' ear-splitting environment, was an impersonality that simultaneously depersonalized residents, stripping them of their status as proper, valuable, and deserving recipients of care.

Indeed, even when tenants tried to frame the problems that they were experiencing within the terms and language that those in authority would understand, they still reported bitterly frustrating experiences. Tenants spoke of unresponsive officers, of being sent from office to office, of files being lost and passed around different departments and institutions, from their landlords to environmental health units to the local authority's crime and nuisance action team and to the police. It took Brian and his fellow tenants two-and-a-half years of phoning the local housing association about Jay before they finally found out that their complaints had been going to the wrong person. Even once they managed to reach the relevant official, tenants found that they were asked to submit onerous proof of their neighbours' wrongdoing. The most common mechanism for collecting evidence was through so-called 'incident diaries'—booklets with pre-specified columns asking the author to log any nuisance that they were experiencing, including when it had taken place, the duration of the activity in question, and its impact on their lives. Nasiru had been given an incident diary after he had made a complaint about noise. He described how the process of having to take notes—his only means of redress—had started taking over his life. He became obsessed with the noise, listening out for it and trying to catch the culprits in the process, making living in his flat even more miserable than it had been before.

'Incident diaries' were not always considered sufficient proof of nuisance. In Brian's case, he filled in approximately thirty incident diaries about Jay's activities over a period of several months before he submitted them to the local housing association. He was told that it was insufficient evidence, that an environmental health officer would have to pay him a visit to take a recording of the noise. The environmental health unit was located in a different department, run by the local authority and not the housing association, and consequently took another few weeks to process. Eventually, an environmental health officer contacted him, a woman Brian described as utterly 'frustrating' and 'condescending'. She brought a recorder along that looked like it cost 'fifteen pence and was from a car boot sale'. Jay happened to be quiet that time and the officer insisted that she would have to come back on another day. Torturous weeks followed, during which Brian tried to catch Jay in the moment and get the environmental health officer to get to his house in time to make the recording. Eventually, they succeeded to capture the noise on the recorder, only to be told afterwards that the noise was not continuous and hence not 'against the law':

At 4.30 a.m., 8.30 a.m., and then, look, 4.45 to 5.05 very loud bass [music], then it stopped, and then it'd start up again 10 min later, and then it would go on for an hour and thirty minutes, and then it stopped, and then it comes back on 12 minutes later, and go on for 10 minutes, and then stop, and then come on 15 minutes later, and so on: off, on off, on off, on off, all over the place. So, when environmental health [officer] did come around, a couple of times they did, there was nothing. [But then] out of the door they go, and it starts again. Boom, boom, boom.

Brian was told that there was nothing that could be done to help him. In other situations, frustrations flared once fault had actually been acknowledged. In Nasiru's case, the housing officer who had obtained a noise recording of his next-door neighbour's activities was finally forced to admit that 'there is a structural problem with these flats'. She suggested that Nasiru try taking sleeping pills or, alternatively, try to resolve the problem with mediation. Mediation was routinely promoted as a solution to neighbour disputes; it involved a process whereby quarrelling tenants were asked to discuss their problems in the presence of a neutral third party, the mediator, and to reach a consensual outcome. However, I did not meet a single tenant who endorsed this idea. Nasiru summed it up: 'It's just stupid!', he said. 'Mediation works if there is something to talk about, but in my case, with the problems that I am experiencing, there is nothing to talk about. There is only one solution: make the noise stop!' In fact, it was after the housing officer had told both Nasiru and his neighbour to go for a mediation session that the situation became unbearable. Now, when Nasiru asked his neighbour to turn down the radio noise or to stop littering his balcony with cigarette butts, the neighbour told him to 'call the housing officer or the police; he says that because he knows that nothing will happen!'

When talking to the local authorities, however, including to housing officers and the police, it was clear that official views of neighbour 'trouble' were different from the experiences described by social housing tenants: the authorities spoke of unreasonable and pushy tenants, of people who did not know how to look after their own problems and who were wasting the authorities' time. Often, tenants' actions were framed in infantilizing terms. We saw in the opening vignette that Val already anticipated that tenants would turn up with their 'one-person's problems' when her housing association called a public meeting on 'anti-social behaviour'. In the same conversation, she complained that tenants on Park End suffered from 'apathy' and did not like 'community': she personally liked it, she said, when she could hear her neighbour's children play in the garden or rehearse their instruments in their rooms next-door because this is 'what community life is all about'. What is missing from Val's statement, however, is an acknowledgement of choice, possibilities, or an alternative future: for social housing tenants like Brian, Nasiru, or Priya what made the unpleasant situation unbearable was precisely the fact that they could not leave, even if they wanted to go. Other housing officials I interviewed likened neighbour disputes to 'cat-and-mouse games' and to 'adults acting like children'. Some officers also invoked broader images of a dependent population that we already encountered in the last chapter in relation to benefit recipients. This attitude is clearly in view in the following quote by a male police community support officer I interviewed about neighbour disputes:

There are disputes that go on: 'And so-and-so's daughter fell out with somebody else because she went out with so-and-so and he was my sister's boyfriend.' Sometimes it's just like ... it is like an episode of a *Jeremy Kyle*[5] show sometimes. You turn up, and there is twenty, thirty on the street, shouting at each other, nothing real criminal going on. But, you know, it's like because the police turns up, they wind themselves up even more, knowing that it won't resort to ... it won't result in violence because we're there but they get to shout. And they will: 'I want him fucking arrested, fucking arrested!'; 'I pay your ... I pay your wages, I'm paying your wages!' And you just think to yourself: 'No you don't: You're on the dole; you don't pay my wages ... '

While from the point of view of this officer, tenants' behaviour was often evidence of their infantile and dependent attitude, the experience could be deadly serious from the point of view of those affected. Brian reported how his inability to secure any enforcement action against Jay had only resulted in a deterioration of his neighbour relations. The situation finally came to a head when a housing official accidentally dropped off an incident diary intended for Brian at Jay's house, inadvertently alerting Jay to Brian's formal complaint. In response, Jay mobilized his cousin, who was living on the same street, to intimidate Brian: Brian described how, one day, he saw Jay's cousin through his kitchen window, making threatening gestures and claiming that he would

---

[5] *Jeremy Kyle* is a British tabloid talk show.

'slice his throat' if he did anything against Jay. Brian described how he finally 'lost it' with Jay:

> One night he had the music on, and I went out with a hammer, and I fucking hammered the door, whacked the door with a hammer, that stopped him. I was like a fucking animal that you push in a corner so far that it's just gonna turn around and bite you—he did it again, and I went out and went fucking lamas [crazy]. I smashed the door, I picked up stones and put them through the windows, I picked [up] this tile and threw it at the roof, so he came out, and basically, I grab hold of him—I'm not a violent man, you know I mean? [But] I could have fucking battered him with a stick or smashed his face, other people would've killed him, but I didn't do any of that—but I ended up grabbing him by the shirt, ripped it off, and he was just bearing it, d'you know what I mean? [...]

The police turned up. Brian was not arrested but he was told to come back to the police station the following day. He spent the night feeling anxious and unable to sleep. The next morning, before his meeting, he took 'loads of pills' to calm himself down before he went into the police station: 'You basically think you can't lose the plot because if you lose the plot, you gonna end up being fucking arrested; you end up getting done.' Brian was lucky that other neighbours had made complaints against Jay's behaviour which had been logged in the police system. He was let off with a warning on this occasion. However, the situation nonetheless revealed a grim irony: by refusing to recognize the seriousness of the problems that tenants were experiencing and by abdicating their responsibility to address it, the authorities contributed to the very disorder that their policies and presence were supposed to prevent.

Conclusion

'Decent, affordable housing should be a basic right for everybody', Desmond wrote in his study of America's rampant housing crisis at the lowest end of the rental market (2016: 204). However, for tenants who live in social housing properties today (as for many more in the privately rented sector), decent and affordable housing remains an unattainable goal. As this chapter has shifted the focus from women's attempts to maintain their family homes to social housing tenants' daily engagements with neighbours who live in the same street, apartment block, or row of houses, it has drawn with it the theme of this tense and unstable interaction between citizens and the state which simultaneously claims to represent them, neglects their concerns, and deals out its censure. We saw in the last chapter that Park End mothers experience their engagements with the benefit system as a practical impediment, unpredictable danger, and direct affront to their own aspirations for family homes. In ways all too similar to the fathers of their children whose violent or erratic behaviour they are trying to escape, the benefit system—ostensibly established precisely *for their benefit*—turns a deaf ear to or silences their complaints, where it does not criticize, or even criminalizes their living arrangements and family homes. Similarly, social housing tenants who consider renting with social landlords to be preferable to the vagaries of the private rental sector experience a comparable trade-off. Not only can the building quality be poor in the socially rented sector, but tenants who report problems with next-door neighbours find that the responses they receive from their respective social landlords can aggravate the problems for which they sought a remedy.

An ethnographic analysis of tenants' 'trouble' and their experiences of housing providers complicates the narrative of how contemporary housing policies reproduce classed control. The shift towards tenants' self-management and policing has been described as an example of 'advanced liberalism' in contemporary governance (Bijsterfeld, 2008; Hyatt, 1997; Rose, 1996), as part of a broader shift towards a Foucauldian style of governance whereby social housing tenants are turned from being objects of policy into active fighters of crime. In so doing, responsibility for structural problems is diverted from housing authorities and reconstructed as narrow problems of individual misbehaviour. Park End tenants might be seen to exemplify this process when they learn to use the tools of 'anti-social behaviour' to control, restrain, or punish their neighbours. However, to reduce tenants' behaviour to governmental technologies whose object are their own expansion would mean to lose sight of tenants' moral expectations of what makes a good person and neighbour that reflect, above all, localized and fluid understandings of care. It would also mean to overlook tenants' acute awareness of the authorities' responsibilities towards them and their expectation for better housing. Thus, when Park End tenants use the language of 'nuisance' and 'anti-social behaviour,' they are not merely conduits of government policies. Rather, my argument has been that even where tenants come to appropriate the state's simplifiying 'language of statehood' (Hansen and Stepputat, 2005), they pursue complex moral demands.

For many social housing tenants, it is precisely in light of their dependence upon their landlords, and in the absence of alternative mechanisms for voicing demands, that they come to personalize the state. Indeed, ethnographers and historians have identified the potential for environmental suffering to become repoliticized along more radical lines. For example, in her study of nuisance complaints in early-twentieth century Netherlands, Bijsterveld (2008) has noted how left-wing activists used complaints over radio noise between next-door neighbours as a ground for advancing a class-based politics. Similarly, in the case of a public housing project in inner-city Chicago, Fennell (2015) identifies how a focus on environmental problems, including faulty buildings and bad maintenance work, acted as a way of mobilizing political clout, with positive effects for the inhabitants of the project. And in a community mediation centre in Southwark, south London, Mulcahy observes how mediators encouraged disputant tenants 'to recognize the common source of their concerns and the need to call state agencies to account for service failures which encouraged hostility between residents' (Mulcahy, 2001: 518). Here, mediators were active in conceptualizing tenants' problems in such a way that placed responsibilities on the state for the conditions of social housing tenancies. However, on Park End, such alternative channels for expressing, and mobilizing citizens' agendas, are weak, if not outright absent. In the next chapter, I will turn to yet another situation where people's ability to make their voices heard are similarly restrained: with respect to Park End residents' experiences of violence and serious crimes, and of the police—as the most tangible representative of the criminal justice system—in mediating these experiences.

5
Dangerous Streets: Encounters with the Police

In the autumn of 2015, I received an invitation to participate in a public lecture on gangs and alternative social orders at a London university. I had not really spent much time thinking about these issues before, so on my next trip to Park End, I decided to ask Lindsey about gangs. I had expected her to talk about youth violence. To my surprise, she immediately turned the question on its head: 'What do you even mean by the word?' she retorted. 'The police are like a big gang. They all protect each other and they support each other and so they become untouchable because they have all the power and they can just do what they want.' She proceeded to tell me how her 15-year-old daughter Kyra had recently been taken into custody by the police: she had been crossing the estate on the main road at 9 p.m. in the evening on her way to her friend's house when she was stopped by two police officers in a car. Shortly thereafter, Kyra was arrested allegedly on account of disorderly behaviour (something she strongly denies) and driven to a police station in a nearby town. It was after midnight when Lindsey received a phone call from the police station telling her to come to pick up her child. Lindsey was one of the few people I knew on Park End who actually had her own car, so she was able to drive to the police station and get her daughter. Kyra was very distressed when she finally arrived to pick her up.

In the last two chapters, we looked at how Park End residents' attempts to create homes and neighbourhoods that are adequate and safe for living are undermined by a range of hazards they confront in their daily lives. We saw that it was through the authorities' selective interventions in, and enforcement of, policies and practices that classed control is exercised, exposing residents on Park End to a range of threats that are both formal and informal, both exercised at the hands of intimate partners,

Personalizing the State: The Anthropology of Law, Politics and Welfare at the UK's Margins. First Edition. Insa Koch. © Insa Koch 2018. Published 2018 by Oxford University Press.

next-door neighbours, as well as the officials they come into contact with. This chapter moves to a third aspect of citizens' daily lives that both suffuses everyday social fabric on Park End and draws it inevitably into a classed conflict with the state: residents' exposure to violent threats and the role of the police in mediating this. In their daily attempts to protect themselves from various threats, residents experience the police and predatory threats as being intimately linked. Lindsey, for example, worried that after the experience her daughter had had with the police, she might now start using back streets rather than the brightly lit main roads when visiting friends on the estate. Lizzy was caught between a rock and a hard place: between the threat of what both mother and daughter perceived as police harassment, on the one hand, and potential victimization at the hands of dangers lurking in dark alleys, on the other.

This chapter offers an ethnographic analysis of Park End residents' experiences of, and interactions with, the police and other agents of the criminal justice system, as they try to protect themselves from a range of both predatory and state-sponsored threats. It asks how do residents experience living in high crime surroundings? What role do the police play in containing serious levels of crime? And what expectations do residents have of the police and the criminal justice system writ large? We saw in Chapter 1 that Park End is portrayed in the public imagination as a place of disorder and crime. Images of gang-infested neighbourhoods have been recycled in the local media that see young, and typically black or ethnic minority citizens as directly responsible for problems of drug dealing and violent crime. And as policies have shifted to endorse the 'crime victim' as the idealized citizen of policy-making, so policing tools have been expanded to respond to these perceived problems. Young men, and to a lesser extent, young women on Park End are routinely stopped and searched by the police and given injunction orders for alleged disorderly behaviour. But perhaps less known is the collateral effect of increased policing on people's intimate lives. Law enforcement officials also intervene, rearrange, and modulate the lives of those associated with young men, including their close friends, kin, and household members.

The aim of this chapter is to offer an alternative perspective; one which contrasts the state's language of 'gangs', 'crime', and 'disorder' to residents' own talk of the 'streets'. Young people growing up on Park End learn from a young age that the 'streets' they call home are full of unexpected threats. Virtually everybody I spoke to has had personal experience with, or know of others in their networks of family members and friends who have been exposed to serious violence and crime. Often, this is committed at the hands of people living in close surroundings: a local drug dealer who is creating a climate of fear and menace; an abusive ex-partner or a lover who wants revenge (Chapter 3); or, a next-door neighbour whose daily acts of intimidation strangle any possibility of well-being (Chapter 4). These informal threats are not opposed to the role of the state, however. The expansion of policing under the New Labour government's turn to 'tough on crime' mirrors, if not exceeds, the threat of informal violence. I argue that this 'security gap' (Miller, 2013)—the threat of both victimization and insufficient or predatory policing—produces a range of responses on the part of citizens, ranging from selective personalization of the police into mundane dispute situations with kin, neighbours, and lovers to demands for self-protection in the face of serious threats that bypass the state altogether.

Recent work on the punitive turn has focused on the racialized and class consequences of expanded policing in the United Kingdom and beyond (Barker, 2016; de Koning, 2015; Fassin, 2013; Goffman, 2014; Lerman and Weaver, 2014; Wacquant, 2008). As policing is rolled out into poor and often immigrant-dominated neighbourhoods across much of the Euro-American world, the pursuit of 'law and order' leads to the controlling of the most vulnerable and poor. This chapter investigates how Park End residents across racial and gender divides both challenge and reproduce the state's own logic of domination in their daily engagements with the police. As we have seen in the previous chapters, those dependent upon the state invoke distinct archetypes of the *bad* person and the specific consequences for a polity which tolerates or fails to adequately redress the bad citizen's offences—categories distinct, that is, from the state's own ordering of crime and vice, its tactics of prevention, and its practices of punishment. Extending this insight, this chapter argues that residents' responses to the police capture a desire for authority that is not easily collapsed with that of the state, as they conjure a moral or political order that does not place the state's own categories of order at its centre. And yet, when residents personalize punishment to suit their own purposes, they also risk getting drawn further into the remits of state control, as their actions legitimize further expansion of criminal justice measures. The guiding motive of the last chapters—the complex pattern of resistance and reproduction—emerges once more, then, with respect to people's engagements with the criminal justice system.

Policing, Crime, and Security as a Collective Public Good

The British police force was established in the nineteenth century as the specialised organization charged with the maintenance of order and entrusted with the capacity to deploy the legitimate force that the state monopolizes (Reiner, 2010: xiii). Reiner writes, 'policing inherently operates with dirty hands. It uses morally dubious means to achieve the overriding imperative of preserving and reproducing social order' (ibid.: xiii). But the extent to which the police's 'morally dubious means' have been integrated into a broader societal and political apparatus has changed over time. If the police force was originally established in the face of widespread opposition in the nineteenth century, it was in the post-war decades after the Second World War, alongside the establishment of the welfare state (considered in the last few chapters), that 'policing by consent' became the guiding principle. This reflected the aspirations for a different kind of policing institution, one which idealized the police as a crucial emblem of 'English identity and social order' (Loader, 1997: 16), personified in the fictional character of PC George Dixon (Newburn, 2008: 3). Various policies which resonate with the 'welfarist consensus' considered in Chapter 1, including an emphasis on non-partisanship, accountability, the rule of law, preventive policing, and strategies of minimal force, were also central to this endeavour (Reiner, 2010: 71–8). This book, however, has cautioned against any linear narrative of 'consent' in the post-war decades and its opposition to 'coercion' in the decades that followed (Chapter 1): the post-war social contract was always premised on its own forms of classed, gendered, and racialized coercion, and, indeed, considerable police malpractice continued to exist in working class neighbourhoods during this period (Reiner, 2010: 68).

While 'consent' was never a simple principle of post-war policing, it was in the 1980s that the police's legitimacy was brought under attack in the public realm. Reiner (2010) situates this shift from 'plods to pigs' in macro developments in the political economy of British capitalism, the rise of neoliberalism, and the decline of the post-war social settlement (see also Chapter 1), all of which had the effect of 'uncapturing' large sections of the population, chiefly its working classes, from the post-war consensus (Nugent, 2012). At the same time, internal problems pertaining to the police force—including issues of discrimination, corruption, abuse, and particularly racism—were becoming increasingly apparent (Bowling, Parmar, and Philipps, 2008; Newburn, 2008; Reiner, 2007). Hall et al. in their 1978 account *Policing the Crisis* revealed this legacy of classed and racialized policing. Riots in Brixton, south London, and other minority-dominated areas brought this racial tension into the open and resulted in violent confrontations between the police and the black community. Violent stand-offs with the police also happened in former mining communities affected by economic crisis and the closure of the mines, as well as among middle-class liberals around questions of counter-culture and anti-nuclear movements. Government policies responded, in turn, by politicizing 'law and order' (Downes and Morgan, 2007). Under Thatcher, military-style policing was first introduced to fight internal enemies, now increasingly stylised as 'folk devils' (Cohen, 1972) from whom the nation needed protection.

But it was only in the early-1990s that a cross-party consensus formed around issues of 'law and order', accompanied by sharp partisan conflict about delivery. For Reiner, this marked the beginning of a new period that moved policing 'beyond legitimation' (2010: 96). The last chapter already considered the implications of this shift for social landlords under the Labour government between 1997 and 2010. But changes were also introduced during this period to the police. The Crime Reduction Programme and the Crime and Public Order Act of 1998 required the police to work in partnership with local government and other social agencies to produce evidence-led analyses of local crime and disorder problems, and to develop 'joined up' solutions to solve them. The Police Reform Act 2002 further introduced an 'extended police family' (Newburn, 2008) that included the establishment of community police support officers (PCSOs) into neighbourhood policing teams, which are dedicated police teams responsible for policing single neighbourhoods. The introduction of PCSOs, as well as private sector bodies and civilians into the police force, exemplify the process of what Newburn (2008) has referred to as the 'pluralisation of policing' and is evident in places like Park

End where a myriad of law enforcement officials patrol the streets (Chapter 1). While the police budget has been cut like other public services with the shift to austerity politics since 2010 (Chapter 7), policing and police power remain visible, particularly in poor and ethnic-minority dominated neighbourhoods today.

Anthropologists of policing and scholars of punishment have argued that the expansion of the iron fist of the state has not been a simple response to crime per se, but an attempt to 'enforce order' (Fassin, 2013). It reflects a way of governing insecurity through a 'neo-liberal Leviathan' (Wacquant, 2009, 2010) at a time when the state's authority is increasingly called into question (see also Garland, 2001; Simon, 2007). Wacquant argues that 'much like the "long sixteenth century" saw the birth of the modern Leviathan in Western Europe, [so] our own century's turn has witnessed the fashioning of a novel kind of state' (Wacquant, 2012). From poor neighbourhoods in Paris (Fassin, 2013) and Amsterdam (de Koning, 2015) to both North (Goffman, 2014) and South America (Auyero, Bourgois, and Scheper-Hughes, 2015) to the supposedly more inclusive Scandinavian countries (Barker, 2016), scholars have investigated the effects of increased policing in the most disenfranchised neighbourhoods. In Britain, the classed and racialized dimensions of policing are illustrated with respect to the categories of 'gang' and 'gang violence' that invoke popular images of poor, black, and ethnic minority youths involved with serious drug offences and violence (Lammy, 2017; Williams and Clarke, 2016). Only in 2017, the Lammy Review[1] was published which argued that 'stop-and-search' is often linked to 'suspicions of gang offending, including drug dealing—with Black boys more than ten times as likely as White boys to be arrested for drug offences. This links together two prominent narratives about urban crime: that the war on drugs must be won and that gangs cannot be allowed to terrorise communities' (2017: 7).

Policing practices create new forms of exclusion, legitimize further police violence, and inflict punishment on some of the most disadvantaged sectors of the population. This has inspired some to speak of the emergence of differential citizenship patterns in the United States—of 'semi-legal' (Goffman, 2009) or 'custodial'

---

[1] The Lammy Review, chaired by Labour MP David Lammy, is an independent review into the treatment of, and outcomes for black, Asian, and minority ethnic individuals in the criminal justice system.

forms of citizenship (Lerman and Weaver, 2014). But semi-legal or custodial citizenship also exists alongside an uncomfortable and often less-acknowledged fact: the same people who are victims of increased policing are also most in need of protection from threats to serious harm, often committed by people who live within their own neighbourhoods or even within their own homes (Forman, 2017; Koch, 2017a; Miller, 2013, 2016). Informal or extra-legal violence is unevenly distributed, and its effects are concentrated in disadvantaged communities. Park End, for example, was consistently identified as a 'crime hot spot' by the authorities (Chapter 1). Miller has referred to this situation as a 'security gap' (Miller, 2013): a gap that opens up where marginalized communities face both the threat of victimization by criminals and insufficient or even discriminatory policing. The 'security gap' gives rise to what Meares (1997) has referred to as the 'dual frustration' argument among poor African–American citizens in US neighbourhoods: they express their frustrations both with respect to high levels of crime and drug dealing in their neighbourhoods as well as with police misconduct (Kennedy, 1997; Meares and Kahan, 1998).

It comes as no surprise, perhaps, that popular desire for effective law enforcement constantly runs up against fear and mistrust (Comaroff and Comaroff, 2016: 38), producing complex forms of state–citizen engagement beyond either outright consent to the police's authority or simple antagonism. In poor urban neighbourhoods in the United Kingdom and the United States, this is expressed in the co-existence of popular demands for tougher interventions (Forman, 2017; Kennedy, 1997), selective appropriation of the police (Bell, 2016; Goffman, 2014; Koch, 2017a), as well as reliance on self-policing and vigilante justice (Davey, 2016; Davey and Koch, 2017; Girling, Loader, and Sparks, 1998; Karandinos et al., 2014; Koch, 2017a; Smith, 2017a; Super, 2016). And yet, while 'order is constituted through punishment', Steinberg reminds us that 'who, precisely, is authoring the ensemble is not easy to say' (2016: 527). Thus, African-American mothers in impoverished US neighbourhoods involuntarily contribute to the criminalization of black and marginalized citizens when they deploy the police in intimate disputes with lovers, sons, and neighbours (Bell, 2016). Citizens in Nigeria and South Africa find that once drawn into their lives, the police often harness a power that they cannot control, sometimes even with lethal effects

(Cooper-Knock and Owen, 2015). And both Hornberger (2013) and Caldeira (2002) show in South Africa and Brazil, respectively, that popular demands for punishment can also be redirected against the most vulnerable and poor.

In this chapter, I draw upon these insights to analyse how Park End residents both engage but also reproduce police control in their daily struggles over neighbourhood safety. On Park End, the police force is part of a broader landscape that includes both state-sanctioned and more informal or predatory threats of violence. This generates a complex picture of engagement and disengagement, of personalization and rejection. Many of my interlocutors say that they are 'anti-police'. But they also appropriate the state into their everyday lives, sometimes in ways that align with the law but more frequently for purposes that escape the official representatives—and representations—of law and order. What is more, where the state fails to provide residents with the protection they want (which is frequently the case in situations of more serious threat), residents can fall back on their own informal mechanisms that surpass the state's own desires and forms of punishment and hence get condemned as unlawful violence by the state. I argue that, far from a ratification of the legitimacy of the means and ends of state power, calls for 'more punishment' reflect popular desires for a personalized state, one whose moral and political order is of a very different nature to that imagined by those in power. In what follows, I first describe the informal violence on Park End that residents confront; second, their experiences of the police; and third, I consider the ways in which residents mobilize their own resources in dealing with violent threat.

'You Do or Get Done'

During my fieldwork, I met Vicky, a white mother in her mid-thirties with an infectious smile and a friendly disposition. Vicky had moved to the town at the age of five and had lived on Park End for many years. There, she had raised her teenage son as well as her niece, a teenage girl, who had come to live with her after her mother (Vicky's sister) had suffered a mental breakdown. Unlike many of the other mothers I met, Vicky described herself as someone who was interested in education and in learning. Vicky had dropped out of school early when she had fallen pregnant, but she had finished her high school qualifications as a mature student and, when her son was a bit older, even completed a higher education degree. When I met her, she was working as a teaching assistant in a local secondary school. On the face of it, Vicky had all the outward signs of respectability: she had a job that allowed her to be financially independent (although she would lose the job further down the line), she was supporting herself and her son and niece even as she struggled as a 'single mother.'

But her attempts to be 'respectable'—to have a stable life sheltered from the trauma of her earlier marriages, as she once told me—were easily thwarted. As I got to know Vicky more closely, I realized how quickly normality could slip into unexpected disaster, a point that we already came across in the previous chapters. Threats of violence loomed beneath the surface of her well-organized home. Her partner at the time, a local man who was charismatic and generous, would also beat her up and lock her in a kitchen cupboard when he was intoxicated. He also had shifty friends, who had come to Vicky's house before and left syringes, used for drugs, lying on the floor. Her teenage son was prone to commit violence too. He had been in and out of young offenders' institutions from a young age. On one occasion, he appeared in court on a joint enterprise charge for a violent stabbing. Her 15-year-old niece was suspended from school for a number of weeks when she had gotten into a fight with another girl, necessitating medical treatment.

From the outside, these incidents could be seen as extreme cases of 'difficult family behaviour', which is how the school made sense of the children's behaviour: I once accompanied Vicky to a meeting with the school headmaster who told her that she would have to change her parenting style to prevent her son from getting involved in more criminal activity. People like Vicky could be given a parenting order—a civil order which would place her under the close supervision of the authorities and require her to attend so-called 'parenting classes' under the threat of penalty in the case of non-compliance. But the cursory glance at Vicky's life also revealed a social fabric of threats and crime that young people in Park End were socialized into from a young age. The same people who at one moment were prone to violence could at other moment be victimized at the hands of someone else. Young people—particularly boys but girls as well—grew up in an environment where they quickly learn to accept that the unexpected was to be expected. They lived in streets taken over by dealers who sold drugs openly from their premises and intimidate passers-by. They grew up in families where the threat of domestic abuse at the hands of violent men was commonplace and sometimes expected (Chapter 3). And stabbings, sometimes with fatal results, were a regular occurrence in their social circles, particularly among young men and teenage boys who spent more time 'on the streets'—a term used at once to describe a geographical location as well as a space that connoted danger, shiftiness, and informal violence.

Park End residents had built up intimate topographies of danger (Koch, 2017a). This was made evident to me one day when I accompanied Alice, a 14-year-old girl, on a walk from her house to the bus-stop. Alice was the daughter of Linda and Tony, a couple in their early thirties who were living with Linda's two daughters in a small two-bedroom socially rented house on the edges of the estate. Linda was originally from Portugal, while Tony had grown up on a neighbouring estate in town. He worked as a bus driver when I met him. As we walked along, Alice spontaneously told me about the places around us: at the corner of her street, a neighbour was killed last year. He had been followed by a group of young men from a different part of town and was stabbed to death just in front of his house; Alice had been coming home from school when she saw her street blocked off by police tape. A bit further along the main road, Alice pointed out where a van had caught fire: her stepfather's ex-wife had heard the explosion and come out to watch. It turned out to be an arson attack. Then again, over the other side was a part of the estate she avoided going to altogether: her baby sister's father lived there, but the family was estranged from him. Two years ago, he had stolen her mother's dog and sold it to another resident on the estate. Alice missed the dog but nobody in the family dared to ask for it back for fear that her sister's father would retaliate. 'Lots of stuff is happening here', she commented, 'I don't know why people still come out.'

Residents often spoke of 'the streets' to capture the landscape of predatory threats. Like the term 'trouble' that we encountered in the last chapter, the 'streets' was an emic category used by residents to describe violence and threat, in ways that were broader and more diffuse than the state's own categories of disorder and crime. And like 'trouble', protection from the streets necessitated a honing of particular forms of knowledge and skills. Ethnographic engagements with poverty and crime have often favoured the perspectives of young, particularly black men, who are at risk of both being the victims of crime and of perpetrating disorder (Bourgois, 1995; Goffman, 2014; Wacquant, 2008). But less attention has been paid to how women, in particular the mothers and girlfriends of young men, developed a range of coping mechanisms. Let us come back for a moment to Vicky. Women like her put a huge amount of effort and time into keeping their children 'out of trouble', often in gendered ways. Vicky had taught her niece where she could and could not go on the estate, including the place where her ex-partner lived. She also taught her who 'she could talk to and who she had to blank'; that is, to deliberately exclude someone by acting like they did not exist, and hence mirroring some of the practices of 'keeping oneself to oneself' that we already encountered with respect to next-door neighbours. By contrast, mothers might feel less able to tell their teenage sons how to act. Instead, Tracey told me that the most important thing was to make friends with her son's girlfriend so that she could keep an eye on him.

More important than refraining from particular relations and nurturing others, however, was the development of an attitude of toughness and a reputation for violence. I once fell prey to the threatening activities of a next-door neighbour for reasons unknown to me: he had started throwing rubbish into my backyard, had trampled on the flowers that my housemate at the time had planted in the front, and behaved in other menacing ways towards me. I told Linda, Alicia's mother about it. 'You are too nice', Linda said in response. 'People take advantage of you. You have to find a way for people to fear you, otherwise they will never stop!' What this meant in practice was illustrated in the way Linda herself raised her two teenage children. From a young age, she had insisted on sending them to karate classes where they would learn to 'defend themselves on the streets'. 'They teach them self-defence', she said to me once, 'but it's a self-defence that can kill!' Linda's partner, Tony, was sending his 6-year-old son, a son from a previous relationship, to boxing classes. He told me once, proudly, that 'boxing was the sport of the working class'. Linda had also bought a Staffordshire bull terrier—the one her ex-partner stole from her and sold—when the children were young, with the idea of having a dog that would protect them, and the house. Not unlike the boxers in South Chicago studied by Wacquant (2008), the crack dealers in Harlem (Bourgois, 1995), or the working-class residents in Bermondsey, southeast London (Evans, 2006), it was through the cultivation of physical capital that people sought to protect themselves from being attacked by those living in close proximity to them.

We saw in the last chapter that where neighbourhood peace had been unsettled by the persistent nuisance behaviour of someone living close by, a spiral of decline could rapidly deteriorate social relations; situations of acute danger and threat dramatically inflamed these tensions. By encouraging their children to be 'tough' in the face of danger, by cultivating a reputation for violence and not being, in the words of one friend, 'a pussy', Park End residents became complicit in perpetuating the climate of danger and fear. 'Here, it's a world where you do or get done'; 'you kill or get killed'; and 'what goes around, comes around' were statements I heard used. What this meant in practice is vividly illustrated in the unfolding of events following the murder of a young black man called Jordan from Park End in May 2010. Jordan's death was not the first killing that had been reported in the local news that year, but it was the first one that involved 'one of our boys' from the estate. Both the murderer and the victim were local, and their families well connected on Park End. Jordan was a mixed-race man, in his early twenties, who had grown up on the estate. He was also a father of two. The murder had happened in a night club in town; Jordan had been out with some friends, when he was knifed by another hooded young man, aged sixteen. The murderer had handed himself into the police station later that night. Meanwhile, Jordan had died in hospital, with his closest friend and his father sitting by his bed.

The day after the murder, Jordan's death was the subject of everybody's conversations in the neighbourhood. My phone kept ringing as Tracey kept me posted whenever she found out more details. A Facebook tribute appeared online, with a picture of Jordan, and the tag line: 'You really didn't deserve this our thoughts are with your family and loved ones. God bless Jordan.' Only a few hours later, over 1,000 people had already 'liked' the page and left comments on it, expressing their shock at what had happened; the number of 'likes' and comments continued to grow over the following days. But among the grief and mourning that residents expressed on the Facebook page, others also worried about the implications and the retaliations that might follow. 'Revenge is sweet', one mother of two teenage children wrote on the page, 'but when will it end? It leads to a vicious cycle of revenge'. Serena, a local resident of mixed-race Afro-Caribbean descent, was one of the mothers who was deeply concerned: her own son Ty, seventeen, was a close friend of the killer. While Ty had been at home on the night of the murder, she feared that Ty might be a target of retaliation and be drawn into yet further violence to show allegiance with his friends. Serena's fears were realized shortly after: Ty was arrested for having intimidated a key witness with a knife during the trial process. He was charged with contempt of court and sent to prison. His girlfriend was eight months pregnant with his baby.

In short, on Park End, violence and threat were the weave in the social fabric of daily life. Danger often stemmed from those who were intimately known to oneself, including lovers, neighbours, and, in the case of young people, other peers. But while the threat of violence was something that was denounced when one was on the receiving end, its command became a desirable quality where it enhanced one's own powers: in a world where 'fight is preferable to flight' (Girling, Loader, and Sparks, 1998), where 'you do or get done', 'doing' was a prerequisite for survival and protection. How did the official enforcers of law and order fit into this picture? What role did the police perform in containing violence and crime?

'The Police are the Biggest Gang of All'

If life on Park End was full of unexpected danger, then the current of risk to which residents were exposed flowed not only from next-door neighbours, ex-lovers, and gangs; but also the police, who were often portrayed as the 'biggest gang of all'. Indeed, we saw above that when I asked Lindsey about what she thought of 'gangs', wanting her to talk of youth violence on the estate, she immediately turned the question on its head, telling me precisely that the police are 'like a big gang'. When I started spending more time with teenagers, I realized how much the ever-present risk of being stopped-and-searched, interrogated, and possibly arrested framed the daily movements and consciousness of young people. One young mixed-race man told me that he had been stopped by the police more than twenty times in five months walking home in the evening after work from the bus-stop to his mother's house. Another white man in his twenties described his first interaction with the police as a 14-year-old: he had been walking home from a friend's house when a car pulled up next to him, and not realizing who it was, he had smiled: 'then the car pulled up to me, two guys jumped out, "who the fuck are you, we're the police, why you fucking look at us like that?"—that was my first interaction with the police'. There was a strong sense that being from Park End meant that they were exposed to prejudicial treatment: 'They look at you, and they think "monster"! Just because you're Park End', one young person said. Yet another recounted what it was like for him to grow up as a man from Park End:

> I was coming home from work, on two, three occasions, I got stopped by police. I've been arrested twice at 2 o'clock in the morning, just going through the estate, from one side of the estate to another. 'Hello sir, hello. What you doing?' 'Just left so-and-so.' 'Where you going?' 'Home.' If you fit into the description, you end up getting arrested and get taken to [the city's central] police station [downtown], you realize—you didn't realize [at the time]—their shift used to finish 3 o'clock—so they wanted an excuse to go back to the station. Then, five minutes before their shift ends, they said, 'no charge', drop you off at front door [of the police station], 'see you later', walk home [about 4 miles]. I had that happen to me twice.

This particular man was white, and he put the police's antagonistic attitudes towards him down to the fact that he was 'Park End'. Black or mixed-race men sometimes related police attitudes to their own ethnic backgrounds. I was sometimes told that the police are 'racist', a language that Park End's neighbourhood policing team—that was composed of exclusively white officers—strongly denied. Callum, who was convinced that the police were treating him differently because he was of mixed-race origin, once said: 'The police are pigs, they are our enemies. They just hound you, they hound you, they hound you.' On this particular occasion, I had been walking home with Callum and a group of three other young men—two of them mixed-race and one white—from the youth club at around 10 p.m. in the evening. Callum was working as a youth worker and had been running a session for the other young men. As we were walking along the estate's main through road, a police car drove past and slowed down as they saw us. Then, they turned around a few metres later and went back up the road, again, slowing down as they drove past us, eyeing us from behind the windscreen of the car. We watched them in silence as they repeated the show a couple more times. 'Watch it—they will jump out now', Callum predicted. Callum was wrong on this occasion: after eying us for a few more seconds, the car suddenly sped up and drove away.

Being arrested, stopped and searched, and taken back to the police station were regular occurrences in the lives of young people on Park End. But the police's powers extended far beyond that: they could also intervene in, modulate, and re-arrange people's most intimate social relations in more insidious and disruptive ways. An anti-social behaviour order (ASBO), introduced under the Blair government and superseded by the Injunction, was a civil injunction against non-criminal behaviour, issued under the civil evidentiary standard of a balance of probabilities (rather than the criminal standard, beyond reasonable doubt), that upon breach turned into a criminal offence (Chapter 1). ASBOs banned individuals from associating with certain people or going to certain places, including the homes of family members and close friends, debarring legal, even routine, activities under penalty of criminal conviction. Cindy was a local woman in her forties of Afro-Caribbean descent who had been given an ASBO for allegedly disorderly behaviour against Park End residents (Cindy insisted that she was merely responding to her ex partner's own abusive behaviour by sticking up for herself). As part of the ASBO, she was banned from going to certain parts of Park End, including an area where close family members lived. Should she breach her ASBO, her order would turn into a criminal offence punishable by up to five years in prison. Cindy recalled how, at the time when her ASBO was first passed, the police had also widely publicized pictures of her on social media. Strangers had come up to her on the streets and made rude remarks to her face.

Unwanted police intervention could impact people's lives in other, less direct ways, such as when it acted as a basis for other authorities to become involved in any given situation and escalate the force of punitive interventions. Jane, for example, the mother in my first host family who was introduced in Chapter 2, constantly worried about her then 15-year-old son Tyron 'getting into trouble' with the police. Sometimes she joked that he had to be careful not to get an ASBO for 'being an idiot', and even played tricks on him. One time, she had bought him a card in a discount store with the words 'An ASBO for ...' printed on it. Jane had finished the sentence with her son's name, 'Tyron Dyer'. On the inside of the card, it read that he had been given an ASBO 'for talking bullshit all the time'. Jane left the card on the kitchen table for her son to see when he came home. It worked: when her son spotted the card later that evening, his face went white with fright, while his mother burst out laughing in the background. But joking about ASBOs also belied a more serious reality, receiving an ASBO could have serious repercussions on family member's life: as we already saw in the last chapter, Jane's entire family could get evicted from their social housing tenancy for having a member of the household found to act in an 'anti-social manner'. If evicted, the local authority would consider the family to have made themselves 'intentionally homeless', thus also absconding from any responsibility to rehouse them again. Even worse for the mothers I worked with, an eviction from one's home would almost certainly engender the intervention of social services and the threat of having one's children removed into care.

Women sometimes interpreted the threat of unwanted police attention through a lens of gender. Like in the case of welfare recipients considered in Chapter 3, the police's ability to instigate contact by housing providers, social workers, teachers, and even employers put them on a par with the men who women could not trust. Kayley, a white woman in her late twenties, was dismissed from her job at a local nursery the day after her partner had been charged with a violent crime: this was not stated explicitly, but Kayley was convinced that 'they [the police]' had been in touch with her employer: 'So I end up getting punished for his [her partner's] crime!', she said. But while women carried the collateral effects of police involvement in the lives of their partners or sons, they also complained that the police were not there when needed. Once, I was sitting in the community centre with Tracey, having a cup of tea when her friend Mandy came in, looking pale and obviously distressed. She came over to us, sat down quietly and whispered in a quiet voice so that nobody would hear: her son had just seen her ex-partner leave the pub. This meant that he had been released on bail and was walking around freely in the neighbourhood. The police had not said anything to her about the bail release. Mandy was worried because of his history of abusive behaviour towards her and her son. 'If that was you or me, we'd have our kids taken away from us, we'd be kicked out of our houses and he's just let free to do as he pleases', Mandy said in a bitter voice. She added that she had already told her son, 'I'd really like to go around to his [her ex-partner's] flat once in a while and do some damage to it'.

While Park End men complained of the police's heavy-handed approach, women feared the police's ability to disrupt their homes often in more indirect ways, through the intervention of other authority figures, like social services, housing providers, and employers. Either way, these experiences did not establish the police as figures of protection and support but rather their opposite: as yet another set of actors who commanded raw power over their lives and who could modulate, re-arrange, and dispossess the things and persons they held the dearest and nearest. Matt, a young man from Park End, once said to me that the police have 'all the man power' and that they 'can just do what they want because they are the police'. In the last two chapters, we saw that the homology which residents drew between informal sources of threat and the authorities—whether these be agents of the benefit-system or social housing providers—also predisposed them to disengage from those they did not trust and to cultivate a similar attitude of 'blanking' and avoidance that was common in situations of informal enemies and threats. This was no different with respect to the police: I was often told that Park End residents 'are anti-police', that they 'do not collaborate with the police', and that people 'do not want to be seen talking to the police' on this estate. One young white and English Police Community Support Officer confirmed this view in a recorded interview. When asked if he felt there was an 'anti-police' attitude among Park End residents, he replied:

Is there an anti-police attitude on the estate? Massively, Oh God, yeah. It's a huge problem for us. Kids are told not to talk to us, and these are kids who have no reason to dislike the police—they have never been in trouble or had any problems with us, but they don't talk to us, whether it is because they don't want to be seen talking to us or … Sometimes, outside the shops, you get a group of youths, and then you get an older guy walk past them and he goes at them: 'Why are you talking to the police?'. A lot of the older people as well, they don't wanna talk to us on the streets. Sometimes they come and see us here or they ring us, but they don't want to be seen talking to us on the streets, harassed by us, and they say things like 'we [the police] are sad' or 'we [the police] got nothing better to do'.

Even worse than being seen to be talking to a police officer on the street was having a relationship with them: when a young black woman, a mother of three, started going out with a 'copper', Tracey and her friends judged her harshly, asking 'how much is she getting paid for it?', thus insinuating that she had to be a police informant and could hence not be trusted.

In short, from the point of view of Park End residents, the police were not the antithesis of the danger and threat that permeated the social atmosphere on Park End: on the contrary, just like enemies eager for one's downfall, who could threaten and intimidate, so the police could be seen, to invoke Lindsey's words once more, as 'the biggest gang of all'. There was hence an interchangeability between predatory or informal threats and the violence that was formally sanctioned by the state, giving rise to a strong sense of the police's arbitrariness in its use of force. How else did residents respond to the police in their daily lives? To come back to the key theme of previous chapters, how and when did they personalize the state? And what were the limits of personalization?

Personalizing 'Law and Order'

It was a rainy Monday morning when Tracey, Mandy, and I were sat around the table in the community centre, drinking tea and talking. Both Tracey and Mandy had teenage sons, and often gave each other advice on how to handle them when they were misbehaving at home. Today, Mandy had to console Tracey whose 17-year-old son had turned her life into 'a living hell'. For the past three months, her son had been dating a local girl who had now become pregnant. Her son had not dealt well with the news: he had dropped out of his college course, taken a job working shifts at a local bar, and often came home late at night, drunk. He also refused to contribute any money towards paying the rent in the house, making Tracey feel like she was running a hotel for her son and leaving her with a shortfall in rent payments at the end of every month. Tracey had tried to reason with him on several occasions, and she had sent his godmother and various family members to talk to him. All to no avail. He was still misbehaving at home, and if anything, his bad behaviour had gotten worse. Mandy was firm in her advice: 'kick him out of the house ... and call the police if he comes back late, making a noise!'

Noticing the surprised look on my face, she relayed how she had done the same a couple of years ago to her own son Luke, when he was 15 years old. On that occasion, Luke had been rude to her in front of his younger brother, swearing and threatening to break the TV. Luke and Mandy had started a loud argument, but when Luke 'refused to back down', Mandy had eventually lost it with him. She had shouted, 'if you wanna fight, you and me will do it in the street!' and dragged him out of the house. In the meantime, Luke had rung 999, claiming domestic violence because, as Mandy said, 'he was scared that I would beat him up'. When the police arrived a little while later, the two had indeed been out in the street, fighting. Mandy relayed how she had been able to convince the police officers on that occasion that Luke had been rude to her and was at fault. While nobody was arrested, Mandy was satisfied that she had turned the situation around, and that she had taught her son who the 'boss' was in the house. After that incident, Luke had gone to live with his dad, from whom Mandy was separated. This had been two years ago; 'And now, he is a lovely boy', she said, 'and we get on so well'. A few weeks after this conversation had taken place, Tracey acted on her friend's advice. She told me that her son had come home late at night, banging on the front door and causing noise. She had called the police, accusing him of vandalism and asking them to come and pick him up. Her son left before the police arrived, but Tracey was confident that she had taught him a lesson.

The incident at first surprised me a great deal: why would mothers like Tracey or Mandy, who did not have much faith in the police, who complained that it 'criminalized kids for being kids', and who did not trust them to do 'any good' call upon them in negotiating intimate disputes? What explained this seemingly popular consent with, and desire for, authoritarian interventions? Over time, as I got to know the mothers better, I realized that the incident had in no way been unusual: people routinely threatened, and sometimes acted on their threat, to call the police on those they knew intimately: a next-door neighbour, a lover, a teenage child, or a family member. Sometimes, residents would use their knowledge of another person's engagement in criminal activities as a pretext to call the police: an aggrieved girlfriend might report her partner for drug dealing or handling stolen goods; a teenage girl once reported her mother's partner who was on bail for staying in their house against police rules (Chapter 2); and a young black woman reported her white partner for being a 'racist' in the midst of a heated argument. At other times, socially offensive behaviour was constructed to make it 'fit' a criminal charge: as we have seen above this was the case with Tracey, for example, who claimed that her son had committed 'vandalism', or in the cases we considered in Chapter 4, when social housing tenants constructed their next-door neighbours' activities to make them fit the legalistic definition of 'anti-social behaviour'.

The popular desire that residents showed for authoritarian interventions in these mundane or intimate scenarios might be seen to fit the general narrative of a punitive turn: as I outlined in the Introduction to this book, according to this narrative the public are characterized by punitive dispositions and a desire for authoritative reassurance in the face of rampant insecurity. But this narrative did not neatly fit the ethnographic situations that I had witnessed. Whatever the nature of the charge was that residents were relying upon, there was a common pattern across the situations: people were using the police as personalized tools in the pursuit of their own daily relations; relations that were morally prior to, and more important to them, than, the state's own understanding of 'law and order'. The aim of calling the police in these situations was then not to confirm an abstract state authority, less even its own categories of right and wrong, or of lawful and unlawful behaviour. Like the African-American mothers studied by Bell (2016) or the Soweto residents analysed by Hornberger (2013), Park End residents rather invoked a 'situational' legitimacy of the state by using its powers to bring about a change in status or relations with each other.

The decision to call the police into an intimate situation was always fiercely contested: what to one person was an act of justice, something that they felt entitled to do because they had been wronged by another party was also harshly judged as an act of immorality by those at the receiving end of police attention. Tracey's conflict with her son exemplifies the point. As we saw above, Tracey called the police on her son when, one night, he came home late at night drunk, and was banging on the door. When I saw Tracey the day after, she justified her decision by saying that she had wanted to make her son realize who the authority in the house was: he was 17 years old and he was 'acting like her home was a hotel'. Further, she was worried about what the neighbours might think of the late-night banging on her front door (see Chapter 4) and she did not want her son to implicate her in any more gossip. In this situation, then, she felt morally justified to call the police because it served the purpose of disciplining her son and ensuring that relations with her neighbours would not become strained. Contrast this, however, with how severely affronted she was on her friend Helen's behalf, when Helen's ex-partner reported her for benefit fraud a few months later. It turned out that he had reported her after a particularly nasty argument over parenting duties. Tracey's opinion was that 'he is a class A wanker' and called him a 'grass', a prerogative term that was frequently used to refer to those who collaborated with the police.

Being a 'grass', however, was also an invitation to attack. The potentially dangerous repercussions are illustrated in the following case. Vera, a woman of Caribbean descent in her early forties who had three children, had called the police after her pet cat had been taken and killed by a fighting dog. The owner of the dog was a local teenager who was well known to the police for his 'anti-social behaviour', namely, his involvement in petty crime—although many residents also believed that he was a local drug dealer (a suspicion the police did not investigate, residents complained). Vera subsequently gave a witness statement in court that resulted in the culprit receiving an ASBO banning him from entering certain parts of the estate, including areas where his family and friends lived. The day after the court hearing, residents stopped Vera on the streets: 'It took me hours to do my shopping', she recalled, 'because everyone congratulated me for speaking up.' However, the tables turned when Vera left for a short holiday. In her absence, her house and front yard were vandalized and someone had spray-painted 'grass' on the front door. Neighbours confirmed Vera's suspicion that the attack had been orchestrated by the cat-killer's family. This time, Vera decided that she would not go back to the police. She explained, 'I don't wanna do nothing, I am scared. I don't wanna call the police anymore.'

Vera decided, then, to abandon police involvement half way through the process of managing her relations with her culprit's menacing and criminal behaviour. She was 'too scared', she had said, of further retaliation and did not trust the police to sufficiently protect her. But not everyone chose that course of action, that retreat. In many situations I witnessed or heard about, a felt inability to call upon the police as a personalized resource motivated a different set of responses: reliance on informal action and sometimes direct violence. As we saw above, showing toughness in the face of more serious threat was not only considered necessary but also a virtue. 'If the law can't finish him off, I will!',

Tracey once said to me. As I got to know her better, I saw her dispensing similar advice to other residents: when Helen was dealing with her rogue landlord who was refusing to pay back the deposit (Chapter 4), Tracey suggested she get help from the citizens' advice bureau and, failing that, find out where her landlord lived and pay someone to go around and vandalize his home. When Silvia had been dismissed from her workplace as a kitchen help in an expensive and well-known gastro pub (Chapter 6), Tracey advised her friend to report the restaurant for failing food hygiene with the relevant government authority enforcing food and trading standards. But she also entertained the possibility that someone might want to find her employer's car and 'smash it up'. In yet another case, her friend Mandy was upset because her younger son had been sexually assaulted by a man on his walk home from school. While the man had been arrested and charged, Mandy told Tracey that she knew someone who would be happy to find the man, put him in a van, and take him somewhere to 'teach him a lesson'. Tracey approved of this possibility should 'the law fail'.

What stands out in each of these instances is residents' willingness to take the law into their own hands. I will come back to this point in the next chapter with respect to the activities of a local political party that mobilized its own politics of vigilante control. Implicit in residents' actions was a recognition that the state's own violence was not good enough and that they needed more, or better, protection from the law. Indeed, this criticism of the criminal justice system's failures to protect people in the manner they considered fit was constantly voiced in daily conservations, sometimes instigated by events reported in the media. For example, in December 2009, a news story broke on the estate that caused much uproar among residents. A group of three men had been caught red-handed trying to break into a family home. The home owner and his brother had responded with violence, beating one of the intruders with a baseball bat, which left him with a fractured skull and severe brain damage. The court convicted the two batterers for grievous bodily harm: in passing the judgement, it declared that the extra-legal violence they had exercised was a direct affront to the rule of law. Judge Reddihough, whose words were widely reported in the tabloid media, stated: 'If persons were permitted to take the law into their own hands and inflict their own instant and violent punishment on an apprehended offender rather than letting the criminal justice system take its course, then the rule of law and our system of criminal justice, which are hallmarks of a civilized society, would collapse.'[2]

The court's image of a civilized society and a rule of law that had been put under threat was familiar to residents on Park End. Police officers, local authorities, and the media regularly complained about what they saw as Park End residents' disrespect for the law. However, residents had their own perspectives on what constituted both the nature of the threat to civilized society, and the means of its redress. For them, the case of the burglars was proof that the system had 'swung too far the other way', that it was 'too liberal', and 'too lenient' on offenders. Some also complained that this evidenced a 'culture of human rights' that had been allowed to go too far. Residents made comparisons with their own lives, saying they would have acted in the same way as the batterers who had defended the family home; that they had done nothing wrong and that the system was protecting the wrong kinds of people. Serena, a local youth worker, and a single mother of three mixed-race children, was particularly outraged. 'If someone comes into my yard uninvited, I should be allowed to do with them what I want', she said. Indeed, she took pride in the fact that she kept a baseball bat behind the door and had recently acquired a Staffordshire bull terrier who was constantly at her side. Tony perhaps summed up the moral outrage felt by residents about a system that was 'too liberal', when recalling how he had dealt with a drug-dealer, a next-door neighbour, by calling on his 'mates' and threatening the neighbour with a baseball bat. He recalled:

The point is he came on the bus the other day and he saw me and he went white, he is black, but he was so frightened, he couldn't look at me, but the thing is we taught him respect, we put manners on him. But he is from a family where nobody would do anything, and the social workers would say, 'who are you to make a complaint'? And you're thinking, what kind of world do they live in, it's absolutely bizarre, the majority of the working-class people who are not even educated as well will just grasp that like that and say, hang on, you have to protect them, if you leave them in that environment that will turn them into the death penalty.

---

[2]See, for instance, http://www.dailymail.co.uk/news/article-1235782/Millionaire-Munir-Hussain-fought-knife-wielding-burglar-jailed-intruder-let-off.html.

Tony makes himself clear that the need to 'go heavy-handed' on his next-door neighbour is a matter of common sense for working-class people in general, even those who are 'not educated as well' in the university of life, as it were; but that this is a recognition that set them apart from the world of institutions, personified here in the figure of the social worker. Moreover, he reverses the horrified astonishment evident in the media and court's reaction to vigilante justice, evident in the reported case above, when he exclaims, 'you're thinking, what kind of world do they live in, it's absolutely bizarre'; he points to a profound gulf in the social realities on and off the estate, and across class structures in general. And this divergence in the social fabric is painfully visible in the consequences imagined for the breach of its principles of morality and justice; Judge Reddihough declared that to permit 'persons to take the law into their own hands and inflict their own instant and violent punishment' would destroy 'the rule of law and our system of criminal justice, which are hallmarks of a civilized society'; Tony contends that 'if you leave them in that environment, [it] will turn them into the death penalty'. In short, then, a discrepancy is revealed between residents' own conceptions of moral order, one that placed at its forefront the need to protect their homes and those dearest to them, and the legal order projected by the state that saw residents' acts of self-protection as unlawful and hence immoral violence.

Conclusion

In this chapter, I have shifted the focus from residents' engagements with the benefit system and the housing authorities to their experiences of, and responses to, the police. My focus has been on how Park End residents experience and engage with these officials as they try to protect themselves from the dangers of violent threats and crime. Daily life on Park End is marked by the omnipresent threat of victimhood and violence: children on Park End are socialized into this environment from a young age, learning that they live in a world where 'you do or get done'—where you have to be willing to mobilize the force of violent threat unless you want to risk being victimized yourself. But it is not just the risk of victimization that they confront: the police are also perceived as a source of potential danger as they intervene in, act upon, and often re-arrange people's intimate lives. Once more, we can see a homology between different sources of threat that was so central to the discussion of neighbour relations and the home in the two preceding chapters. Just as the welfare state takes on 'man-like' qualities for the women who escape domestic violence and threat, and just as tenants experience social landlords' responses to neighbour disputes as an aggravation of danger, so for Park End residents, the police are often the most dangerous and biggest 'gang' of all.

Ethnographic attention to daily experiences of victimization and crime moves towards resolving the punitive paradox I addressed at the beginning of this book: the paradox of popular support for seemingly anti-democratic policies and measures. As we saw in the Introduction, this paradox has perplexed contemporary scholars of punishment who have seen the resurgence of illiberal feelings and passions as a contradiction to liberal democracy. However, popular support for more 'law and order' cannot be divorced from how democracy is experienced in the first place. On Park End, people's criticisms of a system that has become too liberal and soft, that has taken human rights too far, and that does not punish harshly enough, are not experienced as a contradiction with democracy at all. On the contrary, the democracy they inhabit is one that is marked by a profound security gap. Park End residents experience not only police repression but also the daily challenges of keeping themselves safe from serious forms of violence and crime. This, in turn, produces a variety of different responses: at times people withdraw from the authorities, at others they personalize them into their intimate disputes, and at yet other times, they bypass the state's own claims to have a monopoly over the use of force. To the extent that people articulate support for 'law and order', this support does not capture a straightforward support for state authority. Rather, it captures a situational demand for justice where the state routinely dismisses or even criminalizes people's attempts to keep themselves safe from multiple risks.

Scholars of vigilantism and policing have cautioned against dominant narratives that see popular attempts at self-policing as a threat to the democratic order, or, as Judge Reddihough said in his judgment, to the 'hallmarks of civilisation'. Vigilantism is not the antithesis of order, but rather an attempt to reassert the possibility of its conditions (Abrahams, 1998; Goldstein, 2003; Johnston, 1996; Steinberg, 2006; Super, 2016). Where the state not only fails its burdens of protection and security but participates in its own projects of jeopardy, people's support for more punishment cannot be reduced to the existing system. In a well-known formulation of such a critique, Abrahams (1998) conceptualized vigilantism as a 'moral or political action that challenges state legitimacy, not to overturn the state but rather, in a classical Hobbesian fashion, to recall its legal obligations, its social contract with citizens'. But what constitutes the social contract between citizens and the state is far from set: the moral and political frameworks that guide responses to danger among Park End residents do not place the state's own categories of legality and illegality, of justice and impunity, and of right and wrong, at their centre. Popular desires for punishment and vengeance (to the extent that they are expressed) cannot easily be collapsed with a desire for the order imposed by the state. In the next two chapters, I will further unpack this discrepancy between Park End moral and political frameworks and the order of the state by turning to residents' daily engagements with grassroots politics (Chapter 6) and with electoral processes and democracy writ large (Chapter 7).

6
Political Brokers: Active Citizenship

In 2015, Pat Evans died, after a long battle with cancer. The news of her death spread like wildfire as people shared the information over cups of tea, in passing on the street, and, of course, in the estate's community centre. The funeral was one of the biggest local events of the year. The street outside the church—and a major through road on the estate—had been cut off for traffic. A screen had been put up outside the church live-streaming the service for those who would not fit inside the church. The community centre, located next to the church, had been decorated for the day: the wake would take place after the church ceremony in the big hall in the community centre that normally accommodated the youth club and summer projects for young people. The local newspaper reported that over 700 people had been present; but to others it felt like 'thousands had come out'. These people had lined the streets, breaking into spontaneous clapping as the procession came past en route to the crematorium on the other side of town. Tracey told me afterwards that the local pub on Park End had been heaving—the only other times when the pub was this busy was when the town's football team, the Lions, were playing a home game in the stadium located on the edge of Park End estate.

Pat Evans had been a long-standing resident on Park End, well known by many people in the neighbourhood. But she was also a local politician, having served as a Labour councillor in the council for over twenty years. Her husband was also in politics. He was the local Labour MP, who had represented the estate for an uninterrupted period of nearly three decades. Pat had been a strong woman with a broad smile. As residents often told me when she was still alive, Pat was unafraid to speak out for estate residents. I had met Pat on a number of occasions as she had sat on various community boards and sometimes held her surgeries around the large table in the community centre where I worked. But many residents had known her for much longer, and related to her as a neighbour, as a community activist, and as someone who had fought for their estate. In the days that followed her death, people affirmed what she had done. 'She was determined that the people of Park End estate would not be dumped on', one long-standing community worker told me, 'that we could get the best she could get us. She was a community champion'. Memorials were set up for her around the estate, including a bench in a local school that she had supported for decades; a community garden in the centre of the estate; and a memorial on the site of an old people's home where she had done voluntary service.

People's mourning of Pat's death and the celebration of her life that followed demonstrated how people on Park End thought of individuals who had played their part through effort, work, and commitment as 'community champions', in the words of the resident above, who were afforded a special place and memory within local histories of Park End. In this chapter, I focus on precisely these figures to foreground some key questions that have not been considered so far: what forms of local activism and community work are present on Park End? How can brokerage work be understood as a form of grassroots level politics? And what is the scope of brokers' actions? Asking these questions means to critically interrogate dominant images of Park End residents as incapable of having a 'community' and engaging in their own forms of grassroots activism, and, indeed of, politics. Park End residents do not fit neatly with the images of the 'active citizen' invoked by the New Labour government policies, and, more recently, the Conservative government's take on the 'Big Society'. Moreover, where Park End residents do engage in their own forms of participatory politics, local authority officials can dismiss their practices as 'difficult', corrupt, and even 'antidemocratic'. Everyday forms of activism, as well as the kinds of relations that residents form with politicians become evidence, on this account, of an unhealthy politics that constitutes a threat to the allegedly more transparent, reflexive, and open practices valued by professionals.

The aim of this chapter is to move beyond dominant portrayals of 'active' citizenship through an ethnographic study of brokerage relations as a form of alternative politics. On Park End, local authority-sponsored initiatives that encourage citizens to become active in their own governance do not fit with

Park End residents' own understandings of what makes good government in their daily live. As the work of political brokers (Koster, 2014)—community activists as well as locally elected politicians—shows, 'active' governance from Park End people's point of view is not about complying with official rules and entering partnership agreements with authority figures. Rather, it is about getting involved in the daily struggles that residents face through the pursuit of what I have called elsewhere a 'bread and butter politics' (Koch, 2016). However, the personalized relationships that political brokers have to build with residents in the pursuit of such a politics can also become the object of attack. Those in power are prone to view these relationships with suspicion and even a sense of outright threat as they see them as evidence of inappropriate and potentially even criminal behaviour. In the end, brokers' struggles to keep up with residents' demands, let alone build a platform for sustainable action, can also end up reinforcing deep-seated feelings of betrayal among Park End residents.

Anthropologists of policy and citizenship have begun to investigate the workings of 'active citizenship' under conditions of heightened neoliberalism or what Rose (1996) has called 'advanced liberalism' (see also Hyatt, 1997; Koster, 2014; Shore and Wright, 2003; Chapter 4). In these accounts, practices of participatory governance have been identified as Foucauldian techniques of governmentality that place the burden of managing structural problems, including urban decline, growing inequality, and crime, onto citizens themselves. This chapter builds on and extends these insights by investigating how Park End residents' engagements in their own forms of political brokerage both challenge dominant images of 'active citizenship' but also make them more vulnerable to further stigmatization and control. Park End residents, and the political brokers they build relations with, do not simply give in to official understandings of 'active' governance. Paradoxically, however, as brokers struggle to realize their own claims to governance, the work that they do can end up feeding into precisely the same mechanisms that also encourage mistrust, disengagement, and civic withdrawal. The last three chapters showed how residents' attempts to personalize the authorities end up reproducing a classed logic of state control: this chapter takes this argument to the case of local governance on Park End.

Active Citizenship, the Third Way, and Alternative Politics

We have seen how specific policies and practices—to do with the benefit system, housing authorities, and policing—work on specific individuals who come into contact with them. But policies also entail broader visions about how citizens should relate to each other and to government in a civic society. While the mantra of post-war welfare was one of paternalism and governing through a hierarchically organized body of professionals and experts, more recently a focus on self-governance and citizen participation has become central (see also Chapter 4). 'Active' citizenship has been part of government language and initiatives since the 1980s, although its form and moral content has shifted over time. Margaret Thatcher embraced a mantra of individual responsibility that expected citizens to stand on their own two feet. As Ramsay points out, the first duty of the active citizen under Thatcherite government was 'to look after themselves and only then to concern themselves with others' needs and their civic responsibilities' (2012: 99). For Thatcher, the substantive content of the active citizen's duties was to be found in the Victorian values of work, family, neighbourliness, and private charity, the sources of which lay in traditional sources of Christian teaching (2012: 100). A citizen's relation to public services was no longer seen as a matter of entitlement granted to the worker–citizen but more as a question of moral duty in a neoliberal market.

In the decades that followed Thatcherite government, active citizenship was morphed into a language of vulnerability to crime. In *The Insecurity State*, Ramsay traces how the incoming Major government in the 1990s shifted the focus on the 'active citizen' away from a Victorian ethic of morality to that of the consumer 'who was active in the provision of welfare services, given rights to choose and a responsibility to choose wisely' (2012: 102). But elided of its traditional morality, this citizen–consumer was also vulnerable to the uncontrollable and insecure marketplace in the way that the Thatcherite citizen with its grounding in moral duties had not been. For Ramsay, it was precisely this 'legitimacy gap' that the Conservative government was unable to meet and that the incoming New Labour government sought to fill with its shift towards Third Way politics, which emphasized a mantra of 'no rights without responsibilities'. In a society that had lost the old tractions of custom and tradition, individual self-fulfilment was to be maximized by ensuring social cohesion among diverse subjects through reflexive behaviour (Ramsay, 2012: 102 ff.). As earlier chapters showed, citizens came to be seen as vulnerable in their mutual interdependence and therefore required to be active in their attention to each other's need for reassurance (2012: 86–96).

The New Labour government's mantra of vulnerability was realized through its 'anti-social behaviour agenda', which implied a specific vision of a desirable civic society, one which foregrounded mutual respect and responsibility at its centre. In 2004, the Home Office Campaign *Together* stated that 'it is the foundation of a truly civil society that we respect the public spaces we share, the property of our neighbours, and the right of people in our communities to live free from fear and harassment' (Home Office, 2003b: 1). Coupled to this notion of respect was the idea that members of a community all share a sense of responsibility. As then Home Secretary David Blunkett stated in the foreword to the Home Office White Paper for the Anti-Social Behaviour Act 2003, *Respect and Responsibility*, 'as a society our rights as individuals are based on a sense of responsibility we have towards others and to our families and communities' (Home Office, 2003a: 4). It followed from such a vision of civic society as a 'something for something society' (2003a: 4)—in which rights are always tied to responsibilities—that anti-social behaviour was any form of behaviour that demonstrates 'a lack of respect for values that almost everyone in this country shares—consideration for others, a recognition that we all have responsibilities as well as rights, civility and good manners' (Blair, 2006) and that shows a 'selfish inability or unwillingness to recognise when one's individual behaviour is offensive to others and a refusal to take responsibility for it' (Home Office, 2003a).

Garland (2001) has coined the term 'responsibilization' to describe the processes wherein the state abandons the exclusive reliance on its own government functions in favour of an approach that solicits the help of non-state organizations and individual citizens in governing civic society. This approach, which exists alongside the state's continued reliance on expressive modes of punishment (Chapters 4, 5), is most commonly instituted through campaigns that are 'aimed to raise public consciousness, interpolate the citizen as a potential victim, create a sense of duty,

Active Citizenship, the Third Way, and Alternative Politics 167

connect the population to crime control agencies, and help change the thinking and practices of those involved' (Garland, 2001: 125). The previous chapters have already begun to outline examples of what this 'responsibilization' looks like in places like Park End: an expansion of the 'police family' to agents like police community support officers (PCSOs), civilian officers, street wardens, and park rangers; partnerships and 'joined up' thinking between social housing providers, local authorities, youth services, social services, and the police; and crucially, initiatives that are designed to draw ordinary citizens into the art of daily governance. On Park End, this included the setting up of so-called 'Neighbourhood Action Group' (NAG) meetings that involved the above-mentioned authority figures as well as selected invited residents; the street pastor scheme mentioned in Chapter 1, and a host of other local initiatives involving partnerships with PCSOs, local residents, and street wardens.

It is also noteworthy that since 2010, with the election of a new Conservative government, active citizenship has continued as a central theme, albeit once more under a new guise to that of Third Way politics, namely that of 'civic conservatism' (Ramsay, 2012: 105). On 19 July 2010, then Prime Minister and Conservative Party leader David Cameron launched his plan for a 'big society'. Cameron (2010) argued that 'the big society is about a huge culture change, where people, in their everyday lives, in their homes, in their neighbourhoods, in their workplace, don't always turn to officials, local authorities or central government for answers to the problems they face but instead feel both free and powerful enough to help themselves and their own communities'.[1] Instead of 'big government', 'big society' asked citizens to take control of their own lives by relying upon mediating institutions from families through to local churches, clubs, and cooperatives that govern the space of civic society. Although the rhetoric was used to denounce Third Way politics for its over-reliance on the state, there were important continuities with the former: both were concerned to ensure 'social cohesion through mechanisms of civility, respect and conditionality of rights' (Ramsay, 2012: 109), and those who failed to do so could be punished accordingly.[2]

---

[1] See https://www.gov.uk/government/speeches/big-society-speech.
[2] For Ramsay the shift in emphasis from big to small government is illustrated in the shift from Anti-Social Behaviour Orders (ASBOs) to Criminal Behaviour

The concept of 'Big Society' did not survive the first few years of Conservative government, but the rhetoric of active citizenship remains central to a host of policies today, as wide-ranging public sector cuts and the shift to 'austerity politics' have called on citizens to carry the burden of wide-ranging public sector cuts (Chapter 7).

Anthropologists of policy and citizenship have analysed 'active' citizenship as a central feature of neoliberal governance across much of Europe and beyond. Within the existing literature, Foucauldian paradigms have tended to dominate (Hyatt, 1997; Koster, 2014; Shore and Wright, 2003; Chapter 4). For example, Hyatt (1997) has analysed the resurgence of informal networks of crime control in the United States, including neighbourhood watch schemes, as an example of how citizens come to internalize techniques of self-governance that hold citizens responsible for the consequences of urban degeneration and decline (see also Chapter 4). Similarly, Koster (2014) in his account of 'participation society' in the Netherlands, observes that policy reports regularly use the label of 'informal' citizenship to describe a range of different partnerships and civic initiatives, ranging from voluntary and amateur care services to citizen networks for crime prevention, including neighbourhood watch schemes. This is not to say that citizens cannot engage with these initiatives creatively. In a deprived urban Dutch neighbourhood, persons who are active in these new spaces of governance act as 'political brokers' who exert agency as 'they rework state policies, push the boundaries of such spaces, or use them for different purposes' (2014: 50). Yet, their performance of active citizenship is ultimately understood in terms of techniques of governmentality, as 'part of the subtle workings of the conduct of conduct' (2014: 50) through which citizens are taught to govern themselves and each other.

In this chapter, I focus on 'political brokers' (Koster, 2014) or 'intermediaries' (Symons, 2018) to investigate how local actors on Park End engage in their own forms of politics that both challenge

Orders (CBOs) and Crime Prevention Injunctions (CPIs): 'The Home Office's complaint about New Labour's antisocial behaviour strategy is not that people should not be restricted and punished for failing to reassure others. It is that an interfering, hyperactive central government has overcomplicated the enforcement "toolkit" and made it impracticable for communities to get the results they need' (Ramsay, 2012: 109).

but also make them more vulnerable to further stigmatization and control as they fail to be 'active citizens' in the way imagined by the authorities. My starting point is the proliferation of civic society initiatives aimed at crime control issues that require Park End citizens to become active in local forms of governance. But what constitutes good governance is contested. As the case of local political brokers shows, for Park End residents, active governance is about getting involved in their daily struggles for security and safety. However, the personalized relationships that brokers build with residents also become the object of attack; brokers find that they are vulnerable to being called difficult, corrupt, and even anti-democratic by those in power. In what follows, I will develop the points by first turning my attention to the landscape of participatory governance as it is sponsored and supported through institutional frameworks; second, contrast this to the kinds of governing activities that local brokers engage in; and finally, turn to the struggles that local brokers face. Throughout, my focus will be on two types of brokers: community activists, like Tracey, who are at the forefront of providing advice and services to residents on Park End, and elected politicians, like Pat Evans, who represent Park End residents in local government.

Responsibilization and Participatory Governance

As described in the Introduction to this book, when I first started planning my ethnographic research, my initial thought was to access both residents and officials through the various partnerships and civic initiatives addressing 'local issues' that had sprung up on Park End and neighbouring estates in the same town. I had initially contacted a local authority official responsible for coordinating the Neighbourhood Action Group (NAG) meetings in the town. This was Tom, a white and University-educated twenty-something-year-old man with a master's degree, who described himself as a 'liberal' with a passion for community empowerment and participation. He also took an interest in my research and promised to take me along to the next NAG meeting which was scheduled in the community centre run by Bob on one of the town's smaller estates. This estate was to become my first field site in the months to come (see Introduction). The day of the NAG meeting, we met at the bus stop near the townhall and went on the twenty-five-minute-long bus ride together. During the ride, Tom briefed me: the NAG meetings were designed 'to bring stakeholders and the community together', he explained, and to make everyone 'active' in identifying and addressing issues that were of local concern. Naturally, many of these issues focused on 'anti-social behaviour' and 'crime', but the purpose of the meetings was broader and 'anything' could potentially form part of the agenda. Tom also explained that the meetings had been successful at bringing people around the same table who do not normally meet and talk.

When we arrived at the community centre, about fifteen people had already gathered around the tables that were arranged in a rectangle in the community hall. At the head of the room, the neighbourhood sergeant was sat, flanked by two PCSOs on either side. A brief round of introductions quickly established that most other members present were there in some official capacity or another: there were two local councillors, two street wardens, one park ranger, members of the city council's crime and nuisance action team, representatives from the nursery, school, and youth club services, as well as Bob, who was the de facto manager of the community centre where the meeting took place. In the corner, a bar area had been set up where a woman in her fifties (Bob's wife) and a teenage boy (Bob's grandson and Jane's own son, Tyron) were standing around. Tom invited me to sit down next to him and introduced me as a 'research student' working on 'anti-social behaviour', which was well received by the chairing sergeant who welcomed me to the meeting. An agenda was passed around on a printed A4 page, with minutes from the previous meetings attached. It read:

1. Closure of dark alley ways around different parts of the estate
2. Drug dealing in the Park
3. Drug taking outside the shops and associated anti-social behaviour
4. Needles left lying around
5. Parking issues—wasteland should be turned into parking spaces
6. Installation of CCTV outside shops [on the estate] in areas with increased anti-social behaviour
7. Police stall at upcoming community fair
8. Youth congregating outside [local] supermarket which intimidates people
9. Youth cycling their bicycles on the pavement

10. Garden item thefts, mainly involving bicycles
11. Parking issues at school area
12. Graffiti around the tower blocks and garages behind the flats

This agenda was typical for a NAG meeting, not just on this particular estate but also elsewhere in the same town. While in theory the scope of the meetings was broader than just 'anti-social behaviour' and 'crime control', the bulk of the time was taken up talking about precisely these issues, albeit in a framework that represented the authorities' own concerns with youth-related behaviour (Chapter 5). Issues typically involved teenagers acting in 'anti-social ways' (items 6, 8, and 9 on the agenda). Even where issues were not directly concerned with youth-related behaviour (as in the case of items 1, 2, 3, 4, and 12), they invariably ended up invoking conversations about young people and issues to do with loitering, low level drug dealing, and their pursuit of 'anti-social' leisure activities (e.g. graffiti spraying). Only two items on the list—to do with insufficient parking outside the local primary school and reported thefts from people's gardens (items 10 and 11)—did not invoke any discussion around the behaviour of young people, but the sergeant also stated that these issues would best be dealt with in a different forum. During the meeting, the neighbourhood police sergeant would take the lead in introducing the individual items of the agenda, but emphasize collaborations with agents in the room: the youth worker was asked to 'have a word with the lads' about their anti-social behaviour; street wardens and PCSOs were tasked to 'keep an eye' on parking and graffiti issues; and the police were to investigate the drug dealing and work together with other agents to 'nip any problems in the bud'.

Perhaps most striking to me at the NAG meeting was the absence of residents from the estate: while in theory a NAG meeting was designed to bring local stakeholders and civilians together, the meetings operated in practice with an 'invite only' policy. Tom explained to me why, mirroring the concerns that were already voiced by Val, the housing official, in Chapter 4: if residents were invited to come along indiscriminately, they would end up focusing on 'one person's problems' rather than broader issues that were of interest to all residents on the estate. But what constituted 'broader issues of interest' was contested. As I got to know Bob, the centre's manager over the following months, I realized just how big the gap was. Bob was in his sixties, white, and an overweight and wheel-chair bound man who was suffering from severe diabetes, with bright blue eyes and a grumpy smile. As the de facto manager of the community centre, he was invited to the NAG meetings but he told me that he only went to be 'nosy'—the meetings were 'boring' and 'tedious' in his view. In fact, Bob did not refer to the NAG meetings by their official name but merely as 'police meetings'. Perhaps most offensive to Bob was the fact that 'the police' were not acting in the same way as any other community group would who wanted to hold a meeting in the community hall: they did not pay the hiring fees for the hall; they expected Bob to set up the tables and chairs in advance; and they never cleaned up after themselves.

Bob's litany of complaints about the NAG meetings might seem trivial but I soon came to realize that they were representative of how many residents felt about partnership initiatives in the institutional landscape of neighbourhood life: namely that they were far removed from what actually mattered to them. This was the case even with initiatives that were ostensibly more citizen-controlled than the NAG meetings. Take the example of the Parish council on Park End. Parish councils are the lowest tier of government, representing smaller geographical areas than those of local government with limited funding for local projects which are raised through a precept. Park End had its own Parish council that was elected every four years and comprised of twelve councillors. One day, I had been sitting with Tracey and her friend Helen in the community centre, when Fred walked in. Fred was an elected member of the Parish council, a white man in his sixties with a background in trade union politics. He told us that the Parish council was 'desperately in need of new members', and that he had come in the hope of recruiting interested residents to join the monthly meetings. Helen and Tracey seemed unimpressed. When asked by Fred why they thought there was so little interest in the Parish council, Helen replied that she did not 'really know what they are about'. Then she added: 'It's the kind of why-should-I-bother-type-of-thing, people don't think that at the end of the day, they can have an impact on whatever decision will be taken.'

Helen's premonition turned out to be correct. After Fred had visited us that day, I convinced Tracey to give it a go. When the time came for the next Parish council meeting, we went along to the small portakabin[3] on the edge of the estate on a disused bit of land where the Parish council met once a month. We entered a small room that was equipped with a large table and some plastic chairs. By the time we arrived, about fifteen to twenty people were sat in the small room, all of whom were white older men with the exception of two white elderly ladies, as well as Tracey and myself. Two male PCSOs and a female street warden, also white, were sat in a corner. We were greeted warmly by the chair of the meeting who told us that they needed 'fresh blood'. He opened the meeting with an agenda that covered a range of matters, including updates on upcoming events, funding applications from various local groups and residents, and a discussion on whether the Parish council should change their website to spend an extra £8 on it. Then, the chair invited two PCSOs and the street warden to give their monthly report about 'the important work they are doing'. The PCSO spoke first, talking about the activities that the team had been involved in: they had successfully dealt with all incidents of anti-social behaviour, we were told, and all of the offenders in question had been identified and banned, some through housing, some through the police, and others through social services. 'We would like to thank you for all you do. Everybody is very grateful for your presence on the estate and for all your hard work. I know we say it every month but a big thank you to you!' the chairman said in response.

After the PCSO had spoken, the female street warden took over. Like the PCSO who had spoken before her, she was white, perhaps in her forties. Tracey told me later that she had recognized her face from 'round here'. The street warden introduced herself as the new team leader of the street wardens on the estate. Then she moved on to the different schemes street wardens were getting involved in, including a 'can't get out scheme' set up for elderly people who needed assistance with daily activities and found it hard to leave their house. The final part of her report was an update on local policing: over the last few weeks, she and her team had identified areas polluted by fly-tipping. Fixed penalty notices (FPNs) had been issued to various individuals held responsible for it. FPNs are notices that can be issued by law enforcement officials for disorder, environmental nuisances, or noise that require an

---

[3] A portakabin is a temporary building, comparable to a prefab hall.

individual to pay a fine. Failure to do so within a specified period of time results in a court proceeding being initiated. 'Most importantly', the street warden said, she 'had issued a resident with a fixed penalty notice for dog fouling as well, and if he doesn't pay his fine within a reasonable period of time, it will go to court'. The street warden finished by encouraging members in the room to continue 'working together' on these issues and thanking 'residents' for being brave enough to speak up about local issues. The PCSOs and the street wardens left and the meeting was wrapped up soon after.

Walking home from the meeting, Tracey was fuming. 'No wonder', she exclaimed as soon as we had walked around the corner, 'that nobody wants to get involved with the Parish council, if all they do is get excited about petty policing. They want to speak truth to power, but they don't do anything!' she said. The PCSOs were no more than 'plastic police', she said, who had no interest in getting involved in real issues of crime, while the street wardens were 'just a joke'. This section has shown how NAG meetings, collaborations between the Parish council and local PCSOs, as well as the 'good neighbour scheme' are all examples of a proliferation of civic initiatives and partnerships that illustrate what Garland has called the 'responsibilization' of crime control agendas, and the broader processes of active citizenship associated with it. But as much as they seek to turn citizens into participatory agents, the reactions of people like Tracey, Bob, and Helen, also speak of the discrepancies that open up between citizens and officials in this process. How then did citizens themselves think about 'good governance'? What forms of participation did they favour and how do these depart from those recognized by the initiatives considered thus far? The next section will turn to an analysis of the local brokerage functions that community activists like Tracey engaged in.

Community Champions as Political Brokers

When I first started working in the local community on Park End estate, I had little understanding of what my role as a volunteer would entail: I had simply been instructed by Tracey, who ran the socializing area with charisma and warmth, that she could 'do with a hand' because 'there is always much to do'. The socializing area was no more than a large table that seated about ten people, a small kitchen area, and Tracey's desk, located in the main entrance area of the community centre. Residents dropped in there to access an IT hub, as well as a local credit union that was acting as a community bank for Park End residents. Tracey's own position was paid for by the community centre's association, a locally elected board, that was managing the modest proceeds the community centre made from hiring out space for functions and to local service users. I soon realized that Tracey's repertoire of daily tasks was huge and extended beyond what the job description of a part-time staff at the community centre might involve. One day, as we saw in Chapter 2, she would help women write their CVs for job applications or for the Jobcentre, the agency administering public welfare assessments. Another time she would call a rogue landlord, pretending to be a council officer and put pressure on them to pay a deposit that they owed a tenant who was leaving the property. And yet another time, she would give residents advice on how they might want to circumvent the authorities altogether and deal with problems in an 'informal way' (Chapter 5). In between, she always had time for a cup of coffee and a 'natter' (a chat) with friends who dropped by and sat around the large table in the community hall.

One particular occasion stuck with me: Silvia, a black woman of Afro-Caribbean descent and a mother of three, came into the community centre, looking distressed. Tracey had known Silvia for years and, while she said she did not want to be too closely involved in Silvia's life, she always made a point of chatting to her when the opportunity presented itself. 'Somebody told me that you can help me with this', Silvia said to Tracey as she walked into the hall that day. Silvia explained what had happened: she had recently started working as a kitchen help in a renowned gastro restaurant a few miles out of the city. When she started working, no written contract had been made. Instead, Silvia had reached an oral agreement with the head chef about working hours and pay—something that was not uncommon in the local service industry. Shortly after her first shift, the head chef started changing her hours and expecting her to work overtime for which she would not get paid. Silvia went along with this at first but after a couple of double shifts told the head chef that she wanted to leave early that night: she had to get home to look after her grandchildren because their mother would be out. The head chef shouted at her and told her that if she did not comply with his orders she would be sacked. Silvia decided that moment to walk out of the kitchen and did not return to work her remaining days.

All of this had been about four weeks ago. Since then, the nightmare had started. Silvia had not been paid for any hours she had worked, which amounted to almost three weeks of full-time work, not counting the over-time she had done. What is more, the Jobcentre had instructed her that if she wanted to get her benefits reinstated, she would have to supply a P45 (her working tax form) and a proper wage slip as proof of her work history. They also wanted a formal note of dismissal. But when Silvia returned to the restaurant to get the required documents and outstanding payments, the head chef told her that she had 'walked out of the job' and would not be entitled to any wages for the shifts she had already worked. As for the P45, she was given a dirty piece of paper with some random numbers scribbled on it without a date or signature. Silvia also tried to speak to the manager of the restaurant, but was told that there was nothing they could do about the situation because the catering had been outsourced to a private company. Now she was worried: for as long as she did not have the required documents in place, she would not be able to get back on welfare benefits, thus potentially leaving her in a state of indefinite limbo. Silvia did not know how she would be able to cover food expenses this month, let alone pay her rent payments to the housing association that she was renting her social tenancy with.

Tracey was appalled by what had happened and agreed to help where she could. Over the following weeks, Tracey and I invested our energies into Silvia's case. Tracey suggested that Silvia speak to advice agencies first to find out what her legal rights were. There was an independent advice centre in town, the Citizens' Advice Bureau (CAB) that gives advice on employment disputes. Silvia and I went together one day and were told that liability lay with the management and that we would be entitled to take legal action after fourteen days. We wrote to the restaurant informing them but never heard back. In the meantime, Tracey decided to go in on the offensive: she found a number for trading standards and phoned up the 'food and safety people' to make an anonymous complaint about food hygiene in the restaurant: 'Just to scare them a bit', she said (see also Chapter 5). She told me to come dressed to work 'smartly' the next day: we would go to the restaurant and confront the management in person. The next day, when I turned up in smart black trousers and a black shirt, Tracey joked that we were dressed like we were going to a funeral or to court—the only times when she would dress in black. She told Silvia 'to keep your mouth shut, don't give them none of that gangster talk again' (at least until all other avenues had been exhausted). At the restaurant, we took the manager by surprise as Tracey threatened them with legal action if they did not comply with the requests. A few days later, the problem resolved itself as a wage slip and P45 arrived through the post to Silvia's house.

'We can do this professionally, Izzy. Blaggars are us!' Tracey said the day after we had gone to the restaurant. While she was saying this as a joke, Tracey's words revealed a more fundamental point: how she had mobilized her resources, wit, and skills by acting as a broker. Tracey was one of a handful of community activists who were situated at the front line of public services on Park End providing assistance to those in need. Even just a cursory glance then at one small aspect of Tracey's activities in the community centre reveals a very different account of 'active citizenship' to that portrayed by the agencies in the NAG meetings, Parish council, or other initiatives: one that made her 'active' in people's daily struggles for security and survival, that made, as one person once said, 'politics real for them'. This is not to say that Tracey rejected the kinds of partnerships favoured by the official frameworks of governance, including, say, working with PCSOs or housing authorities as and when needed. But official partnerships only mattered to her to the extent that they helped her advance specific causes on behalf of residents. She was a political broker par excellence. Brokers have been described as intermediary actors, people who occupy 'a veritable in-between position, deriving their legitimacy from their seeming proximity to the common people while also possessing specialist skills and knowledge that the latter lack' (James and Koch, n.d.). They sit at the interstices of the people, the market, and the authorities, often stepping in where traditional welfare agents are withdrawing or have left (Forbess and James, 2017).

But Tracey's work extended beyond mere brokerage functions: she was also prepared to take on the authorities, when other routes had failed, and to mobilize the 'community' on behalf of such collective causes. For example, in 2010, Tracey decided to organize the annual community fair on Park End which, in previous years, had been organized and managed by a city council official who had good working relations with local groups. Now, however, the local authorities had cut the funding for his post which, in turn, called the future of the community fair into question. Tracey decided to put on 'the biggest and largest celebration' the estate had ever seen. Within days, she had organized a committee of interested volunteers, including staff from the local library, and she started holding meetings once every fortnight; we discussed where to get funding from, what local groups to contact, and how to organize the day. She phoned members of the Parish council to find out how to apply for community-funding; she got in touch with local authority officials to see if they had any money to spare; and she mobilized local groups to contribute activities, services, and performances on the day. Perhaps most importantly, she was concerned to make sure that as many people as possible would turn up on the day. Her idea was to make our own posters: we would take pictures of local individuals and print them on A4 pages with the slogan 'Your community needs you'. The slogan was a play on words on the well-known phrase 'your country needs you', used by Lord Kitchener in the First World War as a recruitment campaign for soldiers. They would be put up in public spaces on the estate: in the windows of the fish and chip shop, the Chinese take away, the local grocery shop, as well as the schools, gym, and nursery, and community centres.

'People will recognize the faces on the poster and they are more likely to come out because they feel connected and they will bring their mates, neighbors and family', Tracey explained, and added, 'here it's not what you know, but who you know'. In this instance, she was mobilizing 'claims to connectedness' (Edwards, 2000) to organize a wider collective and to conjure a feeling of togetherness and community on Park End. On the day before the event, we made our tours to drum up some final support, walking to the school, shops, and community centres to tell people about the event and to remind them to come out. Tracey's efforts were rewarded: the day of Park End's community fair was a success, as hundreds of people came out to listen to reggae music, eat locally cooked food, watch youth groups perform on the stage, and catch up on news and gossip with other residents and friends. Afterwards, Tracey would look back and remember the event as a day when 'the whole community had come out', when 'Park End had stood united', and when 'everyone was there'. She was happy that Park End had shown the council that 'they could not do to people whatever they want'. While this was no doubt an exaggeration, her words captured the sense of collectivity that the event had conjured, a collective that had energizing effects for her as she became involved in a range of other protests against austerity cuts in the months to come. A few days after the event, I came into the community centre when I saw her typing into her laptop. A while later, she passed me a printed copy of what she had written:

The health & well-being of our community is affected by the health and well-being of every individual in it. As long as there are individuals suffering from physical, emotional, mental or fiscal hardship, then we too as a community suffer. Similarly, if even 1 or 2 individuals lives improve, then the general health & well-being of our community improves also. Park End has approximately 14,000 residents, so the question is, what can we do as a community to support ourselves, our locals, especially in this economic climate?

The community must unite and take responsibility in supporting those of us who cannot have the ability to respond, to reduce inequalities and break the cycle of deprivation. We (the community) know better than anyone what it is like to live here, what challenges we face and what we need; we need to voice these issues very loudly and very clearly, to those who have been placed in a position to make these changes. Rather than sit back on our laurels, let us talk, shout, vote, march ... even strike if we must, in order for change to begin!

Service providers, community leaders and activists; young people, old people and those-in-between: the system might be wrong and unfair, but what will you do to make a difference? For so long, it's been easier to point the finger and blame others—let's use the same energy to bring about a REVOLUTION!

As this letter shows, the kind of 'active citizenship' and participatory governance that Tracey engaged in was very different from that imagined by the institutional frameworks of governance considered in the last section. As a broker, she was mediating, translating, and, in her words, 'blagging' on behalf of other residents, as well as mobilizing support against the authorities where residents had been wronged. In so doing, she engaged in what I have called elsewhere a 'bread and butter politics' (Koch, 2016): a politics that is about getting involved in the pursuit of people's daily material struggles and demands and the everyday networks of mutual reciprocity that frame them. But what were the limits of such forms of alternative citizenship? And what happened when they came into contact with the kinds of institutionalized practices recognized and enforced by outsiders? The next section will turn to these questions and in so doing, move the focus to a second set of political brokers: locally based politicians who represent Park End residents.

Personalizing Politics

If their perceived proximity to 'the people' was a necessary condition for brokers' pursuit of a 'bread and butter politics', it was not a sufficient condition for their success. People like Tracey also needed the backing, or at least tacit consent, of the authorities and outsiders, with whom they negotiated and upon whom they often depended in practical and financial ways. These dependencies are illustrated in what happened subsequently to Tracey's job, about a year after I had started volunteering with her. Her own position was contingent upon the city council's continued willingness to let her operate in the community centre: the building was local authority owned, even if an independently elected committee oversaw its daily running. One day, in 2011, the city council announced 'restructuring' plans in the local community centre. It objected to the ways in which the community centre had 'run itself' more or less independent from the council and been allowed to operate in informal ways. Tracey's own position, until now paid for through the community centre's committee, would be replaced by a council-paid employee who would be directly accountable to the council. The reasoning was one that I had heard many times before: the city council argued that the community centre had been allowed to run for too long 'without guidance', that there was not enough transparency in its financial matters, and that too many people had been able to get keys and hence unauthorized access to the building. Tracey was invited to apply for the new post that would replace her position with the more streamlined position of a centre manager, who would be expected to work in close relationship with the local authorities, reporting back to the council on regular intervals.

Tracey could have applied for the post but decided she would not do so, even if this meant facing significant personal hardship, including the prospect of unemployment or employment in low-paid service sector jobs as well as the loss of her role as a hugely respected community activist (indeed, she went to work on the shopfloor of a large supermarket chain after she left the community centre). For her, the restructuring was yet another attempt on the part of the city council to encroach on people's lives on Park End and to solidify its control over them. Their plans to formalize the management of the community centre were a direct affront to the way she had run the centre's space for the past few years. 'They just want to get rid of our community centre', she said, 'it's the beginning of the end.' When the day came when candidates for Tracey's old position were to be interviewed by the city council, Tracey packed up her things—a small laptop, some pens, her favourite mug from the community centre's kitchen—and walked out of the community centre forever. 'My community days are over, I'm going to pack up', she said to me. She insisted that she did not want to be implicated when the 'council are destroying our community'.

There was some truth in her words: shortly after she left and a new person was hired, a big wall was inserted into the middle of the room, creating a separate space to give the new community worker a private office space. The wall caused much controversy. For weeks after it had been erected, people would refer to it as a physical statement of how the community centre had changed. Council officers, usually white, suited men, would also regularly drop by (something that would never have happened before when Tracey was running the space), sitting behind the office desk and busying themselves at the computer. 'It just feels like a council building now', one resident commented to me. When I returned to the community centre in 2018 to do an interview with Tracey's successor, I could see how Tracey's fears of the post being 'controlled' by the council might have come true. I was interested to speak about an impending regeneration project that was very controversial for residents. While Tracey's successor was a local resident who deeply cared about the community on the estate, she was reluctant to speak to me on tape about the council, apologizing several times that she had to be 'careful' about what she could say. Around the same time, I saw Tracey post a note on social media that openly attacked the council's regeneration plans as an attempt to gentrify the neighbourhood and, she feared, to displace local people.

Community activists faced what Symons' has called a 'tautological contradiction': on the one hand they were exhorted to be independent and self-determining but, on the other, their lives were intimately intertwined with state policies and representatives

(Symons, 2018: 216). Being situated at the frontline of local services, they were in precarious positions as they feared having funding sources withdrawn, their physical base taken away or be ousted by competition. Take the example of another council-led regeneration project on a neighbouring estate where I started my research in 2009, prior to my arrival on Park End (see also Introduction). There, the community centre's association had been largely run by a single family—Bob who was already introduced above, his wife, and their close friends. Over the years, relations with adjoining institutions, including a nursery, a primary school, and the youth club had gone sour and services were being duplicated across the sites. The regeneration project would involve pulling down the existing facilities and replacing them with a single multi-purpose structure that would accommodate all of the service providers on a principle of shared spaces. In an informal interview carried out with the head of the regeneration unit, she complained of what she saw as an unhealthy culture of favouritism and clientelistic relations that had developed in the community centre. Bob and his family were operating the community centre like a little 'clan', benefiting their own and excluding others from using the spaces. One official also worried that services and groups were not being run in accordance with official procedures: Bob's son, who cooked meals at the Monday lunch club, did not have food standard certificates; Lynn, who was running a mother and toddler group had never even completed an accredited caring course; and Bob was given 'too much power' to do what he wanted.

From Bob's point of view, the local authorities' talk of 'regeneration', of 'culture change', and of 'joined up thinking' were dangerous threats. Like Tracey, he felt that the regeneration plan was a direct affront to his work. He knew that under the new plans, his own role and that of the community association would be made completely redundant in favour of a council-led multi-purpose board of different service providers and institutions. While the city council set up a 'community panel' linking the different service providers in the months that followed, Bob, his family, and friends decided to oppose the regeneration plans. They refused to collaborate in joint meetings, organized their own public events to 'inform' the 'local community' about the regeneration plans, sought out press attention and pressurized local councillors and even the MP. In the end, their resistance to the regeneration plan only acted as further proof to the city council that Bob and his committee were 'difficult' and only interested in their 'own agenda'. Eventually, nine months after Bob had first started the campaign, I went to see him. It was the day before his community centre would shut its doors forever. Sitting in a bare room that had already been stripped of its furniture, heaters, and decorations, Bob said to me: 'You came to study our community, but now you can study its downfall'. A few weeks later, the news arrived that Bob had died of a sudden heart attack. 'He was heartbroken', a mutual friend said. After his death, Bob's family started a campaign to have a memorial put up where the old community centre had stood. To my knowledge, this never happened.

The death caused by regeneration can be seen as an extreme example of how local authorities came to act on what they saw as evidence of corruption with Bob running the place like his own 'fiefdom' or 'clan'. It also spoke of a more general problem that I came across again and again: the engrained suspicion with which the authorities treated local community activists and the personalized relations they maintained with their bases. To combat this suspicion and to afford them a level of independence and legitimacy, some activists decided to become involved in local politics as elected councillors. In Chapter 7, we will look in more depth at how decisions to become involved in electoral politics took place against the backdrop of widespread electoral withdrawal. Here, my focus is on how individuals who did become involved in local-level politics did so by replicating, and in some cases even surpassing, the kinds of brokerage activities that community activists engaged in. Take the example of a local political party, the Free Workers Party (FWP) which was active on Park End and two other estates in town in the 2000s. Until 2010, Tony, Alice's stepfather introduced in Chapter 5, was one of their four councillors who had been voted into the city council. I have described the political history of the party in depth elsewhere (Koch, 2016). Suffice to say, it was founded by activists dissatisfied with the New Labour government, which, the party argued, had betrayed the working classes. Locally, their politics were focused on issues of crime control. Arguing that the local authorities were turning a blind eye to problems of serious drug-dealing and crime, the party decided to 'take the law into their own hands' by collecting their own CCTV evidence against drug dealers, patrolling the streets, and setting up picket lines outside the homes of known drugdealers. Fred, a white resident and former trade union activist in his fifties, was one of the residents who recalled the FWP's work on Park End with fondness:

> Well, yeah, they were vigilantes, and why not? Near where I live, there was a drug den. And one of the neighbours, she complained about that quite a lot. And she gets in touch with the police, ol' odd 'CANACT' [acronym for the Crime and Nuisance Action Team]—you mean 'DON'T ACT'! You know! Basically, what you gotta do is bang in the door, shut the place down, kick them bastards out. But it took them bloody months, and months, and months! And [the FWP], they was good, they really helped to get things moving.

The FWP had taken 'bread and butter politics' to a different level by claiming de facto state powers for themselves. While Fred referred to the FWP's party's activities as 'vigilante' politics, the party's support for extra-legal action was entirely justified in his eyes: they had done what needed doing to protect residents from the serious threat of drug-dealers and criminals by moving beyond the state's own claims to have a monopoly over the use of legitimate force (see also Chapter 5). Fred's views were mirrored by other residents who spoke of the FWP as a 'localist party', as a party who had been 'for Park End'. Importantly, it was precisely the personalized link that the party had established with local residents through the pursuit of its politics of crime control that also explained its electoral success. As we will see in Chapter 7, against a backdrop of electoral withdrawal where participation in local elections had fallen to levels of less than 20 per cent, they mobilized votes as part of a personalized relationship with Park End residents. When asked why they had voted for the party, residents emphasized that they had done so because they knew Tony and they supported his work; because they knew of others who had been helped by Tony or simply because he was 'local' and from the estate (Koch, 2016).

The example of the FWP was not unique: as we saw in the opening to this chapter, other locally based politicians—including Pat Evans, the local Labour councillor and her husband, the MP—had built similarly close-knit relations with residents through their long-standing residence and engagement in local-level community work. But as local politicians, they were also constrained in ways that community activists like Tracey were not: in their daily case work, they were expected to work with, not against, the authorities, and to abide by official etiquette and rules. They also had to manage expectations from residents that they would be able to help them and improve their lot. And where they failed to do so, their legitimacy was at stake. Take the example of the FWP again. Almost immediately after the FWP had managed to be voted onto local governance, they encountered a great deal of resistance to their work. The local Labour party accused the FWP of being 'an extremist organization', with ties to terrorist organizations in Ireland. In interviews I carried out with housing officials and local authority figures, the FWP were described as a 'vigilante' party, as 'anti-democratic', and as being too 'anti' and 'angry'. Val, for example, the local housing official introduced in Chapter 4, described the FWP as 'a bunch of angry men'. 'I see my job as giving housing to people, not taking housing away from them', she said in response to my question of how she had felt about the FWP's campaign to get certain persistently troublesome neighbours (including Jay, the drug-dealing neighbour in Chapter 4) evicted.

Community activists like Bob, Tracey, or Lindsey were accused of being 'too close to their own', of pursuing clan-like ties, and of failing to adhere to standards of transparency and openness. Local politicians like the councillors of the FWP, in turn, risked being seen as anti-democratic, angry, and corrupt. Either way, the antagonism that activists encountered, combined with the daily stresses of having to keep up with never-ending case work, could prove too big of a challenge to master, especially for small political parties or independent councillors. This is how David, a former FWP supporter and active member summed up the history of the FWP: 'at one stage, we had four councillors. And then we got absolutely annihilated by Labour: they get the students in and they canvass and they do it for a living. But we have to work fulltime and fit it all in. And then you are in council and you are being out voted all the time.' David underestimated the stronghold that Labour councillors had on the estate, not primarily through their connection with the party and party politics but through the dedication and commitment that individual Labour party members like Pat Evans had put in. Be that as it may, however, from the point of view of Park End residents, the FWP's inability to respond to their demands for help, let alone expand into a broader movement, was yet more proof, that those they had trusted were liable to let them down. Thus, David continued, 'after these years, the people who have been voting for you say "You are not getting anywhere", and then people lose faith in you and you lose them forever'. Indeed, in 2010, ten years after the FWP had their first councillor voted in, the party had lost of all of its seats again. In his final interview with the local newspaper, Tony, the last remaining councillor, spoke with pride of what the FWP had achieved on Park End but also acknowledged the people who had voted them into power had come to see them as part of the system that the FWP had tried to change.

Conclusion

In this chapter, I have moved my attention from residents' daily engagements with the authorities to the work of community champions as 'political brokers' (Koster, 2014) who mediate, campaign, and sometimes fight on behalf of residents. Political brokers are agents situated at the intersection between the people and outside institutions, whether these be state authorities, those the government has outsourced its responsibilities to, or the market. They derive their legitimacy from their perceived proximity to the people and their knowledge of the struggles that people confront. But what makes them different from ordinary residents is their relative potency and power. Political brokers engage in a variety of practices that residents cannot do on their own. These range from mediating and translating between particular domains and spheres of activities that are commonly held separate (in the case of Silvia's employment problems), to mobilizing residents in an oppositional fight against local authority-induced changes (in Tracey's campaign against public sector cuts) to bypassing the state altogether (in the case of the vigilante politics practised by the FWP). By engaging in these activities, the significance of brokerage work extends beyond individualized acts of assistance as they also conjure feelings of unity, belonging, and togetherness on Park End which can be mobilized against those in power.

An ethnographic analysis of local actors as brokers complicates the narrative of a new Foucauldian turn towards modes of 'active citizenship'. 'Active citizenship' has been a central trope of government policy since the 1980s (Hyatt, 1997; Koster, 2014; Ramsay, 2012). Citizens are expected to become participants in their own governance, often at the expense of more structural or welfarist solutions. But residents like Tracey or local politicians like Tony who become active in these spaces of governance do not just give into official logic of 'active' citizenship-making. As we have seen in the previous chapters, Park End residents actively personalize their engagements with the state as they act in accordance with their own priorities in and outside the home. Similarly, the kinds of activities that brokers like Tracey or Tony engage in constitute everyday attempts to personalize politics and the spaces of participatory governance that are open to them: through their daily acts of translating, of bridging the gaps, of fighting the authorities, and of taking on government-like functions, brokers seek to bridge the gap between an 'us' and a 'them'. In so doing, they conjure a different relationship with state, one which foregrounds the daily realities and relationships that matter to people on Park End.

There is nothing particularly unique or noteworthy about personalized politics. Personalized politics resembles the activities of brokers that have been investigated across marginalized settings (Alexander, 2002; James, 2007, 2011; Lindquist, 2015). Lazar (2004), for example, has argued in the context of electoral politics in Bolivia that while liberal representative democracies see political agency as individualized, and citizens' participation as organized via a set of rights and obligations (such as voting), Bolivian citizens destabilize both the abstraction and individuation. By developing personalized relations with politicians, they overcome the depersonalization of electoral politics and create a more direct, less delegative local democracy than that envisaged by their political architects. However, while personalized politics might be a well-established and even thriving feature of South American polities (e.g. Ayuero, 2000; Braconnier, Dormagen, and Rocha, 2015; Grisaffi, n.d.; Koster, 2012; Lazar, 2004) as well as in the Mediterranean area (e.g. Alexander, 2000), 'there is a dominant assumption … that politics in Northern Europe are much more formalized' (Koster, 2014: 53). This is despite important evidence to the contrary (Forbess and James, 2017; Koch, 2016; Koster, 2014; Tuckett, n.d., 2018). This assumption is shared by officials and authority figures on Park End who routinely stigmatize, if not punish, Park End activists' behaviour as evidence of clientelistic politics and non-transparent ties when these do not fit with their own understandings of what 'active citizenship' should look like. The next chapter will continue with this theme by looking at the broader democratic implications of the gap between the people and those who govern them.

7

Democracy as Punishment: Brexit and Austerity Politics

When British citizens voted to leave the European Union by popular referendum on 23 June 2016, the country changed forever. Overnight, Britain's economic, legal, and political life, governed by a supranational framework since 1973, was thrown up in the air. In the week leading up to the event, I had been in contact with my friends on Park End via social media and over the phone. Some of the responses I received about my questions relating to the EU referendum already anticipated the results. Tracey was a good example. Having told me that she had decided to vote in favour of 'leave', she countered my (poorly disguised) unease by justifying what made her feel that way. 'Something needs to change', she told me. Having myself been unable to vote in the referendum as a non-British citizen, I replied that to me the vote felt like an affront to who I was—a foreign national from the EU who had come to live in Britain a decade earlier. 'Don't be silly', Tracey instructed me, and told me that this had nothing to do with me. I was reminded of Tracey's own immigrant background and the pride she took in it; her parents had come from Jamaica as teenagers in the late 1960s; and she herself had always interacted with people from different countries in her work as a community worker. For her, the vote was not motivated by anti-immigrant feelings, it was rather a call for 'change' as she put it, both on Park End and perhaps beyond.

Tracey's response contrasts with common portrayals of the 'leave vote' in much of the liberal media and public discourse in the direct aftermath of the referendum. The referendum on leaving the EU drove a rift through a country that had been unprepared for its result: while those who had voted in favour of 're-main' mourned the loss of the European Union, expressing their incomprehension and anger at those who had voted in favour

Personalizing the State: The Anthropology of Law, Politics and Welfare at the UK's Margins. First Edition. Insa Koch. © Insa Koch 2018. Published 2018 by Oxford University Press.

of leaving, those who had cast their vote to 'leave' felt victimized and misunderstood. In the months that followed, much of the tabloid press presented 'remainers' as traitors of the people, while the liberal media and public figures saw 'leave' voters as misinformed, and worse, as racist and bigoted. To give just one example, almost six months after the EU referendum, on the eve of her by-election in Richmond Park, a wealthy West London constituency, Liberal Democrat Sarah Onley, a staunch Brexit-opposer, declared: 'Richmond Park was full of people like me, who felt the country was going wrong, that the politics of anger and division were on the rise, that the liberal, tolerant values we took for granted were under threat.' She added, 'Today we have said no. We will defend the Britain we love. We will stand up for the open, tolerant Britain we believe in' (Walker, 2016).

Dominant narratives that have crystallized around Brexit voters portray images of an autocratic mob. These images are typically linked to a growth in 'popular authoritarianism' or 'authoritarian populism' among Brexit supporters said to reflect an increased appetite for coercive state measures. This is expressed through a number of different but interlinked assumptions: the public's appetite for harsher punishment and anti-human rights stance; its call for tougher anti-immigrant policies; and a popular leaning in favour of strong foreign and defence policies (Dearden, 2016; Stewart, 2016; Swales, 2016; Twyman, 2016). However, ethnographic engagements with Brexit voters have begun to show that they do not form a unitary group, driven by punitive desires for tougher state controls, whether these are framed along xenophobic lines or not. Rather they have been motivated by a variety of different causes (Edwards, Haugerud, and Parikh, 2017), including disaffection with government at the margins (Koch, 2017b); a nostalgic longing for the past (Balthazar, 2017); anger and despair among the 'left out' (Mckenzie, 2016); anxieties about downward mobility among an intermediate class (Antonucci et al., 2017), as well as among the wealthier end of the spectrum, a tradition of anti-immigration and anti-European views (Peston, 2017).

The aim of this chapter is to provide yet another angle by moving from particular accounts of Brexit voters to the broader context of a crisis of representation and the failures of liberal democracy as they are experienced in Britain's socially abandoned neighbourhoods. I ask: how did Brexit constitute a vote long overdue for those who feel that they have been abandoned and neglected? If, say, Richmond Park saw one way 'the country was going wrong', then what kind of Britain were Park End residents saying 'no' to? And what does the Brexit vote reveal about people's views of government and democracy, more broadly? In England and Wales, some (although by no means all) citizens who decided to vote against the EU come from the country's most marginalized socio-economic groups. The anger unleashed by the EU referendum stands in stark contrast to evidence of widespread withdrawal from, and disenchantment with, electoral processes in Britain and beyond.[1] Park End typifies these developments. Electoral turn out has been low on the estate for decades, falling to levels below 20 per cent in local elections. And yet, some of my interlocutors, like Tracey, who had not voted in a long time, came out to vote on 23 June 2016. Many of them did so in favour of 'leave': Park End was a majority leave area, compared with the over 80 per cent of the city that voted in favour of 'remain'.

At the core of this chapter is an apparent paradox that needs explaining: how high levels of electoral withdrawal and alienation from formal politics sat alongside citizens' engagements with the EU referendum. On Park End, residents routinely think of politics and politicians as the antithesis of ordinary sociality that is so central to everyday personhood making on Park End. Within such a context, withdrawal from electoral processes becomes a protective response, one which residents present as an active choice to keep the world of politics and political dealings at bay. But what made the Brexit vote different for at least some of my interlocutors is that the referendum on leaving the EU was perceived as an attempt to moralize politics. I argue that people personalized politics by inserting everyday moralities into electoral processes by pouring their aspirations, hopes, and frustrations into their respective votes. Some Park End residents perceived it as an event that would make a difference to their lives in a way that standard electoral processes do not. For them, the referendum was an opportunity to say 'no' to a government tout court by rejecting the constitutional framework that they have come to associate with repressive governance for so long. While not everybody on Park

---

[1] At 77.2 per cent, voter turnout for the referendum was higher than for the general election that preceded it in 2015, in which 66.1 per cent of eligible voters participated.

End chose this course of action, those who did—like Tracey—were not vilified within their own communities.

Let me be clear. In shifting the analytical focus from dominant narratives that have tended to pathologize the voter–citizen to a broader crisis of representation, my aim is not to replace one singular narrative with another, less even to deny that authoritarian feelings—be they xenophobic or otherwise—have in some instances motivated people's choices in favour of 'leave'. On the contrary, a growing and important body of ethnographic work has started to track the rise of populist voices on the far-right, both in the United Kingdom (Evans, 2012, 2017; Rhodes, 2010; Smith, 2012a) and beyond (Gingrich and Banks, 2006; Holmes, 2000; Kalb, 2009, 2011; Szombati, 2018). In the United Kingdom, the 'leave campaign' powerfully mobilized a language of anti-immigration around tropes of regaining 'local control' in the lead up to the referendum. Some people in Park End undoubtedly identified with this language that placed blame with foreign workers. However, not everyone did (reflecting the reality of multi-cultural estate life that cuts across any straightforward racial or ethnic divides), and among the people with whom I spoke, more complex narratives prevailed. By focusing on these narratives, as well as by highlighting the broader context of a democratic crisis, I then aim to draw attention to an aspect that has received less attention in the liberal media and commentary: namely, the failures of government to be accountable to the people on their own terms. In the end, 'Brexit' on Park End crystallizes the ethnographic reality that the book as a whole has sought to capture thus far: how citizenship is experienced as punishment by those at the margins.

Anthropologists of class and neoliberalism have explored the current political conjuncture as one of a constant narrowing down of political options and institutional mechanisms for voicing class-based demands (Carrier and Kalb, 2015; Friedman, 2003; Kalb, 2009; Narotzky, 2016). With the decline of received channels of political representation that were once central to the post-war social democratic state (as imperfect as these channels were), working-class citizens are not only experiencing economic and social dispossession but political dispossession too. In the last chapter, we already saw how this dispossession plays out on the level of localized politics as citizens find that their agendas and own forms of governance are sidelined if not criminalized by those in power. This chapter takes the analysis to people's relations with the broader democratic polity, and it investigates how votes like 'Brexit' become a 'critical juncture' (Kalb, 2009) that links everyday experiences of abandonment, anger, and dispossession to the political system writ large. Judged in this light, Park End residents' engagements with electoral processes, Brexit included, have the potential both to critically disrupt, but also to further legitimize a political status quo that has silenced working-class demands.

Brexit, Popular Authoritarianism, and the Crisis of Democracy

Downwards trends in electoral participation over the last three decades indicate that electoral democracy is in crisis. This is certainly how policy-makers and academics have spoken of the state of government in the UK and beyond. Politicians and academics have routinely pointed to low levels of electoral turn out and other forms of civic participation to depict a picture of a civil society marked by apathy and decline. Prominent sociologists have similarly linked apathy and withdrawal to a loss of trust and social capital in late modernity (Putnam, 2004) and to an unravelling of received structures of class, family, and status and the correlating 'individualization' of lifestyles in 'second modernity' (Beck and Beck-Gernsheim, 2002). The old collective institutions upon which political and social life was once founded have given way to the 'asocial, free or alternatively isolated individual' (Hey, 2003: 329) who has become estranged from received channels of political representation. As sociologist Beck has put it, 'we are witnessing today an actively unpolitical younger generation which has taken the life out of the political institutions and is turning them into zombie categories' (Beck and Beck-Gernsheim, 2002: 203). 'Zombie categories' are defined by Beck as 'living dead' categories which 'govern our thinking but are not really able to capture the contemporary milieu' (Beck and Beck-Gernsheim, 2002: 262).

For Beck, civic and political processes such as elections—and even representative democracy itself—are an example of 'zombie categories': while formal electoral processes continue to exist, an increasing number of citizens are withdrawing from participation in voting and other forms of civic participation, thereby hollowing democracy out of its meaning. This narrative resonates with 'post-democracy' accounts put forward by Crouch (2004) amongst others, according to which democracy has moved increasingly towards more managerial and technocratic modes of governance at the expense of substantive decision-making and debate. Widespread electoral withdrawal and disenchantment with the institutional procedures of democracy is seen as the outcome of such processes. Similarly, Loader (2008) has coined the term of the 'anti-politics of crime' to identify the link that has been made between a harshening of 'law and order' policies considered in the last few chapters and an alleged decline of political visions and ideologies. In the works of people like Ericson (2007) and Simon (2007), crime and punishment 'make up the ideology of the post-ideological age, their regular appearance on the surfaces of political life and social consciousness obscuring the manner in which they have been bound up—as cause and effect—with the rise of what one might call "anti-politics"' (Loader, 2008: 400).

Against dominant readings of 'zombie democracy' (Beck and Beck-Gernsheim, 2002), of a 'post-democratic' (Crouch, 2004) or post-political (cf. Loader, 2008) era, the result on the referendum on leaving the European Union can be easily interpreted as evidence of a growing punitive, illiberal, and anti-political electorate. This is, indeed, how much of the liberal media and public policy think tanks have made sense of the 'Brexit vote' by invoking images of the 'authoritarian voter'. As mentioned, Brexit voters are presented on these accounts as being driven by their affinity for more coercive state interventions and policies, ranging from anti-immigration policies to anti-human rights propaganda and support for more and stronger state defence policies (Dearden, 2016; Stewart, 2016; Swales, 2016; Twyman, 2016). The head of the research think tank Nesta told the BBC shortly after the referendum that Brexit voters attitudes to punishment are a much more likely indicator of their voting preferences than more traditional categories of class: questions about citizens' attitudes towards policies like the public whipping of criminals or the death penalty delivered a reliable result in over 70 per cent of the cases as opposed to only about 50 per cent in cases where indicators of class and income were favoured (Burton, 2016). Portrayals of the authoritarian Brexit voter also sit with media narratives that have portrayed the British electorate as being divided along the lines of a growing 'culture war' between so-called internationalist or cosmopolitan liberals and those who come to be portrayed as the defenders of socially conservative values (Bush, 2016; Dunt, 2016; Stewart, 2016).

Unitary portrayals of the 'punitive' or 'authoritarian' voter–citizen and their associations with an anti-political or post-democratic age run the risk of feeding into purely pathologizing accounts of the people. In so doing, they also divorce people's decisions from the structural conditions that engulf their lives and the broader crisis of representative democracy that those at the margins confront. The denial of class (as evident in the statement given by the head of Nesta) as a relevant factor in understanding the results of the EU referendum is telling in this respect. Already four decades earlier, Hall and his colleagues (Hall et al., 1978), argued that the rise of what they called 'popular authoritarianism' among the British working-class public necessitated close attention to the state, including its attempts to insulate certain policies and institutional practices from social and political dissent from the 1970s onwards. The then Labour government's inability to respond to these issues through traditional social democratic means created a window for the right and a moralizing discourse of the 'nation' that legitimized a new and socially conservative 'common sense' that made Thatcher appear to be with the people. This book has militated against any unitary portrayals of a 'punitive' or 'authoritarian' common-sense among working-class people, to the extent that Park End residents display a range of attitudes towards the authorities that cannot be easily collapsed with straightforward consent for 'more' state power. Notwithstanding this, however, Hall and his colleagues alert us to an important point: the failures of democracy to deliver just government for its people.

Hall and his colleagues were concerned with the crisis of the post-war social democratic state. But since then, neoliberalism's ever-tighter 'authoritarian fixes' (Bruff, 2014) have heightened the crisis of legitimation and political representation that was already becoming apparent in earlier moments. We have already seen that Thatcher in the 1980s smashed the unions, introduced widespread privatization, and hastened the financialization of Britain's economy and made 'active citizenship' a core tenet of political governance (Chapter 6). All of this left working-class people bereft of their livelihoods as their voices and concerns became increasingly delegitimized in the political sphere. Yet, Evans has argued that neoliberal restructuring under the Thatcher years paled in comparison with what was perceived to be the Labour Party's neglect of its traditional support base (2012: 26). In her analysis, central to this betrayal was the turn in the mid-1990s to New Labour politics, with its emphasis on multiculturalism, meritocracy, and the expansion of the middle classes. Moreover, we have seen that the party's turn to 'law and order' did not translate into the policing and protection that residents in crime-ridden communities need, thus failing to incorporate the most marginalized sectors through its notion of 'vulnerable' citizenship (Ramsay, 2012). As explained in more depth later, since 2010, successive Conservative governments have heightened the crisis of political representation through their drive to 'austerity politics' that according to Fetzer (2018) played a crucial role in producing the 'Brexit result'.

Bruff has suggested that 'authoritarian neoliberalism simultaneously strengthens and weakens the state as the latter reconfigures into a less open and democratic polity' (2014: 124). Examples of such weakening and, consequently, also of signs of resistance, include declining voter turnout and party membership, increasing electoral volatility and growing mistrust of the political elite (2014: 125). Bruff's account allows us to begin placing responses among the electorate, including with respect to the recent EU referendum, within an analytical frame that moves away from singular notions of 'post-democracy', of a 'post-ideological age', or of 'zombie democracy' by uncovering alternative framings. However, as anthropologists of class and neoliberalism have shown, in a situation where the channels for expressing dissatisfaction, let alone for proposing political alternatives, are largely absent or take on purely defensive means, subaltern critiques can also be sidelined or co-opted by more powerful actors (Alexander, Hojer-Bruun, and Koch, 2018; Kalb, 2009, 2011). Social justice claims can become trapped in a 'moral rather than a politico-economic framework for mobilization, one which is not predicated on class, that is, on the awareness of the structural positions within the unequal ownership of the means to reproduce a livelihood' (Narotzky, 2016: 87).

In this chapter, I engage with this dilemma by analysing how Park End residents' engagements with electoral politics have the potential both to disrupt but also to reproduce a political status quo that has silenced the language of class. Park End residents are not trapped in, but rather consciously embrace, a moral and political framework that is consonant with the political–economic realities that they confront. Their emic political theory is one that sees formal government and elected representatives as the antithesis of ordinary sociality that is so central to everyday personhood making on Park End. Withdrawal from electoral processes becomes a protective response that keeps the polluting influences of politics at bay. Against such a backdrop, for at least some of my interlocutors, the referendum on leaving the EU was perceived as an attempt to moralize politics. It was an act of refusal to be governed by the framework they associate with hollowed-out promises of representative democracy. Yet, in the absence of institutional mechanisms that can channel their demands, the 'Brexit' result is also likely not to alleviate, but rather to reinforce, deep-seated feelings of abandonment, thus further cementing an ideological gap that is conducive for populist actors who want to tap into working-class frustrations (Kalb, 2011). In what follows, I will develop the points by first taking a closer look at the recent turn to austerity politics; second, how this has fed deep-seated feelings of betrayal on Park End; and third, return to the Brexit vote.

Austerity Politics

'The kind of punishment that is laid on people is unbelievable and the bedroom tax is just another part of it, added on top of it, totally unnecessary.' This is how Rose, a white woman in her late fifties, described the government's under-occupancy policy colloquially termed the 'bedroom tax', when I met her in the summer of 2014. I had returned that year to Park End to carry out interviews with residents on the estate and surrounding neighbourhoods about austerity politics and how this had been affecting their lives. The bedroom tax came into force on 1 April 2013 alongside a host of other so-called welfare reforms. The policy works by reducing housing benefit payments to working age tenants in social housing who are considered to under-occupy their dwellings: tenants get 14 per cent of their housing benefits reduced for one spare bedroom and 25 per cent for two or more. Rose was one of the half million residents who in 2014 had been affected by the tax: she was occupying a two-bedroom council flat on her own after her partner had died of a heart attack two years prior. Her son was grown up and had moved out and was living in sheltered housing nearby, after spending some time in prison for a drug-related offence. Rose had been signed off on disability benefits since she had suffered a brain haemorrhage the day after her partner had passed away and she had to quit her work as a library assistant.

The bedroom tax in particular, and austerity reforms, in general, are associated with the most recent period of governance that began in 2010, when first a coalition government composed of Liberal Democrats and Conservatives, and then, in 2015 again, a Conservative government (confirmed in the general elections of 2016) were voted into power. Under their reign, fiscal policies and financialization, under the label of 'austerity', have once more reconfigured state-market-and-society relations as they have taken the ideal of the consumer–citizen to new extremes. Reflected in public sector cuts across much of Europe and beyond (Bear and Knight, 2017; Cohen, Fuhr, and Bock, 2017; Knight, 2017b; Knight and Stuart, 2017; Muehlebach, 2016; Narotzky and Goddard, 2017), austerity has been described as a 'full frontal assault on the Keynesian proposition that cutting spending in a weak economy produces further weakness' (Krugman, 2013). In Britain, austerity has engendered the biggest cuts in the history of the post-war welfare state, as housing (Wilde, n.d.), social welfare and debt (Davey, n.d.), immigration (Tuckett, n.d.), and legal aid (Forbess and James, 2017) to mention just a few, have been affected. The human costs are large: deaths among those who, under the new regime of welfare-to-workfare are deemed 'fit to work', rose exponentially in 2016 (Butler, 2015), while policies such as the 'bedroom tax' have driven some people to suicide (Koch, 2014).

The case of Rose, introduced above, illustrates the strains that austerity politics is putting people under. She invited me over to her house on a sunny June morning. While we were sitting opposite each other in the bright and comfortable living room of her post-war council flat, she told me how the bedroom tax was pushing her to the brink. The local authority had taken £70 off her monthly housing benefit payments for having a spare bedroom in the house. Under the new arrangement that she was facing, Rose was living on £85 a week, which had to cover gas, electricity, water, her phone bill, food, clothes, and a small pension to pay for death costs that she did not want to give up for fear of passing on the burden of her funeral costs to her family 'when I am not there anymore'. She dreaded the winter, she confessed, when her heating and gas bill would go up and she feared she might not be able to afford it anymore. But even now, it was simply not enough to get by. Rose told me that she had £4 left in her wallet to live off until her next benefit payments were due in four days' time. And that was only because her neighbour had lent her £20 earlier in the week. And she had fallen into rent arrears with the council, owing them over £200. Rose explained how the 14 per cent reduction in benefit payments was a qualitatively different experience for her than for the middle classes for the disproportionate effect it was having on her life:

> When you say to people, sort of the middle classes or whatever, 'oh they pay 14 per cent out of their benefits for their spare room', they think 'oh that's good value because it sounds as though that's not all that much' and, you know, they would happily pay 14 per cent for a spare room that they have. But that's not the issue, is it? The fact is they are asking for 14 per cent of money you just haven't got! I just have no money whatsoever.

Never mind that the second bedroom for which 14 per cent of her housing benefit payments had been reduced was anything but spare: Rose explained that the bedroom (a tiny boxy room that had just about enough space for a double bed) was vital for keeping her family together. One of her grandsons, who suffered from autism, would come and stay with her two nights a week when his mother was working. For another of her grandsons, Rose's flat was the only place where he could come to spend time with his father. Since his father had been to prison, he and the mother of the child had broken up and he was not allowed to take his son to the sheltered housing where he was staying. Rose would organize for her grandson to be dropped off at her flat at least once a month for a weekend and her son would come and spend two days with them together. But this might no longer be possible in the future. Rose was faced with two options now: either she could 'put up with the tax', and risk accumulating more rent arrears, eventually facing eviction, or she could try to find alternative accommodation, most likely in the private rental sector as the government had repeatedly said. However, we saw in Chapter 4 that renting in the private market was often worse than renting in the social housing market given the problem of insecure tenancies, rogue landlords, and often higher rent payments. For Rose this option was no more than a 'smokescreen':

> I mean that's just a smokescreen—oh they can go to the private sector! Who in their right mind is actually going to give up a social housing place to rent in the private sector? And it's gonna cost more, absolutely,

it's gonna cost the government more [because housing benefit payments will have to be adjusted in accordance with the higher rents], and it's not secure. No! It's not secure. You know, nobody is going to move into the private sector, I have heard politicians say—well, they can just move into the private sector. It's just a smokescreen, it's ridiculous, nobody is going to do that!

For many citizens affected by austerity politics, the public sector cuts are only the most recent 'punishment imposed on top of everything else', as Rose had put it to me in the interview. It is only the most recent attack on their relations and homes in a long-drawn history of domination and control, much of which was relayed in the preceding chapters. Rose's own history illustrates this point once more. There was, for example, the time her application for benefits had been refused following her haemorrhage, because the doctor, who undertook the assessment, had deemed her to be fit to work despite her persistent migraines. It took Rose almost eight months to appeal the decision and to receive her first payment. Or there was the time when her benefits were reduced because she had missed an appointment (she had confused the building that she was expected to go to and had been late), a process referred to as 'sanctioning'. She had to go for weeks without full benefit support, a punishment that seems disproportionate to her own fault in the first place. The delays and interruptions in benefit payments had also caused Rose to fall into thousands of pounds of credit card debt, as she was struggling to pay her bills and make ends meet. When I met her in 2014, Rose had applied for a debt relief order, something she described as a 'personal bankruptcy for the poor'.

Local authorities had put measures in place to help welfare recipients transition into austerity life. Discretionary housing payments were made available to those who proved their efforts to become independent; and, predictably, this imposed requirement gave rise to bureaucratic contradictions. That is, funds were intended to be disbursed principally to those who had the most funds at the same time as claimants were instructed to prove that they did not intend to be claimants and would be financially independent in the near-future; and people who were exhorted to stand, metaphorically, on their own two feet, were frequently applying precisely because of literal disabilities that prevented them from doing so. Rose described how going through the assessment for discretionary housing payment had been an excruciating process: 'I got that discretionary housing payment but I had to listen to a lot before about, you know, about how the council believes that everyone should be self-sufficient and if you can prove to me that, you know, during this time you will be able to find alternative means to pay it, we are more likely to give you that grant and all that rubbish.' Because of a disability that prevented her from entering gainful employment, Rose was unable to prove that she would be able to find alternative means to pay for the shortfall of rent payments. In the end, Rose had been granted the payment because her application for a debt relief order was taken as proof of her intentions to become financially independent.

Even where recipients had been successful in obtaining discretionary housing payments by the authorities to help them with the impact of housing benefit cuts, they did not always find that their lives were better off for the added support. On the contrary, some found that the monitoring, surveillance, and humiliating treatment that they had to endure as a consequence of being the recipients of discretionary help were worse than coping on their own. Take the example of Olifia, a 'single mother' of five who was introduced in Chapter 3. Olifia had been affected by the benefit cap, a policy that caps the maximum amount of benefits that one is entitled to claim, irrespective of personal circumstances. For Olifia, the policy was a disaster. Because she had to rent a house large enough for her family in a grossly inflated private rental market, her rent was over a £1,000 a month. Previously, this had been covered by housing benefit payments while Olifia was studying towards a degree in youth work. In 2013, however, she was told that her housing benefits would be capped, leaving her to cover the shortfall in rent payments out of her own pocket. Olifia received £320 a week in benefit payments for herself and her five children and she had calculated that with the added expenses, she would be left with £17 for weekly food expenses and any other additional outcomes.

Olifia had been convinced by an officer in the city council to apply for a discretionary housing payment, a temporary payment that would cover the shortfall in rent to help with the transition. But in order to qualify for the payment, she had to prove that she was working sixteen hours a week, thus placing her in a situation where she had to juggle her studying and work. For months, she had been applying for jobs 'left, right and centre', getting rejections and being told by the benefits officers that she was asking for too much money and would have to try harder. Eventually, she found a job on a zero-hour contract working for a local authority-run youth club. We saw in Chapter 3 what happened after that: contrary to the initial agreement that Olifia had reached with the employer, she found that her hours were constantly being changed. Every time, Olifia reported the change in hours to the benefits agents, her benefit payments would be stalled and readjusted. This could take weeks to be processed, during which time Olifia was forced to borrow money, leaving her in debt to family and friends. It also made her feel like she was 'a bad mother' because she was unable to manage a home without falling into debt (see also Chapter 3). In the end, she decided that she would rather live without the discretionary payment if it meant that she would be left in peace. But this only made matters worse. Now she started getting phone calls from the benefits officer who expressed concerns about the welfare of her children:

So, she kept contacting me and saying 'can you please come back and see us, we are really concerned, we are really concerned about the welfare of your children, you can't live off 17 pounds a week'. So, then I was like, oh my god, now they are gonna report me to social services, aren't they! Shit. Now what do I do? What did I say? Cos I said kind of a lot to them in anger. So, then I got really paranoid cos I was like, now what do I do? And so I spoke to her on the phone and I said to her, 'you know, look, my situation is this, I love my kids more than anything, the government don't love my kids, you lot don't love my kids, I do. But your pressure is doing this to me, I need to maintain these children, I need to look after them, love them, but you are pressurizing me. And materialistic stuff doesn't really matter'. And then she is like, 'no one can live like that!'

Ironically, then, for Olifia, even her wish to be left alone had triggered still more unwanted attention of the authorities and the threat of social service involvement.

In short, women like Olifia and Rose experienced austerity reforms as a form of punishment: as a sanction or penalty that was imposed on them because they were poor and perhaps also 'single mothers' who survived without the support of men. The punishment operated in different ways: it was financial (by cutting benefit payments); it was practical (by exposing welfare recipients to humiliating encounters with welfare bureaucrats); and it was social (by de facto penalizing the processes of social reproduction central to their lives). And, it was only one of the many examples in which Park End residents experienced the authorities, as preceding chapters have shown. How did these experiences feed into people's views of government and democracy writ large? What responsibilities and obligations did they attribute to the government and how did these fit with the reality of state performance? The next section will turn to these questions.

State Failure

'What do you expect to happen? It's like the young people on this estate, they have kept it in for so long, and then they just don't wanna take it in anymore. You just flip. It's not surprising at all.' Lindsey was one of the residents I spoke to in the aftermath of the London riots in 2012, two years after the Conservative government had been elected into power with its agenda of public sector cuts. Lindsey was angered by the way the media and politicians had responded to the riots: with a sense of unspeakable shock as commentators rushed to stigmatize those who had gone out on the streets as rioters, criminals, and disruptive citizens. For Lindsey, like many other residents on Park End, the events that unfolded in London and over the course of the next few days across the country had been entirely foreseeable, and if not foreseeable then in any case not particularly surprising. 'Look at people here, they are just sick of the backstabbing, the false promises, the lying. They feel forgotten about. What do you expect to happen? At some point they just don't wanna take it no more and that's when shit starts hitting the fan', Fred said, another resident who was introduced in Chapter 6. His voice echoed those of others who spoke of how they felt that they had been 'forgotten about', that nobody 'cared about them', and that people in power wanted to 'get rid of them'.

The riots had happened on the night of 4 August 2011, when the family and friends of a young mixed-race man called Mark Duggon gathered outside the police station on Broadwater Farm, in Tottenham, a predominantly Afro-Caribbean and historically deprived neighbourhood in North London. They were demanding justice over what had happened to Mark the night before: the 29-year-old man and father of several children had been shot and killed by a police officer during an investigation by the London Metropolitan Police. At the beginning, the protest was peaceful but soon hundreds of people had gathered, and the crowds grew larger. Around 9 p.m. in the evening, they started marching to the high street in Tottenham. Some stormed the shops and were reported to have carried out goods—trainers, TVs, electrical equipment, and clothes from sport shops. Windows were smashed, cars set on fire along the way as riot police rushed in to control the crowds and contain the looting. The violence spread in the days that followed to other cities, including Birmingham, Manchester, and Nottingham. More than 15,000 people were said to have been involved. About 4,000 of them were arrested, 5,112 crimes were committed, and 3,800 shops damaged in London. Five people died in association with the riots (Townsend, 2016). The courts sat extended hours initially as they pushed thousands of young people through the criminal justice system and clamped down hard on 'law and order'.

On Park End estate, residents were waiting to see if riots would happen there too. They did not. Callum, a young black man in his twenties, who was teaching young people in the youth club about recording their own music, explained to me why: 'Young people don't wanna riot cos they know what the police are like round here. They would recognize your face straight away, and you'd get done for it, so what's the point.' But the events in London and people's talk of them had laid bare what was brewing under the surface: people's discontent with the authorities and their inability to make themselves heard, understood, and noticed, a discontent that was felt both by young and old. One of the most common themes that I encountered was the sense that nobody 'cared' about people in Park End and their neighbourhoods. I was told that 'they' are not 'interested', that they do not want to know anything about Park End, and even that they want to 'see the likes of us gone'. Different people had different reasons: some, like the rioters that interviewed in the 'reading the riots' study (Lewis et al., 2012), mentioned their anger at perceived police misconduct, including harassment and incessant stop-and-searches. For others, the riots had brought into focus their dissatisfaction with the authorities. Rose, for example, spoke of austerity politics and public sector cuts as an explanation for why the riots had happened. Or here is Olifia, speaking of her own experiences of having to fight her case with the benefit system:

What kills me the most [are] these people, these people in power [who] make these policies, change these policies, according to what they think is okay and there is no reality of what's happening to the real human beings out there who its really affecting. It doesn't really matter to them what

I went through; for them it's not my feedback that's gonna make them change anything; it's their own decision according to what looks good at the time to them. And they don't care. They don't care about the people they really don't.

When people on Park End spoke of how nobody 'cared', of how they had been 'forgotten', and how the authorities were not 'interested', they were not just using neutral language: as we have seen tropes of care, of loyalty, and support were central to daily sociality on Park End (Chapter 2). The sense of abandonment that people articulated expressed a deeper sense of betrayal, one where residents' own efforts to be 'decent' and 'good' against the odds remained unreciprocated by the authorities. In Chapter 2, we saw that in the post-war decades, paternalistic welfare policies were in place that were broadly in line with tenants' own aspirations, giving rise to what I called a fragile (albeit exclusive and highly policed) moral union that placed the nuclear, male-headed household at its centre. Today, this moral union has been thoroughly dismantled, even for those who had originally been included in its core. In oral history interviews, older Park End residents sometimes expressed the loss of this moral union in terms of a nostalgic longing for the past. Molly, an older white resident who had been among the first residents to be offered a house on Park End recalled the presence of rent collectors and housing officials as figures of paternalistic care: 'They were good in them days. They used to check you had done your gardening. And if it wasn't nice, you used to get a letter saying you had to put it right. And if anything needed fixing, they would come. These days no-one comes to check up anymore.' Others placed blame more squarely with Thatcher. Here is another older white resident, a woman called Sheila: 'I still think it's wrong that Maggie Thatcher introduced the right to sell houses. The council just don't care about council houses anymore. And people [who have bought their houses] don't look after their property, they rent it out to people who come in and who don't look after their homes.'

Younger residents, who lacked a living memory of the 'olden days', would still invoke a language of reciprocity that contrasted their own efforts to care to the council's correlating failure to do the same. This was sometimes done with reference to tropes of the 'worker–citizen' discussed in Chapter 1. Take the example of Mark, my first host and a father of four who was working as a lorry driver: 'I would go on telly and tell everyone that I am a married man and I've worked all my life, since the day I left school I worked, and I always pay my rent on the day it's due and they don't even care', he said to me once. But more commonly, particularly among the women I knew, alternative tropes of value and personhood were invoked that emphasized contributions in terms of one's ability to be a good kin member, mother, godparent, or neighbour. We saw this in Chapter 2 when Tracey was making the women in Park End feel valued as 'proper persons' by helping them to write CVs that told narratives about their lives that were meaningful to them. Similarly, women would talk of their own or others' efforts to be good mothers and kin members to contrast this with the government's failure to do their bit. Take the example of Lynn. Lynn was a friend of Lindsey's, and a white mother in her forties. She had two grown-up children but was living by herself in a two-bedroom house that she was renting from a local housing association. Lynn had been moved onto disability benefits following long-term mental and physical health problems that made it very difficult for her to hold down a job. Because her children had left home, she was now considered to 'under-occupy' her property and had been hit by the bedroom tax. One day in 2014, Lindsey, Lynn, and I got together in Lynn's back garden. Lindsey tried to convince Lynn to apply for discretionary housing payment to help her with the transition to the new benefit arrangement. When Lynn said she 'couldn't be bothered', Lindsey began probing her. 'Why do you not want to apply again?', she asked her friend, before she continued:

Maybe you don't want to apply for it because they make you feel that you're not deserving? But you're someone who has worked hard, the fact is you only claim benefit after you got badly hurt in an accident, you are a really good decent person, you've always helped me as a friend, you have always looked after your children and you're a good godmother to my daughter. And I don't feel like it's right for you to have this financial penalty put on you. But maybe you don't see it that way, maybe it's because they don't make you feel like … well, they make you feel like you are not deserving of it.

In this instance, Lindsey explicitly contrasted Lynn's exemplary role as a godmother, friend, and mother, with the government's views of her as someone who was 'undeserving'; she was imagining an alternative, fuller social contract, and constructing 'good' government as an entity that participated in affective and social reciprocities.

Whether residents relied on their own contributions in terms of labour, rent payments, or tax, or their attempts to be good mothers and friends, the purpose of emphasizing their efforts to be decent persons was always the same: it served to highlight the authorities' failure to honour their perceived duty of care towards citizens. And it translated into a deep-seated sense that 'They' had given up on people in Park End. Authors have noted how residents on post-industrial council estates narrate the history of their estate and their relations with outsiders in terms of a series of amorphous actors, institutions, and officials acting on their lives. For example, Alexander et al. (2009) quote a local authority official saying about the residents of a council estate: 'They (estate residents) have long memories. In the end, all the different councils blur together. Maybe there's a short period after a new council comes in. But, in the end, people are just going to see the council as one group of people responsible for all the things that have gone wrong' (ibid.: 18). Harrison also notices that residents in Newhaven, a 'Sussex town' in south-east England, lament the decline of 'community' by putting blame on 'policy actors, primarily those at the local level' (2011: 92). These are often referred to in generic terms as 'the council', 'a term used to cover a range of different levels of government' (Harrison, 2011: 92). And Barke and Turnbull tell us of Meadowell, 'an estate with problems' in North Shields, that residents talk of 'Them' as 'everything outside, everything that conspires in one way or another to treat Meadowell on the ground' (1992: 84).

Similarly, on Park End, talk of 'the council' and of 'Them' provided a way of making sense of the workings of power in all sorts of events and happenings. 'Them' offered an interpretive framework for the past and the present, as people were quick to see local initiatives, funding cuts, or council-led projects as evidence that 'They' wanted to cause 'the downfall of the community': a regeneration project that involved the replacement of an existing community facility on one of the town's smaller estates was seen as evidence that 'They' wanted to get rid of local groups (Chapter 6); the installation of new traffic lights on a major road leading out of the estate was intended to keep local residents 'locked in on the estate'; and the swine flu epidemic which broke out in autumn 2011 was orchestrated by 'Them' to give teachers a paid holiday (by closing down the local schools) and putting parents out of work. Sometimes, the boundaries between reality and fantasy became blurred in people's talk of 'Them'. Thus, for example, when I ran into a Park End resident by chance during a national march in London against austerity reforms, she told me that 'They' had invented austerity politics to 'kill off poor people'. 'They' had started producing white plastic coffins in large underground storage rooms, where the bodies of the poor would be kept. Likewise, in the aftermath of the riots, I heard people talk of how the uprisings had been orchestrated by the authorities to make poor people 'turn on each other' and have an excuse to get 'rid of them'.

Over half a century ago, Hoggart argued that talk of 'Them' was something that pertained to the world of the 'very poor' (1957).[2] But today, it provided an interpretive framework to Park End residents for making sense of their daily relations with the authorities. It expressed not only a feeling of powerlessness with respect to those who governed their lives but a deeper sense of moral betrayal. This, then, is how state failure was experienced: as a failure on the part of those who governed to care and to reciprocate residents' own efforts to be good persons and citizens. But how did these views scale into people's understanding of government writ large? How did it impact on their electoral behaviour? And what opportunities did Brexit represent in this context? The final section will turn to these questions.

Democracy in Crisis

Political theorists Lerman and Weaver (2014) argue that among African-American citizens in the US negative experiences of the state are not separate from people's wider relations to the democratic polity. This is because 'citizens come to learn about their government through their direct contacts with it. Interactions

---

[2] Thus, he says: 'The world of "Them" is the world of bosses, whether those bosses are private individuals or, as is increasingly the case today, public officials. "Them" may be, as occasion requires, anyone from the classes outside other than the few individuals from those classes whom working-class people know as individuals [...]. To the very poor, especially, they compose a shadowy but numerous and powerful group affecting their lives at almost every point: the world is divided into "Them" and "Us"' (1957: 53).

between citizens and the state help form ideas about how government functions ... [and] about the democratic values and norms that it embodies' (ibid.: 10). On Park End, this was no different. Everyday frustrations, experiences of abandonment, and a sense of neglect among Park End residents were also transposed onto politicians, parties, and government writ large. Take the example of Rose again. For her, proof that 'they did not care' was as much in the daily acts of benefits officers as it was in the rhetoric of party politicians and government. It was in the leaflets left by party politicians who revealed the false lies and backstabbings of their competitors. When I visited her, Rose showed me a leaflet put through the door by the Liberal Democrats that blamed the local Labour Party (who run the council) for sending money that was left over from the financial year back to national government instead of helping people like her. 'It's disgraceful, it just shows you how little they care!', she said. But her opinion of the Liberal Democrats was no better: 'they are all as bad as each other', she said. Rose's opinion was shared by others. Thus, in a conversation between Lindsey and Olifia, the two women spoke of what 'government' meant to them:

Lindsey: The government they are always—them. They are disconnected from—us. They make decisions, bad ones, that affect us. And even though like we can vote, we don't have much influence or ... actually feel part of it.

Olifia: Actually, when you vote, you don't know what you are voting for. I really struggle with this voting thing. I know people always say you need to vote, not to vote is worse. But I don't really know. I don't really have any understanding or trust in any of them.

On Park End, many residents had become deeply disenchanted with party politics. Some, like Rose above, were explicit in laying blame with the Labour Party. Like other formerly industrial neighbourhoods across the country (Evans, 2012; Mollona, 2009; Smith, 2012a), Park End had once been a staunch Labour Party heartland. Particularly the older generations had living memories of this, as they recalled a life 'back in the day' when people were working in the factories, trade unions were strong, and everybody voted Labour. This is not to imply some romanticized image of post-war politics. On the contrary, in interviews carried out with older residents, people revealed at best an ambiguous relationship with the Labour Party and the trade unions, and at worst outright suspicion. Take the example of trade unions. People recalled the bad working conditions in the factories, conflict in the union leadership, and worst of all for many, the strikes that left families without an income. Similar to Coffield, Borrill, and Marshall's findings (1986), people of different age groups told me that trade unions were 'closed shops'; they 'just go on useless strikes' and 'they put people out of work'. Fred, who was introduced in the last chapter as a current Parish councillor for Park End, was one of them. He had worked mostly night shifts in the local factory before he was made redundant in the late 1980s. 'The unions had their part to play', he said, 'don't get me wrong, the unions had their part to play, but they should have looked after their membership first and their own little thing afterwards. For a lot of people didn't like work in the factory. You hated going into that place every day, every night of the week.' His narrative went on to contrast the lack of care of the union leadership with the informal support from the community in times of strike action:

Sometimes it was bloody hard. If you was thrown out on a strike, for good or bad reasons. You know. Your family suffered, you didn't get paid, there was no dole money then, 'you're on strike, mate, you don't get nothing', you know. And it was a terrible time, sometimes, for people up here. You had to rely on the generosity of butchers, bakers and shop makers. You used the butcher in the [nearby shopping centre], if a bloke fell out [with with management], was laid off, or out of work because of strike; they'd make bills up. So you'd pay the meat at a lower price.

Today, residents still sometimes claimed that the Labour Party was meant to represent the likes of them. Jade, a woman in her late twenties who had moved to Park End from Trinidad fifteen years prior, once said to me, 'Labour is meant to be for working-class people like me and you, innit. But to be honest, I don't know what they are doing for me'. 'I know some people say you have to vote Labour cos our parents voted Labour and before that our grandparents', Tracey also once said to me, 'but to me this means nothing because what have Labour actually done for us?'. Tracey's and Jade's feelings can be illustrated with reference to how many residents related to the local Labour MP who had represented the estate for an uninterrupted period of nearly three decades by the time I first started my fieldwork. In the last chapter, we already saw that residents sometimes insisted that they voted for him not because he was a Labour politician and represented a particular party but because he was a dedicated individual who they perceived to have made a difference to their estate through his commitment and long-standing residence in the place. This was confirmed to me by a local Labour councillor who explained how canvassing strategies for the local Labour MP in the 2010 general elections had secured his re-election despite widespread disenchantment with the party: 'we told them to vote for [the MP], not because it's Labour but to support him, as a person, because of what he's done for this estate'.

But it was not just party politics and trade unions that were mistrusted as 'closed shops' and 'sell-outs': on Park End, people spoke of the entire system of government and the constitutional framework of representative democracy as something that was not for them. Both young and old, men and women, told me that elected representatives are all 'crooks', 'gangsters', 'vampires', and 'cannot be trusted'. 'Democracy means nothing when you are uneducated and poor' and 'we don't live in a democracy, it feels more like a dictatorship' was something that I was told. The profound sense of alienation that Park End residents felt was perhaps best expressed in low levels of voter turnout, which had fallen to levels below 20 per cent in local elections. During election time, conscious attempts were made to keep the world of formal politics away from the world of 'us'. For example, I once overheard a conservation between Jane and her close friend Kate in the lead-up to the elections in 2010. One afternoon, I was sitting in the living room in Jane and Mark's home, watching TV with Jane, when the front door opened and Jane's close friend, Kate, walked in. As Kate came through the door, she picked up a polling card for the upcoming elections that had been dropped through the letter box. She handed it to Jane. 'Oh, I don't need that', Jane said dismissively to Kate. When Kate remained silent, Jane eventually asked her: 'You're not going to vote, are you?' Kate looked at her. 'No, of course not', Kate replied quickly.

In this particular instance, then, Jane's question if Kate intended to vote was a demand for complicity rather than a simple question: a demand that Kate swiftly met by offering reassurance to her (Koch, 2017c). Through this demand, electoral withdrawal was normalized between friends and family members. Conversely, when people did decide to get engaged in politics then this could sometimes be met with open criticism and suspicion. I was often told that politics just leads to conflict and argument and that it is something that should not be discussed. This applied to periods outside of election time too. Let us come back to Lindsey. Lindsey told me that when growing up on the estate her parents used to tell her that she should stay away from politics and that politics was bad. So strong was the feeling that Lindsey would hide her own interest in current affairs from her parents: she confessed that she used to sneak down early in the morning when her family were still asleep to have a look at the newspaper and read the news section before anybody would wake up and see her. Her family bought the newspaper to read the sports section and celebrity gossip. Today, her sister was still the same, Lindsey told me: she tried to shelter her own kids from being exposed to the news because she did not want to 'upset them'. Likewise, involuntary exposure to politicians and electoral politics could provoke strong reactions. Lindsey recalled one episode from her childhood, when during election time a local politician had come knocking on her mother's door:

I remember, going back to my childhood, again to my mum, that one election when my mum was having it on TV. My mum having a really big moan that she was in a nightie and having a drink and watching *Inspector Morse* or whatever she was watching on TV and these politicians knocked on the door and even offered to give her a lift to the polling station. And my mum said: 'I'm not voting 'cos I'm not well' […]. And she was so annoyed that they tried to pick her up and give her a lift, and she was like: 'How [dare] these people' …!

It is against this backdrop that we can return to the event with which I opened this chapter: the referendum on leaving the European Union on 23 June 2016. Some, although by no means all, of my friends and interlocutors voted in favour of leave: Jane and Mark, Tracey, Vera, and Brian counted among them. Some of them were people who I had never known to be interested in elections before. Take the example of Lindsey and her family. Lindsey had voted in favour of 'remain' because she felt strongly about the 'idea of Europe', as she said, and the need 'to work together'. She explained how she had been exposed to different ideas through her work and friendship circles. On the day of the referendum, Lindsey contacted me in tears about the results. But other family members had voted in favour of 'leave', including her mother. We saw above that Lindsey's mother had taught her as a child not to get involved with politics. Now, however, she had voted in favour of leaving the European Union. When I asked Lindsey what had motivated her to come out to vote on this occasion, Lindsey shrugged, 'she was fed up', she said, 'and she said it was time for a change'.

When digging deeper into people's reasons for voting to 'leave', complex narratives came through. A common factor running through them was that Brexit was an opportunity to rework, even reject, the system that they were in. For some it was an opportunity to express long-standing frustrations with the authorities and their failure to demonstrate sufficient care: Brian, for example, who was introduced in Chapter 4, had come out to vote in favour of 'leave'. He had not voted in the previous general elections, although he did help the Free Workers Party introduced in the last chapter with canvassing in the 2000s. He was fed up with the housing authorities' and the police's long-standing failure to sort out his problems with his next-door neighbour. 'They are all evil', he had said to me in 2009 when I first met him, 'and they will fall when the revolution comes.' For others, the vote was an opportunity to move beyond austerity Britain. This is illustrated in Tracey's vote: we saw in the last chapter that Tracey's own attempts to counter austerity politics and to mobilize Park End residents on behalf of a larger collective had failed. Even worse for her personal situation, Tracey lost the job in the community centre when restructuring happened a few months later and she had to take up a job in a nearby supermarket (where she works to this day). Her opinion on Brexit was that 'it's best for the country right now, no matter what happens'. When I expressed my own reservations about this opinion to her, she advised me to watch the official video sponsored by leave campaigners on YouTube because it illustrated the need to give control back to people who had been long shut out by the system.

For Tracey, the leave campaign provided what Kalb calls a 'critical juncture' (2009) that allowed her to link her own frustrations to larger narratives in a context wherein alternatives were weak or perceived to be outright absent. One of the core messages that was brought home in the leave campaign was the mantra of bringing back 'local control': a message that appealed to Park End residents who felt that their neighbourhoods had been neglected, that their worries and frustrations had been ignored, and that the wrong people (including the elites and those with power) had been allowed to get too many benefits for too long.

A narrative harmony was then established between people's daily experiences and their own vernacular narratives of lack of care, on the one hand, and a broader language of victimhood that was deployed by leave campaigners, on the other. The day after the referendum, Trisha, a local mother of Afro-Caribbean descent with two mixed-race teenage children posted on social media: 'Am I a racist? No! Am I thick? No! Am I ignorant? No! Did I do some research? Yes! Have I watched hours and hours of debates? Yes! Did I vote out? Yes! It's my opinion and my vote!' The post continued: 'What's done is done. Let's try and work together to make our country, schools, housing, hospitals, communities etc a better place for all of us to live in.' Within a few hours, her comment was almost immediately liked by over 100 people, who sent Trisha hugs and kisses and thanked her for her wise words.

Conclusion

In much of the commentary in the media and public policy, the Brexit result has been seen as evidence of a worrying and potentially dangerous development. According to explanations that have dominated the debate on the EU referendum, it is evidence that identity-based politics is hardening. Voters who came out in favour of 'leave' have been portrayed as deficient and as lacking in the qualities that make a good, liberal citizen. There is no doubt that what the liberal media has described as 'authoritarian populism' or 'popular authoritarianism' featured in the discourses, campaigns, and debates that were available to citizens in the public domain. Nor can we deny that at least some people who voted in favour of 'leave' were motivated by racist sentiments and stood behind the xenophobic messages sent out by the 'leave' campaign. But to reduce the election result to such singular explanations also risks ignoring the multiplicity of reasons and motivations that different voter-bases across the country brought to the referendum. Among my interlocutors, to the extent that these different motivations had a common underlying factor, it was not a unitary punitive disposition, whether this be xenophobic or otherwise, but a deep-seated sense of disenchantment with those who govern their daily lives.

The anger, shock, and passion that the EU referendum unleashed among both those who voted to leave and those voted to remain (Knight, 2017a), suggest that it is precisely the moral dimensions of Brexit that deserve closer attention. Yet these dimensions are all too frequently denied or obscured in the rational–bureaucratic dimensions of liberal democracy that sees voting as a neutral and abstracted act (Lazar, 2004). This chapter has argued against such portrayals. On Park End, people's electoral choices are deeply intertwined with their daily experiences of state failure, and by implication also of politicians and government as the antithesis of ordinary sociality and their requirements of care. Electoral withdrawal becomes in such a situation a normalized response, one which meets protective functions that allows residents to keep the perceived polluting influences of politics at bay. What seemed to make the referendum different from an ordinary election, at least for some of my informants, was that it was not just perceived as an opportunity to choose between the lesser of different evils, or worse even legitimizing the political status quo by ratifying a process that had engineered the present situation through one's vote. Rather, it was an opportunity to say 'no' to government *as* government, by rejecting what Park End residents took to be an oppressive system that was controlling their lives—whether this referred to those who sat in local authority, in Westminster, or even further afield in the EU Parliament. For some of my interlocutors, Brexit was at once an indictment of the government's disavowal of its obligations towards citizens as well as an intervention into the moral desert created by its abandonment in places like Park End.

In his account on the 'rise of authoritarian neoliberalism', Bruff had asked whether 'the contradictions inherent to authoritarian neoliberalism [...] have created the conditions in which progressive and radical politics can begin to reverse the tide of the last three decades' (2014: 125). Anthropologists of democracy have made the point that political elections can also become moments of ritual or social transformation that open a window into different futures and political imaginations (Banerjee, 2011; Cook, Long, and Moore, 2016; Grisaffi, 2013, 2019; Paley, 2008). More radically, social movements like Occupy and the Arab Spring, have experimented with alternative models of politics that are not confined to the liberal model of voting, elections, and the system of government that these support (Butler, 2011; Graeber, 2009; Hardt and Negri, 2011; Juris, 2012; Razsa and Kurnik, 2012). And yet, as Shah has forcefully argued, 'fantasies of the future need to be linked with the prosaic material workings of the present in order to analyze and resolve the contradictions in the present which prevent radical transformations from coming about' (2012: 350). On Park End, local elections or referenda, like the Brexit referendum, as well as alternative channels for expressing political dissatisfactions, remain at best imperfect, and at worst, wholly inadequate routes for capturing 'the prosaic material workings of the present'.

There are few signs that the gap between the people and government, revealed by the 'Brexit' vote, will close in the aftermath of the event. Anthropologists of class and neoliberalism have reminded us that where the institutional and political mechanisms for redistributive struggles have been seriously weakened, if not extinguished, there is a danger that people's demands for change will end up being channelled into a divisive politics of victimhood (Friedman, 2003; Kalb, 2009, 2011; Narotzky, 2016; Szombati, 2018). Insofar as the liberal elites and the media have recognized a moral dimension to leave votes, they have tended to construct leave-voters as morally deficient and lacking. At the precise moment then that liberalism has re-appropriated its moral dimensions, it seems to have done so with attacks on the actions and mindsets of people who had long indicted it for its immorality. Meanwhile, it is precisely the far right that represents a political craft that recognizes the centrality of moral valences of statecraft. This was already evident in the lead-up to the EU referendum when the much-publicized leave campaign backed by the rightwing UKIP, stood out for recognizing the centrality of the moral in the political, even as it blamed immigrants for Britain's social and economic woes. While much of this chapter has militated against the idea that we are on an inevitable march towards popular authoritarianism or even full-blown fascism, there is no reason to believe that Park End residents too might end up turning to the far right in the absence of graspable political alternatives.

Conclusion: A Different Kind of Paradox

At the turn of the twenty-first century, commentators have rushed to explain what many see as a worrying development: the illiberal turn that state policies and practices in liberal democracies have taken. In Britain, from tougher criminal justice policies to an ever-shrinking welfare system, and a tough rhetoric adopted by those who sponsored the official 'leave' campaign in the lead up to the EU referendum, scholars have commented on both the punitive *and* the populist aspect of these developments. Within criminal justice and punishment debates, various explanations have been advanced to make sense of 'populist punitiveness' or 'punitive populism'. These have ranged from cultural accounts that locate the root causes of 'law and order' policies in the conditions of late modernity (Garland, 2001; Simon, 2007; Young, 1999) to those who have seen it as an outcome of neoliberalism (Ramsay, 2012; Reiner, 2007; Wacquant, 2009), to yet others who identify the role played by institutional and political–economic factors (Lacey, 2008). This book has offered an alternative perspective. Rather than starting from the question of 'why' state policies and practices in liberal democracy have taken an illiberal turn, it has shifted the focus to the 'how' and the 'what': how can we make sense of liberal democracy in the first place? What can an ethnographic take on state–citizen relations tell us about a legacy of state coercion and control in working class citizens' lives? And what happens to the idea of a punitive public when these aspects are brought into focus?

The purpose of this book has been to go where dominant commentary on the punitive turn has stopped short: to the daily and lived experiences of citizens at the margins and their alleged support for, and engagement with, punitive policies and laws. My focus on some of the country's most marginalized citizens is not

Personalizing the State: The Anthropology of Law, Politics and Welfare at the UK's Margins. First Edition. Insa Koch. © Insa Koch 2018. Published 2018 by Oxford University Press.

an accident. Park End residents and those who live in comparable neighbourhoods have been among those most affected by changes in state policies, not only as recipients of vital services of support, including benefit policies and policing, but also as those who are commonly seen as scroungers, criminals, and outlaws. By taking their lived experiences of the state as its point of departure, the book has brought citizens' engagements with a range of different authority figures—including those of 'law and order' and the supposedly 'softer' arms of the welfare state—into a single framing. Across these domains, the book has uncovered unexpected parallels that emerge between different sources of threat, both formal and informal, or predatory and state-sponsored. A welfare officer takes on a similar role to a violent partner or lover; social housing officials become part of the same landscape of danger that includes threatening next-door neighbours; police officers appear as the 'biggest gang of all'; and politicians and local brokers come to be seen as part of the system they are trying to change.

By tracing the interchangeability of these various forms of both formal and informal threats, the book has uncovered an important point: how official policies and practices, often ostensibly implemented to 'help' the vulnerable and poor, come to frame, modulate, and re-arrange often the most intimate realms of people's daily lives. Park End residents do not experience government as a source of redistribution, support, and protection. On the contrary, even while (or perhaps precisely because) they depend upon its material and practical resources in their daily struggles for security and survival, their experiences of the authorities are invariably interlaced with the ever-present possibility of unwanted coercion. Benefit officers and welfare agents not only guarantee access to social goods but they also require working-class mothers to live by means-tested policies that penalize their processes of social reproduction. Social housing providers protect tenants from the dangers of the market as they provide more secure tenancies at a subsidized rate, but they also expect tenants to become active in policing their own and each other's behaviour in a way that private landlords do not. Police officers do not simply offer protection from informal threats but in many instances come to be the very agents who further threaten to undermine people's homes and the relations that matter within them. And agendas of 'active citizenship' and participatory governance do not simply promote community empowerment but also find the 'bread and butter politics' of local political brokers wanting of these ideas.

And yet, repressive governance is only part of the story. Citizens also engage the authorities on their own terms, as the moral and political frameworks that are important to their lives become a lens through which they view and engage, or often disengage from, the authorities. My key ethnographic finding has centred on the daily engagements between state and citizens, or what I have called, following Alexander (2002), acts of 'personalizing the state': people appropriate officials, institutions, and images of the state and state-like actors, including local authorities, private bodies, and third sector institutions to whom the state has delegated its traditional responsibilities. They seek to tame or domesticate the state's coercive powers and their disproportionately harsh impact on working-class communities by variously rejecting, appropriating, or bypassing the state's language, officials, and institutions. A welfare recipient might learn to 'play the system'. A social housing tenant appropriates the language of 'anti-social behaviour'. A mother co-opts the police's powers of arrest in negotiating domestic conflicts. And residents interject ordinary moralities into the workings of government by personalizing relations with local politicians and rejecting democracy writ large. To the extent that these different examples have anything in common, it is that they de-centre the state's own assumptions to be the harbinger of authority and order. In appropriating the state's powers, Park End residents bring into focus an alternative ethics of personhood and care that contrasts with the categories of citizenship imposed by the state.

Much has been written about the paradox of the punitive turn: the paradox of how, in a liberal democracy, state policies and practices can depart so far from their own liberal aspirations that they cease to be democratic measures (Lacey, 2008: 7–8). This book arrives at a different kind of paradox, one that is historically grounded and ethnographically driven: *the paradox of how the expansion of state power to forcibly control its citizens becomes an inverse to its powers to control the means of its own application or recruitment*. Institutional mechanisms for mobilizing collective demands are often weak, if not outright absent today. Trade unions have lost their stronghold, tenants associations are largely dormant, and grassroots activists are constantly faced with the threat of having funding, resources and above all, their public legitimacy, withdrawn. In such a situation, the impoverished repertoire of social action generated by the state's increased reliance on punitive tactics compels those at their receiving end to rely on those same tactics: citizens often come to frame their demands for justice in the language and frameworks favored by those in power. But in so doing, citizens also personalize the state in unexpected ways as they bring their own reasoning to the picture. Hence, the contradictions we have observed: popular support for more policing co-exists alongside mistrust in the police; everyday 'performances of being poor' in front of welfare officials sit alongside acts of withdrawal from bureaucratic measures; and electoral support for particular individuals, and even for the 'Brexit' vote, happen against the backdrop of widespread disenchantment with democracy. Paradoxically, then, the more the state tries to control its citizens, the more it reveals its lack of authority to govern.

What, then, are the broader implications of this study? What happens to political statecraft when state authority is reduced to hollow claims? And what are the possibilities for the future? In what follows, I will summarize the book's key findings alongside some nascent proposals for engaging critically with 'the state we're in' (Cook, Long, and Moore, 2016). I do this by putting forward three key points that follow the ethnographic paradox stated here. First, I argue that citizenship is experienced as a form of punishment by those at the margins as state power has been expanding and intensifying along classed lines. Second, that this intensification has generated a plurality of contradictory responses that taken together reveal the state's own lack of authority at Britain's margins today. And, third, that citizens' emic critiques of statecraft speak of the state's failure to honour its perceived duties towards citizens, a failure that lies at the heart of political disenchantment today. Each of these conclusions corresponds to, and rejects, dominant assumptions within the commentary on the punitive turn: that the punitive shift at the start of the twenty-first century is an aberration from, and hence an exceptional moment in, the history of post-war British democracy; that popular authoritarianism is indicative of a contemporary Leviathan; and that the rise of 'law and order' reflects an era of post-politics or post-ideology. Taken together, the three lessons aim to recover, to paraphrase Tyler (K. Tyler, 2015), 'people's humanity through ethnographic depth': they are an attempt to bring people's lived realities of the world to debates that have all too frequently been devoid of the human experiences of those at the receiving end of policies.

Citizenship as Punishment: Moving Beyond the Criminal Law

Few would dispute that the exercise of state coercion is a central feature of contemporary governance in Britain. But authors disagree over the nature of these 'authoritarian fixes', to borrow Bruff's (2014) term, and their historical legacy. Within criminal justice and punishment scholarship, dominant accounts have framed the current moment along two axes: first, in terms of a contrast between the post-war moment of social democracy and the forms of government that have developed typically since the 1970s; and, second, in terms of a contrast between the workings of criminal justice and policies adopted in social policy and welfare. Across both of these axes of comparisons, what is shared is a dichotic portrayal of what I referred to in Chapter 1 as a 'politics of welfare' and that of 'lawfare' (see also Koch, 2018): a politics that emphasizes inclusive policies and redistributive solutions to that which is more exclusive in outlook and typically favours a language of individualized responsibility and blame. This dichotomy not only locates a politics of welfare in the past—the 'golden age' of post-war social democracy—but also looks at areas of social and welfare policies for the possibility of its recuperation in the contemporary moment. On this account, broader changes in society, the economy and political ideology since the advent of neoliberal reform have alienated policy-makers (and the electorate) from the older ideal of a social democratic state, one which was committed to principles of social integration, rehabilitation, and relative equality between different classes.

I do not wish to downplay the differences in the social, economic, and institutional capacities of post-war Keynesian welfare and the liberal market economy model that followed in the wake of Thatcherism. Nor do I wish to dismiss the greater capacity of social and welfare policies to address not just the symptoms but, as Miller has argued, the root causes of inequality and crime (Miller, 2016). Rather, the historical and ethnographic narrative in this book has questioned the degree to which the picture is one of abrupt rupture or break as opposed to continuity and a gradual intensification of coercive state powers both across time and different domains of state action. Council estates have served as an example in this book to explore exactly this point: as Chapter 1 argued, far from being just about the provision of material homes, council estates have been privileged sites of state-building and control. In the post-war decades, when the dominant model of the idealized citizen was that of the worker–citizen, paternalistic policies were geared towards the creation of 'respectable' nuclear working-class homes. With the shift to neoliberalism in the 1980s, dominant understandings of citizenship began to shift. As the consumer–citizen became the new idealized citizen (and by extension the home-owning individual), anybody who was unable to participate in the consumerist dream was potentially subject to heightened forms of classed control. From the mid-1990s onwards, the expansion of 'law and order' policing has marked an expansion of the consumerist logic into the realms of the criminal law, as the crime-victim has become the representative subject of governance (Ramsay, 2012).

This story of gradual intensification and continuity, rather than of rupture and crisis, comes even more into focus when different areas of state policy-making are systematically compared. As this book has shown, across different areas of state–citizen relations, dominant tropes of punishment appear. But only a fraction of the examples considered in this book involve punishment in the 'classical' or legal sense of arrests, trials, criminal sanctions, and the threat of imprisonment (cf. Fassin, 2017). More commonly, punishment is experienced in the ways in which state officials and institutions police, modulate, and rearrange the kinds of social relations with those that residents hold the dearest and nearest: their kin, children, and next-door neighbours. For example, Chapter 5 showed that policing targets young, black, or mixed-race men as well as young people of all ethnicities who are associated with stigmatized places, like Park End. But the police do more than that: the force of the law travels along kinship and household lines, imposing what Williams and Clarke (2016) refer to as 'collective punishment' to an entire class of people. Injunction orders ban those who are subject to them from frequenting familiar places or associating with their own family and friends. Young men and women can be charged under the laws of joint enterprise for crimes that they have not committed because they are assumed to be part of a larger group. And mothers find that their social housing tenancies become vulnerable if their teenage sons have been implicated with the law, thus exposing them to the threat of eviction.

The classed exercise of coercive force beyond conventional lines of punishment is even more clearly brought into focus when considering the areas of policy-making that have been seen as representing the 'left hand' of the state (Wacquant, 2012). These areas often target everyday processes of social reproduction, and the women who are at their centre. As Skeggs (1997) reminds us, at the heart of middle-class morality is the ideal of the patriarchal family home. This doubly marginalizes many working-class mothers: for their class position as well as for their failures to live up to dominant family forms. Even today, when benefit policies are ostensibly gender-neutral, they continue to frame working-class women's experiences in gendered ways. Chapter 3 showed that, when becoming dependent on a means-tested benefit system, so-called 'single mothers' not only have to negotiate an extremely complicated benefit system but they also have to live by rules that penalize the household arrangements central to their daily lives. But gender is not the only vector through which classed coercion is exercised. In Chapter 4, we saw that both men and women who lack the means to buy their own homes are policed through social housing associations and local authorities that provide housing for the needy and poor. 'Anti-social behaviour' and 'nuisance' policies have the effect of shifting responsibilities for managing problems from social housing providers to individual tenants by denying the structural causes of environmental suffering.

It is also important to note that since 2010, the election of a coalition government, and then of a Conservative government in 2015 and 2017, respectively, have introduced a new mantra, that of 'austerity politics', into the language of policy-making. Austerity is commonly understood as a withdrawal or withering away of the state because it is based on a reduction of public expenditure and state provisions in favour of the market (Chapter 7). Yet, it also implies a reconfiguration of state–citizen–market relations in more complicated ways (James and Koch, n.d.), and, crucially, an expansion of punitive control on the part of the state into people's daily lives . Austerity has meant that already hard hit and vulnerable social housing tenants find that their lives are rendered even more precarious under the brunt of policy change, while being policed in heightened ways. An example of this is the 'bedroom tax'. Chapter 7 showed that those who are seen to under-occupy their social housing tenancies have their housing benefits cut for having spare rooms (despite the fact that there are often no smaller social housing properties available that these people could move into). This not only pushes people into rent arrears, and eventually, the threat of eviction, but also glosses over the fact that rooms are often anything but 'spare': they provide shelter for one's grown-up children, grandchildren, friends, and kin. Rose, a widowed woman who has been affected by the bedroom tax spoke of austerity as a 'punishment imposed on working class people on top of everything else' (Chapter 7).

We have come a long way then from the repressive workings of contemporary criminal justice policies to a picture of state coercion that is both of a longer duration and more encompassing that conventionally assumed. This, then, is the first conclusion I reach: *the expansion of 'authoritarian fixes' under neoliberal rule reflects a broader legacy of state control in the lives of working-class citizens*. Reconceived in this light, an ethnographic analysis of state–citizen relations challenges one of the most powerful assumptions that have prevailed in debates on punishment in 'late modernity': that the turn to 'law and order' within UK governance constitutes a dangerous aberration from the 'ordinary' workings of state policy in democracy. On the contrary, it allows us to recognize differences as well as continuities with the past, drawing attention to the limits of liberal democracy's own claims to be the protector of progress and freedom (Davey and Koch, 2017). It also militates against the tendency in much existing scholarship to see 'welfare' and 'lawfare' as polar opposites rather than as overlapping arenas in which classed coercion is apprehended, exercised, and multiplied, in often gendered and racialized ways. Finally, my ethnographic analysis cautions against those who have seen the end of New Labour government in 2010 as the ebbing of 'law and order' by drawing attention to the ways in which racialized policing, means-tested welfare, and above all, austerity politics, continue to frame citizenship in punitive terms. But what about the actual experiences of the people who are at the receiving end of state control?

On Popular Punitivism and State Authority: Bringing Down the Leviathan

So far, we have focused on the expansion or intensification of state coercion and control in the lives of working-class citizens. But this is only half the story: this book has shown that people appropriate the state's powers on their own terms as they co-opt officials, institutions, and images of the state and state-like bodies into their daily lives. This leads to what I referred to above as an ethnographic paradox—namely, the paradox of how the expansion of state power to forcibly control its citizens becomes an inverse to its powers to control the means of its own application or recruitment, producing a set of seemingly contradictory responses and forms of engagement with those in power. In other words, the more the state tries to control its citizens, the more scope it might end up creating for those same citizens to re-appropriate its powers for reasons other than their intended purposes and effects. This paradox flies in the face of a second set of assumptions that have been dominant in literature on the punitive turn: that increasingly harsh criminal justice policies are supported by popular consent in any straightforward way. Miller (2016) has referred to this as the 'mob rule thesis'. On this account, the public is being represented as 'panic-prone' and 'irrational' (ibid.: 2), and thus in need of authoritarian reassurance from the state. 'The conventional framework posits', she writes, 'that crime rates do not lead to political salience but political salience leads inexorably to punitive policies where the electorate has many opportunities to influence political outcomes' (ibid.: 12). It would follow that the expansion of 'law and order' does not result in a diversification of popular responses but, rather, their opposite: an ever-closer alignment of popular sentiments with the state's authoritarian measures.

My point is not that the people are not retributive nor that popular support for state-enforced punishment cannot run high: to deny both of these points would mean to fall prey to the romanticizing tendency of the community-centred approaches critiqued in Chapter 2 that idealize 'classical' working-class communities as purely self-contained and kinship-governed entities. And yet, the idea of a singular punitive public who is asking for state-led retribution ought to be rethought. I am, of course, not the first to suggest this need for revision. It has been argued that punitive attitudes towards punishment are not set in stone, but derive in part from an understandable failure to know about the effectiveness of different levels of state intervention (Hough and Roberts, 2002), and are hence a matter of education and adequate information. Although politicians may use opinion surveys to show that the public support specific policies, little effort is invested in exploring the nature of public attitudes to punishment, or even less to improving the state of public knowledge in this area (Hough and Roberts, 2002; see also Hough et al., 2009). Others have suggested that citizens do not merely base their attitudes to punishment on information, but are influenced by the method of inquiry and how issues are framed (Girling, Loader, and Sparks, 2000; Hutton, 2005). Indeed, a 'cognitive deficit model' (Loader, 2005) that supposes that punitive attitudes can be altered by adducing evidence and information rests on a misleading assumption that feelings are separate from cognition (Canton, 2015). As Rossner (2013) has argued, it is precisely by paying attention to how emotions are developed and sustained in restorative justice rituals that genuine alternatives to punishment can be developed that are mindful of all the participants in a criminal justice process.

Whether authors have favoured cognitive reasoning or emotions, or both, they have offered important correctives to the idea that popular punitivism is necessarily the only and dominant response that citizens bring to crime. But less explored has been the question of how popular punitivism, to the extent that it *is* expressed (and, to repeat, this book has shown that it can indeed run high), relates to popular support for state authority: where retributive feelings have been acknowledged, the state's monopoly in being the rightful enforcer of these feelings has been taken for granted. This is perhaps not surprising given that classical political and legal theory sees the state as the harbinger of authority and order (Roberts, 2013). Yet, it is precisely this link between punitivism and state authority that has been questioned in this book. The basis for such a critique was developed in Chapter 2: there, we saw that council estate tenants' understandings of what makes a good person and by extension also a good citizen have more often than not diverged from, rather than dovetailed with, dominant ideologies and official rationalities. We saw that it was in the postwar decades that there was a fragile moral union between council estate tenants and the ideology of the worker–citizen that was centred around the ideal of the nuclear, male-headed household. In the intervening decades this moral consensus was thoroughly dismantled—not by the extension of the fruits of citizenship to racial and sexual 'others' who had previously been placed outside the bounds of respectability, but by the very expansion of the grounds of 'otherness' to an entire class of people. Today, tenants' own pursuits to be 'good persons' who demonstrate care for their family homes and neighbourhoods, are precisely the target of punitive control.

It is against such a backdrop where people's informal attempts to be 'good persons' also mark them out as potentially 'bad citizens' in the eyes of the state that we need to understand the diverse range of responses cultivated by Park End residents with respect to state and state-like actors. These vary between withdrawal, a by-passing of state authorities, to a selective appropriation of its powers, or what I have referred to as personalization. Withdrawal from those who residents know to be hostile and repressive towards them is probably the most obvious response. Similar to the young men described by Goffman (2014) and the housing residents that feature in Davey's (2016) study, Park End residents hide themselves and their homes from those whose punitive interventions they loathe. In Chapter 5, for example, we saw that young people are taught by their parents and peers not to speak to the police, while the social housing tenants in Chapter 4 fail to turn up to meetings and public events organized by the authorities. And Chapter 3 described how welfare recipients disengage from the processes of bureaucratic upkeep and diligence that benefit officers expect from them: letters with official headings from institutions like the Department for Work and Pensions remain unopened, phone lines are unplugged or the sound of a ringing phone is ignored, and requests to turn up for interviews or assessments are 'forgotten' about. Sometimes, the consequences of such disengagement can be severe, leading to eviction from a social tenancy home in the case of a mother who had fallen into rent arrears and not realized because she had not kept up with the official correspondence.

Alongside withdrawal are popular attempts to personalize the state that often interlace in complex ways with desires to by-pass its authority altogether. The mothers in Chapter 3 learn to 'play' the benefit system by acting up to its logic of needs-based entitlement; social housing tenants in Chapter 4 appropriate the language of 'anti-social behaviour' and 'nuisance' to frame intimate violations of their homes at the hands of next-door neighbours; and women in Chapter 5 call the police on their teenage sons and lovers to gain control over them. Sometimes, residents' demands for punitive interventions can even surpass those officially sanctioned by the state as they expect the latter's agents to engage in acts akin to the 'police vigilantism' described by Cooper-Knock and Owen (2015): they expect state institutions to act as allies, to punish and to exclude their enemies, and to be partial to their worlds. But everyday attempts to personalize the state implicate the state's authority in complicated ways. Sometimes, personalizing the state into one's daily lives becomes a way of keeping even more punitive interventions at bay: this is the case of 'single mothers' who play the system in order to be able to protect their family homes from yet further state surveillance. In others, it becomes a means of negotiating or protecting everyday relations that the state may not know or care about. For example, when mothers call the police on their teenage sons, they use the state's own categories of criminality and danger to negotiate intimate relations. And in yet other situations, failure to personalize the state becomes a way of justifying reliance on informal or vigilante policing, as we saw in Chapters 5 and 6, when residents take the law into their own hands.

It is by focusing on these everyday forms of state–citizen engagement that the book complicates any straightforward idea of popular consent to an authoritarian state. On the contrary, in the examples surveyed here, the authorities appear at best as personalized allies, and at worst as public enemies whose coercive powers ought to be kept at bay. Not unlike the residents in Soweto (Hornberger, 2013) or the African American mothers in an impoverished US neighbourhood (Bell, 2016), Park End residents invoke a situational legitimacy of the state, one which is always fragile, shifting, and liable to break down. Indeed, as the ethnography has shown, people's attempts to personalize the state often generate contradictory, or even worse, negative results. As citizens come to re-appropriate the coercive powers and institutions that govern their lives, they also allow themselves to be drawn even more into its remit of control, thus further cementing a climate of suspicion and mistrust and destabilizing the possibilities of collective action. Mothers who play the system find that they make themselves vulnerable to charges of benefit fraud and the threat of imprisonment. Social housing tenants who appropriate the language of 'anti-social behaviour' have their claims dismissed as being petty and infantile. And people's calls on the police in daily conflicts feed into the criminalization of the most disadvantaged sectors of society, while further marking them out as lawless when they come to rely upon their own forms of policing and self-protection.

Ethnographic attention to daily practices of personalization takes us, then, to the second major conclusion of this book: *popular punitivism is not the same as popular support for more state authority, at least not in any straightforward way.* This message directly challenges the claim so frequently made in dominant commentary on the punitive turn that the rise of 'law and order' is also representative of popular desires for an authoritarian project of statecraft making. Yet, once popular punitivism is divorced from popular desires for statecraft, an analytical space opens from within which we can critically question the state's own claims to authority. Ramsay (2012) has critiqued the prominence of images of a contemporary Leviathan in contemporary debates on punishment. For him, the penal laws enacted in the name of protecting an insecure public cannot be indicative of state authority in the Hobbesian sense: this is because 'to justify ... penal laws by reference to the security benefits of the vulnerable is an admission of defeat for Hobbes' sovereign' (2012: 216). Or, to put it differently, lawmakers and politicians admit their own lack of authority when they assume that the law's representative citizen is characterized by their vulnerability—something that Hobbes saw as being a central feature of the state of nature that the state was meant to eliminate. The ethnography offered in this book reveals that, from the perspective of law's subjects too, the return of a Leviathan is a myth.

From 'Law and Order' to Post-Democracy? Reconnecting Moral and Political Statecraft

What, then, are the broader implications for politics and, indeed, the future of democracy? What are the lessons for the future? And what can be done? Asking these questions means to run up against a third thesis that we find recurring in the commentary on the current moment of governance: that we have entered a post-ideological, post-democratic, or post-political state. This notion of a 'post'-era is sometimes explicitly connected to questions of punishment and crime. For example, we saw in Chapter 7 that Loader (2008) has proposed to read important scholarship of punishment, including work by Ericson (2007) and Simon (2007), through the narrative of an 'anti-politics of crime'. On this account, many of the transformations that criminal justice scholars and sociologists of crime have commented upon—such as the harshening of policies and their alleged populist bases—are both the cause of, and effected by, the decline of political ideas since the late 1970s. This argument also resonates with the thesis put forward by political theorists and sociologists that politics is moving, at the turn of the twenty-first century, to a 'post-democratic' state (Crouch, 2004) where democracy has been hollowed out of its substantive meaning (cf. Gallo, 2017). It also speaks to political and media commentary on the 'Brexit vote' that has portrayed citizens who voted in favour of 'leave' as being defined by their authoritarian tendencies, including strong support for more national defence, anti-immigrant policies, and harsher punishment.

To repeat, I do not doubt that authoritarian sentiments exist among the British population or beyond: the resurgence of the far-right in the United Kingdom (Evans, 2012, 2017; Rhodes, 2010; Smith, 2012a) and beyond (Gingrich and Banks, 2006; Holmes, 2000; Kalb, 2009, 2011; Szombati, 2018) acts as the most powerful reminder of this frightening reality. In the United Kingdom, the 'leave campaign' in the lead-up to the EU referendum powerfully mobilized a language of anti-immigration around a language of taking back 'local control'. Some people in Park End undoubtedly identified with this language that placed blame with foreign workers. However, not everyone did, and among the people with whom I spoke, more complex narratives prevailed. Just as Chapter 5 showed that residents' support for punitive state policies cannot be reduced to a singular 'authoritarian' rationale, so Chapter 7 argued that their choices at the ballot box are complex. They are framed through vernacular interpretive frameworks of an 'us' and 'them' that reveal emic realities of state failure. Moreover, Chapter 6 showed that people's own understandings of politics and 'active' citizenship do not assume the primacy of the state; indeed, they can often be constructed in direct opposition to a state-constructed order as local community activists subvert, bypass, or sometimes actively oppose hegemonic agendas.

Gallo (2017) has forcefully argued for the need to incorporate an alternative understanding of politics that decentres the state's claims to political and legal sovereignty. Her plea points to a crucial point: the crux of the contemporary moment is perhaps not so much one of an absence of political ideologies, as theorists of punishment have assumed, so much as that of a widening gap between citizens and the state. On this account, citizens' own narratives of government merit closer consideration. Far from evidencing once more the assumed irrationality of the people, these narratives constitute a moral–political framework that renders legible the injustices that citizens at the margins confront. At their heart, they reveal a strong sense of betrayal that is acutely felt by residents on Park End, as their own efforts to be good persons are not matched by the state's perceived duties of care. They speak of what I have called in Chapter 7 a fuller social contract between those who govern and the governed, one that captures the more affective and social dimensions of Park End daily life. According to this fuller social contract, what makes a good person and by extension a good citizen are precisely their everyday efforts to care: whether this be in terms of more conventional tropes of economic labour (common to the post-war social settlement between the state and the worker–citizen) or the more unspoken, fluid, but crucial acts of care that women (and men) in Park End invest into their daily kin and family relations. The state's failures on this account are not simply political, social, and economic (although they are, of course, all of these things), but crucially also *moral* failures to recognize its own duties of care.

Institutional and political mechanisms that allow for meaningful citizen participation do make a difference, as comparative work on institutions has persistently shown (Barker, 2009; Gallo, 2015; Lacey, 2008; Miller, 2008). And where these mechanisms are weak or absent, like in Park End, there is a risk that localized languages of justice and 'fairness' (Smith, 2012b) will be side-stepped, or even worse, divorced from a political–economic framework (Alexander, Hojer-Bruun, and Koch, 2018; Kalb, 2009, 2011; Narotzky, 2016). The dangers of this happening were perhaps best illustrated with respect to the Brexit referendum. As we saw in Chapter 7, almost immediately after the vote took place, those who voted in favour of 'leave' found themselves stigmatized as racist, authoritarian, and bigoted by the liberal elite. To be clear, I do not doubt that punitive sentiments, be they xenophobic or otherwise, existed among the British public. But I am interested in how liberals, at the precise moment when they came to re-appropriate a moral language, did so with an attack on marginalized citizens who have long loathed liberal democracy for its immorality. Meanwhile, the far-right has represented a political craft that recognizes the centrality of moral valences of statecraft. This was already evident in the lead-up to the EU referendum when the much-publicized leave campaign backed by the rightwing UKIP, stood out for recognizing the centrality of the moral in the political, even as it blamed immigrants for Britain's social and economic woes. While I argued in Chapter 7 that Park End is a long way away from fascism, there is no reason to believe that residents too might end up turning to the far-right if graspable alternatives are not forthcoming.

This, then, leaves us with the book's third and final conclusion: *liberal democracy's disavowal of its moral duties towards its most marginalized citizens reveals the hollowness of its political statecraft*. This disavowal of moral duties is not simply indicative of a 'post-democratic' or 'anti-political' state: as we have seen, according to these meta-narratives, the current moment, with its harshening of penal policies and ever-exclusionary forms of governance, is the outcome of, and effected by, the demise of political ideologies and ideas. By contrast, the ethnographic data uncovered in this book has shown that what we might want to call an 'emic political theory' remains strong in Park End. The word 'theory' is not one endorsed by Park End residents themselves when speaking of their own views of government. However, the diagnostic and critical potential embodied by their own views make it equivalent to, if not a genuine alternative for, any political theory that has been recognized as such. Theirs is a political theory that constructs the current conjuncture not as one of absence of political ideas, but of a growing gap between people and the state. It also contrasts their own efforts to demonstrate care—often against the odds—to the state's correlating failures to extend its own duties of care. And perhaps most importantly, it points to the limits of the state to monopolize the political imaginaries of its citizens, thus also breaking open the possibility of alternative futures (Bear and Knight, 2017), as distant and far-fetched as these might appear.

Where, then, does this leave us? What could the political imaginaries for the future be? No single solution can be found in an instant. But the three arguments put forward in this conclusion also bear the potential for change. Let me return, then, one last time, to each of them in turn. First, acknowledging the legacy of state control provides a starting point for rethinking policy choices. Genuine alternatives to the current system of governance have to recuperate the social democratic capacities of post-war governance, including its emphasis on redistributive solutions, without replicating its historical entrenchment in classed, gendered, and racialized forms of control. Second, understanding the plurality of responses with which citizens respond to the state's own powers challenges policy-makers (and academics) to take as their point of departure the daily relations and processes of social reproduction central to people's lives. Rather than silencing, side-stepping, or even criminalizing these relations, state policies should recognize them as central aspects of citizenship-making. And finally, any project that seeks to move towards closing the gap between the people and the state, and the crisis of political representation that is at its core, needs to start with the challenge that liberal democracy today is failing to achieve: that of connecting the state's moral duties to its political craft. Without this connection, there is a risk that any proposal for change will fail to command the sovereign voice that democracy needs. This book has suggested that it is through closer attention to the emic political theories of those at the margins that we can move a step closer in this direction, but more work needs to be done in the years to come.

Epilogue

Let us come back to Park End one last time. It is 11 June 2017, just over a year on from the referendum on leaving the European Union and roughly the same time since I had last visited Park End. I travelled back to the town and met up with my close friend, Lindsey. I was interested to speak to her about the general elections that had taken place only a few days earlier, on 9 June 2017, which kept the Conservative government in power. Lindsey and I met at a cemetery in the city centre of town. We sat on a bench, drinking coffee, and talked about our fears of the Conservative-rule in the years to come. After a while, our conversation drifted into other matters that were immediate to Park End life: a murder had happened the week before, five young men had been charged with the crime. This had triggered its own violent responses as almost immediately after the event, another young man was stabbed, suffering multiple wounds. Lindsey was distraught. She knew the young men who had been charged and more so, their mothers, many of them were deeply ingratiated in neighbourhood life. The murder was a deeply traumatic event for Park End community.

While Lindsey and I were talking, we noticed a small tent that had been put up on the cemetery amongst the graves. Lindsey was surprised: the homeless community, who had been squatting on the cemetery ground for the previous six months, had recently been evicted by the vicar. While our conversation shifted away from the murder to problems of homelessness which had been exacerbated by recent waves of welfare reforms, a young white man perhaps in his early thirties came out of the tent. He was clean shaven, but his eyes betrayed tiredness and fatigue. Lindsey asked him for a lighter and handed him her tobacco when he asked her for a cigarette, in turn. Then she wanted to know if he had heard about the eviction on the church grounds. He didn't know about it, he responded, he had only been here for a week now and all had been fine but he wanted to leave anyway: his tent had been burgled the other night while out in town, two bags were taken, one with food and one with clothing. It was the clothing that broke his heart, the young man explained, it had been his birthday recently and his sister had given him a brand-new tracksuit bottom that she had bought at TK Maxx for £70. 'That's horrible', Lindsey empathized, as the young man walked closer to us, stopping about 2 metres away and smiling shyly.

He introduced himself to us as James, and we got chatting. It turned out that he was from Park End, born and bred. James told us that just over a year ago, his life had been under control. Back then, he had worked in the factory and lived with his mother. All was going well until his mother got a new boyfriend and, in his words, was 'brainwashed' by him and she kicked him out of the house. James moved into a room above a pub for a few months until one day the landlord decided to raise the rent to £550 a month, almost double the amount of what James had been paying. Unable to afford the payment, James went to live with a friend in a village a few miles away. He was still riding to work on his bike, but eventually, it 'got too much' and he lost his job. Since then, he had been on the streets. Shelter, a homeless charity, was now trying to get him into emergency housing but had told him that he would have to wait for another month because nothing was available. Lindsey who had been listening with empathy to James' story now came in. She asked him if he had been in contact with various local organizations that could offer support. He had, but none had been able to help. Lindsey now started talking to him about places in town where he might be able to squat more easily without making himself vulnerable to both victimization at the hands of fellow citizens and eviction from the police.

In this short incident, many of this book's major themes were revealed: the precarity that citizens like Lindsey and James experience in their daily lives and their exposure to threats that are completely beyond their own control—from the threat of violent crime, such as stabbings and robberies, to insufficient and inadequate housing, to the impact of welfare reforms and precarious employment conditions. Intertwined in these stories are also the numerous failures of the state to protect its most vulnerable citizens from falling through the safety net. Austerity cuts make it impossible for people to find a roof over their head, even if it is just in the form of temporary accommodation; bad relationships with the police further exacerbate cycles of violent crime; and decades of state-led privatization and free market policies have deprived people of the employment opportunities and securities they might have once had. But within this picture of doom, the conversation between Lindsey and James also betrayed the acts of informal care and kindness that continue to persist. A friend who offers their home when a close one can no longer afford the rent on their room; a bag of clothing given by a sister to her struggling brother for his birthday; and a chance encounter at a cemetery when a stranger is sharing a cigarette with another and giving advice on where in town there might be a safe place to squat. These acts of kindness break open the indifference, even disdain, that those at the margins confront.

This indifference is not just a feature of the liberal state. As a society too, we have all too frequently chosen to withdraw our empathy for those who are vilified by policy-makers. Fast forward now to 13 September 2017, a late afternoon, this time, in north London, in a gentrified café in Stoke Newington. On the face of it, the café is a million miles from the lives of people on Park End. The café is buzzing with people who carry expensive laptops and prams; it is catering mostly for young professionals with high disposable incomes—the prices on the food menu of the café are not cheap. I had been sitting inside the café, preparing for a seminar I had to teach in the coming weeks, when I watched a black woman in her forties walk in. Her beauty struck me. She was impeccably dressed, with done up green nails, elaborate make up, and tight-fitting black trousers and a blouse. Her proud face betrayed no emotions. She sat down at one of the smaller tables near mine, and ordered some hot water from a young waitress. When the mug arrived, the woman slipped a brown English tea bag that she had taken out of her handbag into the hot water. The waitress, a young Italian woman, came back. She told the woman politely that she was not allowed to bring her own tea bag. The woman with the tea bag contested it: she had paid for the hot water she said, and so what was the difference? The waitress was firm. She will let it go this time, she said, but next time, it would not be allowed. 'Well, there won't be a next time!', the woman with the tea bag snapped. There was an awkward silence before the waitress turned around and walked away.

A few minutes later, a woman in plain clothes approached the table again. She introduced herself as the manager of the café. With her hands resting on her hips, her body communicated determination. When she started reiterating the café's policy that customers were not be allowed to bring their own tea bags, her voice was calm and firm. The woman with her tea bag listened, looking down at the table, and then sighed. 'You know', she said, 'I wouldn't be here if I had work, if I had something to do. But I just sit at home. I don't have a job and I have nothing else to do, I'm lonely'. Pointing at the waitress who had spoken to her earlier, she added, 'when I was her age, I had my parents, I never thought it would come to this and I would be on my own one day. I don't have a husband, my son is gone. I have three sisters but they have money and they don't talk to me. I am just asking for a bit of compassion'. The manager looked around uncomfortably, as silence fell on the room. She understood, she said, but reiterated that there was nothing she could do and that she would have to ask for the woman to leave. The woman with the tea bag went silent. 'Well', she said quietly, resigned this time, 'thank you. I won't come back again.'

References

Abrahams, R. (1998). *Vigilant Citizens: Vigilantism and the State*. Malden, Massachusetts: Polity Press.

Alcock, P. (1999). 'Poverty and Social Security'. In: *British Social Welfare in the Twentieth Century* (pp. 199–223). Basingstoke: Palgrave Macmillan.

Alexander, C. (2002). *Personal States: Making Connections between People and Bureaucracy in Turkey*. Oxford: Oxford University Press.

Alexander, C., Hojer-Bruun, M., and Koch, I. (2018). 'Political Economy Comes Home: "On Moral Economies of Housing"'. *Critique of Anthropology*, 38(2), 121–39.

Alexander, C., Smaje, C., Timlett, R., and Williams, I. (2009). 'Improving Social Technologies for Recycling: Interfaces, Estates, Multi-Family Dwellings and Infrastructural Deprivation'. *Journal of Waste and Resources Management*, 162 (WR1), 15–29.

Antonucci, L., Horvath, L., Kutiyski, Y., and Krouwel, A. (2017). 'The Malaise of the Squeezed Middle: Challenging the Narrative of the "Left Behind" Brexiter'. *Competition & Change*, 21(3), 211–29.

Auyero, J. (2000). 'The Logic of Clientelism in Argentina: An Ethnographic Account'. *Latin American Research Review*, 35(3), 55–81.

Auyero, J. (2012). *Patients of the State: The Politics of Waiting in Argentina*. Durham, North Carolina: Duke University Press.

Auyero, J., Bourgois, P. I., and Scheper-Hughes, N. (2015). *Violence at the Urban Margins*. New York, Oxford: Oxford University Press.

Auyero, J. and Swistun, D. A. (2009). *Flammable: Environmental Suffering in an Argentine Shantytown*. Oxford: Oxford University Press.

Back, L. and Ware, V. (2002). *Out of Whiteness: Color, Politics and Culture*. Chicago, Illinois: University of Chicago Press.

Balthazar, A. C. (2017). 'Made in Britain: Brexit, Teacups, and the Materiality of the Nation'. *American Ethnologist*, 44(2), 220–4.

Banerjee, M. (2011). 'Elections as Communitas'. *Social Research*, 78(1), 75–98.

Barke, M. and Turnbull, G. (1992). *Meadowell: The Biography of an Estate with Problems*. Aldershot: Avebury.

Barker, V. (2009). *The Politics of Imprisonment: How the Democratic Process Shapes the Way America Punishes Offenders*. New York, Oxford: Oxford University Press.

Barker, V. (2016). 'Policing Difference'. In: B. Bradford, B. Jauregui, I. Loader, and J. Steinberg (eds), *The SAGE Handbook of Global Policing* (pp. 221–5). Los Angeles, California: SAGE.

Barker, V. (2017). *Nordic Nationalism and Penal Order: Walling the Welfare State*. Abingdon: Routledge.

Bear, L. (2007). *Lines of the Nation: Indian Railway Workers, Bureaucracy, and the Intimate Historical Self*. New York: Columbia University Press.

Bear, L. and Knight, D. M. (2017). 'Alternatives to Austerity'. *Anthropology Today*, 35(5), 1–2.

Beck, U. and Beck-Gernsheim, E. (2002). *Individualization: Institutionalized Individualism and its Social and Political Consequences*. London: SAGE.

Bell, M. (2016). 'Situational Trust: How Disadvantaged Mothers Reconceive Legal Cynicism'. *Law and Society Review*, 60(2), 314–47.

Bew, J. (2017). *Citizen Clem: A Biography of Attlee*. London: Riverrun.

Bijsterfeld, K. (2008). *Mechanical Sound: Technology, Culture and Public Problems of Noise in the Twentieth Century*. Cambridge, Massachusetts: MIT Press.

Blair, T. 'Our Nation's Future'. *The Times* (23 June 2006).

Bott, J. (1971). *Social Research in Bethnal Green: An Evaluation of the Work of the Institute of Community Studies*. London: MacMillan.

Bottoms, A. E. (1995). 'The Philosophy and Politics of Punishment and Sentencing'. In: C. Clarkson and R. Morgan (eds), *The Politics of Sentencing Reform* (pp. 17–50). Oxford: Oxford University Press.

Bottoms, A. E. (2006). 'Incivilities, Offence and Social Order in Residential Communities'. In: A. von Hirsch and A. Simester (eds), *Incivilities: Regulating Offensive Behaviour* (pp. 239–80). Oxford: Hart.

Bourgois, P. (1995). *In Search of Respect: Selling Crack in El Barrio*. Cambridge: Cambridge University Press.

Bowling, B., Parmar, A., and Philipps, C. (2008). 'Policing Minority Ethnic Communities'. In: T. Newburn (ed.), *Handbook of Policing* (pp. 611–41). Cullompton: Willan.

Braconnier, C., Dormagen, J.-Y., and Rocha, D. (2015). 'Quand les Milieux Populaires se Rendent aux Urnes: Mobilisation Electorale dans un Quartier Pauvre de Brasilia'. *Revue Francaise de Science Politique*, 63(3–4), 487–518.

Brown, W. (1995). *States of Injury: Power and Freedom in Late Modernity*. Princeton, New Jersey: Princeton University Press.

Bruff, I. (2014). 'The Rise of Authoritarian Neoliberalism'. *Rethinking Marxism: A Journal of Economics, Culture & Society*, 26(1), 113–29.

Burney, E. (1999). *Crime and Banishment: Nuisance and Exclusion in Social Housing*. Winchester: Waterside Press.

Burney, E. (2009). *Making People Behave: Anti-Social Behaviour, Politics and Policy*. Cullompton: Willan.

Burton, A. 'The Link between Brexit and the Death Penalty'. *BBC News* (17 July 2016).

Bush, S. 'Divided Britain: How the EU Referendum Exposed Britain's New Culture War'. *New Statesman* (23 June 2016).
Butler, J. (2011). 'Bodies in Public'. In: K. Gessen, C. Blumenkranz, S. L. Greif, S. Resnick, N. Saval, A. Taylor, and E. Schmitt (eds), *Occupy! Scenes from Occupied America* (pp. 192–5). London: Verso.
Butler, P. 'Thousands Died After Fit for Work Assessment, DWP Figures Show'. *The Guardian* (27 August 2015).
Cabinet Office (2006). *Policy Review: Crime, Justice and Cohesion. Prime Minister's Strategy Unit*. London.
Caldeira, T. (2002). 'The Paradox of Police Violence in Democratic Brazil'. *Ethnography*, 3(3), 235–63.
Cameron, D. (2010). *The Big Society Speech*. London. Online at: https://www.gov.uk/government/speeches/big-society-speech.
Campbell, B. (1993). *Goliath: Britain's Dangerous Places*. London: Methuen.
Canton, R. (2015). 'Crime, Punishment and the Moral Emotions: Righteous Minds and their Attitudes towards Punishment'. *Punishment & Society*, 17(1), 54–72.
Carrier, J. G. and Kalb, D. (2015). *Anthropologies of Class: Power, Practice and Inequality*. Cambridge: Cambridge University Press.
Cavadino, M. and Dignan, J. (2005). *Penal Systems: A Comparative Approach*. London: SAGE.
Charlesworth, S. (2000). *A Phenomenology of Working Class Experience*. Cambridge: Cambridge University Press.
Coffield, F., Borrill, C., and Marshall, S. (1986). *Growing Up at the Margins: Young Adults in the North East Philadelphia*. Milton Keynes: Open University Press.
Cohen, A. (1985). *The Symbolic Construction of Community*. London: Ellis Horwood Ltd and Tavistock.
Cohen, S. (1972). *Folk Devils and Moral Panics: The Creation of the Mods and Rockers*. London: MacGibbon and Kee.
Cohen, S., Fuhr, C., and Bock, J.-J. (2017). *Austerity, Community Action, and the Future of Citizenship in Europe*. Bristol: Policy Press.
Collier, J., Maurer, B., and Suarez-Navaz, L. (1995). 'Sanctioned Identities: Legal Constructions of Modern Personhood'. *Identities*, 2(1/2), 1–27.
Collison, P. (1963). *The Cutteslowe Wall: A Study in Social Class*. London: Faber and Faber.
Comaroff, J. and Comaroff, J. (2004). 'Cultural Justice, Criminal Justice: The Limits of Liberalism and the Pragmatics of Difference in the New South Africa'. *American Ethnologist*, 31(2), 188–204.
Comaroff, J. and Comaroff, J. (2006). *Law and Disorder in the Postcolony*. Chicago, Illinois: University of Chicago Press.

Cook, J., Long, N., and Moore, H. (2016). 'Introduction: When Democracy Goes Wrong'. In: J. Cook, N. Long, and H. Moore (eds), *The State We're In: Reflecting on Democracy's Troubles* (pp. 1–26). New York, Oxford: Berghahn.

Cooper-Knock, S. J. and Owen, O. (2015). 'Between Vigilantism and Bureaucracy: Improving our Understanding of Police Work in Nigeria and South Africa'. *Theoretical Criminology*, 19(3), 355–75.

Crouch, C. (2004). *Post-Democracy*. Cambridge: Polity.

Dahrendorf, R. (1989). 'The Future of the Underclass: A European Perspective'. *Northern Economic Review*, 18, 7–15.

Damer, S. (1989). *From Moorepark to 'Wine Alley': The Rise and Fall of a Glasgow Housing Scheme*. Edinburgh: Edinburgh University Press.

Davey, R. (n.d.). 'Resourcing Debt Advice: The Voluntary Sector and the Financial Industry in the Provision of Social Welfare in the UK'. *Ethnos*.

Davey, R. (2016). *Debts in Suspense: Coercion and Optimism in the Making of Class in England*. PhD Thesis. Cambridge.

Davey, R. and Koch, I. (2017). *Popular Authoritarianism Revisited*. Washington DC: Conference Paper given at Annual American Anthropological Association Meeting.

de Koning, A. (2015). 'Citizenship Agendas for the Abject: The Production of Distrust in Amsterdam's Youth and Security Domain'. *Citizenship Studies*, 19(2), 155–68.

de Koning, A., Jaffe, R., and Koster, M. (2015). 'Citizenship Agendas in and beyond the Nation-State: (En)countering Framings of the Good Citizen'. *Citizenship Studies*, 19(2), 121–7.

Dearden, L. '"Authoritarian Populism" behind Donald Trump's Victory and Brexit Becoming Driving Force in European Politics'. *The Independent* (21 November 2016).

Degnen, C. (2005). 'Relationality, Place, and Absence: A Three-Dimensional Perspective on Social Memory'. *The Sociological Review*, 53(4), 729–44.

Degnen, C. (2013). '"Knowing", Absence, and Presence: The Spatial and Temporal Depth of Relations'. *Environment and Planning D: Society and Space*, 31, 554–70.

Dench, G., Gavron, K., and Young, M. (2006). *The New East End: Kinship, Race and Conflict*. London: Profile Books.

Dennis, N. and Erdos, G. (1999). *Families without Fatherhood*. London: Institute for Economic Affairs.

Desmond, M. (2016). *Evicted: Poverty and Profit in the American City*. London: Allen Lane.

Downes, D. and Morgan, R. (2007). 'No Turning Back: The Politics of Law and Order into the Millennium'. In: M. Maguire, R. Morgan, and

R. Reiner (eds), *The Oxford Handbook of Criminology* (pp. 201–40). Oxford: Oxford University Press.

Dubber, M. (2001). *The Police Power: Patriarchy and the Foundations of American Government*. New York: Columbia University Press.

Duffy, B., Wake, R., Burrows, T., and Bremner, P. (2008). 'Closing the Gaps—Crime and Public Perceptions'. *International Review of Law, Computers & Technology*, 22(1–2), 17–44.

Dunt, I. 'The Brexit Culture War: Brexit is the New Trump'. *Politics.co.uk* (6 June 2016).

Edwards, J. (2000). *Born and Bred: Idioms of Kinship and New Reproductive Technologies in England*. Oxford: Open University Press.

Edwards, J., Haugerud, A., and Parikh, S. (2017). 'Introduction: The 2016 Brexit Referendum and Trump Election'. *American Ethnologist*, 44(2), 195–200.

Engels, F. ([1845]2009). *The Condition of the Working Class in England*. Oxford: Oxford University Press.

Ericson, R. V. (2007). *Crime in an Insecure World*. Cambridge: Polity.

Evans, G. (2006). *Educational Failure and Working Class White Children in Britain*. Basingstoke: Palgrave Macmillan.

Evans, G. (2012). '"The Aboriginal People of England": The Culture of Class Politics in Contemporary Britain'. *Focaal: Journal of Historical and Global Anthropology*, 62(13), 17–29.

Evans, G. (2017). 'Social Class and the Cultural Turn: Anthropology, Sociology, and the Post-Industrial Politics of 21st Century Britain'. *The Sociological Review*, 65(1), 88–104.

Fassin, D. (2013). *Enforcing Order: An Ethnography of Urban Policing*. Cambridge: Polity.

Fassin, D. (2015). 'Governing Precariousness'. In: D. Fassin and P. Brown (eds), *At the Heart of the State: The Moral World of Institutions* (pp. 1–12). London: Pluto Press.

Fassin, D. (2017). 'Rethinking Punishment'. Public Lecture at the London School of Enomics (16 February 2017).

Fennell, C. (2015). *The Last Project Standing: Civics and Sympathy in Post-Welfare Chicago*. Minneapolis, Minnesota: University of Minnesota Press.

Ferguson, J. (1990). *The Anti-Politics Machine: Development, Depoliticization, and Bureaucratic Power in Lesotho*. Cambridge: Cambridge University Press.

Ferguson, J. and Gupta, A. (2002). 'Spatializing States: Toward an Ethnography of Neoliberal Governmentality'. *American Ethnologist*, 29(4), 981–1002.

Fetzer, T. (2018). 'Did Austerity Cause Brexit?'. Working Paper Series. Centre for Competitive Advantage in the Global Economy: University of Warwick.

Firth, R. (1956). *Two Studies of Kinship in London*. London: Athlone Press.
Forbess, A. and James, D. (2017). 'Innovation and Patchwork Partnerships: Advice Services in Austere Times'. *Onati Socio-Legal Studies*, 7(7), 1–22.
Forman, J. (2017). *Locking Up Our Own: Crime and Punishment in Black America*. New York: Farrar, Straus and Giroux.
Forrest, R. and Murie, A. (1988). *Selling the Welfare State: The Privatisation of Public Housing*. London: Routledge.
Friedman, J. (2003), ed. *Globalization, the State, and Violence*. Walnut Creek, California: AltaMira.
Fuller, C. and Bénéï, V. (2000). *The Everyday State and Society in Modern India*. New Delhi, India: Social Science Press.
Gallo, Z. (2015). 'Punishment, Authority and Political Economy: Italian Challenges to Western Punitiveness'. *Punishment & Society*, 17(5), 598–623.
Gallo, Z. (2017). '"The Constitution of Political Membership": Punishment, Political Membership, and the Italian Case'. *Theoretical Criminology*, 21(4), 458–77.
Gallo, Z. (2018). 'Political Ideologies and Penality'. *Oxford Research Encyclopedia of Criminology and Criminal Justice*.
Garland, D. (2001). *The Culture of Control: Crime and Social Order in Contemporary Society*. Oxford: Oxford University Press.
Geschiere, P. (2013). *Witchcraft, Intimacy and Trust: Africa in Comparison*. Chicago, Illinois: University of Chicago Press.
Gillies, V. (2007). *Marginalised Mothers: Exploring Working Class Experiences of Parenting*. London: Routledge.
Gilroy, P. (1987). *There Ain't No Black in the Union Jack: The Cultural Politics of Race and Nation*. London: Hutchinson.
Gingrich, A. and Banks, M. (2006). *Neo-Nationalism in Europe and Beyond: Perspectives from Social Anthropology*. New York, Oxford: Berghahn.
Girling, E., Loader, I., and Sparks, R. (1998). 'A Telling Tale: A Case of Vigilantism and its Aftermath in an English Town'. *The British Journal of Sociology*, 49(3), 474.
Girling, E., Loader, I., and Sparks, R. (2000). *Crime and Social Change in Middle England: Questions of Order in an English Town*. London: Routledge.
Goffman, A. (2009). 'On the Run: Wanted Men in a Philadelphia Ghetto'. *American Sociological Review*, 74(3), 339–57.
Goffman, A. (2014). *On the Run: Fugitive Life in an American City*. Chicago, Illinois: University of Chicago Press.
Goldstein, D. (2003). '"In Our Hands": Lynching, Justice and the Law in Bolivia'. *American Ethnologist*, 30(1), 22–43.
Goldthorpe, J., Lockwood, D., Bechhofer, F., and Platt, J. (1968). *The Affluent Worker: Industrial Attitudes and Behaviour*. Cambridge: Cambridge University Press.

Graeber, D. (2009). *Direct Action: An Ethnography*. Oakland, California: AK Press.

Graeber, D. (2011). *Debt: The First 5,000 Years*. Brooklyn, New York: Melville House.

Graeber, D. (2015). *The Utopia of Rules: On Technology, Stupidity, and the Secret Joys of Bureaucracy*. Brooklyn, New York: Melville House.

Grisaffi, T. (2013). '"All of us are Presidents": Radical Democracy and Citizenship in the Chapare Province, Bolivia 1'. *Critique of Anthropology*, 33(1), 47–65.

Grisaffi, T. (2019). *Coca Yes, Cocaine No: How Bolivia's Coca Growers Re-shaped Democracy*. Durham, North Carolina: Duke University Press.

Gutierrez-Garza, A. (n.d.). '"Te Los Tienes Que Currar": Enacting an Ethics of Care in Times of Austerity'. *Ethnos*.

Hall, P. and Soskice, D. (2001). *Varieties of Capitalism*. Oxford: Oxford University Press.

Hall, S., Critcher, C., Jefferson, T., Clarke, J., and Roberts, B. (1978). *Policing the Crisis: Mugging, the State and Law & Order*. London: MacMillan.

Hanley, L. (2007). *Estates: An Intimate History*. London: Granta.

Hansen, T. B. and Stepputat, F. (2005). 'Sovereign Bodies: Citizens, Migrants and States in the Post-Colonial World'. In: *Sovereign Bodies: Citizens, Migrants and States in the Post-Colonial World* (pp. 1–36). Princeton, New Jersey: Princeton University Press.

Hardt, M. and Negri, A. 'The Fight for Real Democracy at the Heart of Occupy Wall Street'. *Foreign Affairs* (11 October 2011).

Harrell-Bond, B. (1967). *Blackbird Leys. A Pilot Study of an Urban Housing Estate*. PhD Thesis. University of Oxford.

Harrison, E. (2011). 'The Incinerator and the Beach. Community, Activism and "the Big Society" in a Sussex Town'. *Focaal: Journal of Historical and Global Anthropology*, 61(13), 91–103.

Harvey, D. (2003). *The New Imperialism*. New York, Oxford: Oxford University Press.

Harvey, D. (2007). *A Brief History of Neoliberalism*. New York, Oxford: Oxford University Press.

Hey, V. (2003). 'Joining the Club? Academia and Working-class Femininities'. *Gender and Education*, 15(3), 319–36.

High, H. (2014). *Fields of Desire: Poverty and Policy in Laos*. Singapore: National University of Singapore Press.

Hills, J. (2015). *Good Times, Bad Times: The Welfare Myth of Us and Them*. Bristol: Policy Press.

Hoggart, R. (1957). *The Uses of Literacy: Aspects of Working-Class Life, with Special References to Publications and Entertainments*. London: Chatto & Windus.

Holmes, D. (2000). *Integral Europe: Fast-Capitalism, Multiculturalism, Neofascism*. Princeton, New Jersey: Princeton University Press.

Home Office (2003a). *Respect and Responsibility: Taking a Stance against Anti-Social Behaviour*. London.

Home Office (2003b). *Together: Tackling Anti-Social Behaviour. Action Plan*. London.

Hornberger, J. (2013). 'From General to Commissioner to General—On the Popular State of Policing in South Africa'. *Law & Social Inquiry*, 38(3), 598–614.

Hough, J. and Roberts, J. (2002). *Changing Attitudes to Punishment: Public Opinion, Crime and Justice*. Cullompton: Willan.

Hough, M., Roberts, J., Jacobson, J., Moon, N., and Steel, N. (2009). *Public Attitudes to the Principles of Sentencing*. Advisory Panel Report No. 6. London: Sentencing Advisory Panel.

Howe, L. (1990). *Being Unemployed in Northern Ireland: An Ethnographic Study*. Cambridge: Cambridge University Press.

Hutton, N. (2005). 'Beyond Populist Punitiveness?' *Punishment & Society*, 7(3), 243–58.

Hyatt, S. (1997). 'Poverty in a "Post-Welfare" Landscape: Tenant Management Policies, Self-Governance and the Democratization of Knowledge in Great Britain'. In: C. Shore and S. Wright (eds), *Anthropology of Policy: Critical Perspectives on Governance and Power* (pp. 166–82). New York, London: Routledge.

Hyatt, S. (2011). 'What Was Neoliberalism and What Comes Next? The Transformation of Citizenship in the Law-and-Order State'. In: D. Pero, C. Shore, and S. Wright (eds), *Policy Worlds: Anthropology and the Anatomy of Contemporary Power* (pp. 205–23). Oxford, New York: Berghahn Books.

James, D. (2007). *Rights and Property in South African Land Reform*. Cambridge: Routledge.

James, D. (2011). 'The Return of the Broker. Consensus, Hierarchy and Choice in South African Land Reform'. *Journal of the Royal Anthropological Institute*, 17(3), 318–38.

James, D. and Koch, I. (n.d.). 'The State of the Welfare State: Advice, Governance and Care in Settings of Austerity'. *Ethnos*.

Johnston, L. (1996). 'What is Vigilantism?'. *British Journal of Criminology*, 36(2), 220–36.

Jones, O. (2011). *Chavs: The Demonization of the Working Class*. London: Verso.

Joyce, P. (2013). *The State of Freedom: A Social History of the British State since 1800*. Cambridge: Cambridge University Press.

Juris, J. (2012). 'Reflections on #Occupy Everywhere: SocialMedia, Public Space, and Emerging Logics of Aggregation'. *American Ethnologist*, 39(2), 259–79.

Kalb, D. (2009). 'Conversations with a Polish Populist: Tracing Hidden Histories of Globalization, Class, and Dispossession in Postsocialism (and Beyond)'. *American Ethnologist*, 36(2), 207–23.

Kalb, D. (2011). 'Introduction'. In: D. Kalb and G. Halmai (eds), *Headlines of Nations, Subtexts of Class: Working-Class Populism and the Return of the Repressed in Neoliberal Europe* (pp. 1–36). New York, Oxford: Berghahn.

Kalb, D. 'Introduction: class and the New Anthropological Holism'. In: J. G. Carrier and D. Kalb (eds) *Anthropologies of Class: Power, Practice and Inequality* (pp.1–27). Cambridge: Cambridge University Press.

Karandinos, G., Hart, L., Castrillo, M., and Bourgois, P. (2014). 'The Moral Economy of Violence in the US Inner City'. *Current Anthropology*, 55(1), 1–22.

Kelly, T. and Shah, A. (2006). 'A Double-Edged Sword: Protection and State Violence'. *Critique of Anthropology*, 26(3), 251–7.

Kennedy, R. (1997). *Race, Crime, and the Law*. New York: Vintage Books.

Knight, D. (2017a). 'Anxiety and Cosmopolitan Futures: Brexit and Scotland'. *American Ethnologist*, 44(2), 237–42.

Knight, D. (2017b). *History, Time and Economic Crisis in Central Greece*. London: Routledge.

Knight, D. and Stuart, C. (2017). 'Ethnographies of Austerity: Temporality, Crisis and Affect in Southern Europe'. *History and Anthropology*, 27(1):1-18.

Koch, I. '"A Policy that Kills": The Bedroom Tax is an Affront to Basic Rights'. *LSE British Politics and Policy Blog* (23 September 2014).

Koch, I. (2015). '"The State has Replaced the Man": Women, Family Homes, and the Benefit System on a Council Estate in England'. *Focaal: Journal of Historical and Global Anthropology*, 73, 84–96.

Koch, I. (2016). 'Bread-and-Butter Politics: Democratic Disenchantment and Everyday Politics on an English Council Estate'. *American Ethnologist*, 43(2), 282–94.

Koch, I. (2017a). 'Moving Beyond Punitivism: Punishment, State Failure and Democracy at the Margins'. *Punishment & Society*, 19(2), 203–20.

Koch, I. (2017b). 'What's in a Vote? Brexit beyond Culture Wars'. *American Ethnologist*, 44(2), 225–30.

Koch, I. (2017c). 'When Politicians Fail: Zombie Democracy and the Anthropology of Actually Existing Politics'. *The Sociological Review*, 65(1), 105–20.

Koch, I. (2018). 'From Welfare to Lawfare: Environmental Suffering, Neighbour Disputes and the Law in UK Social Housing'. *Critique of Anthropology*, 38(2), 221–35.

Koster, M. (2012). 'Mediating and Getting "Burnt" in the Gap: Politics and Brokerage in a Recife Slum, Brazil'. *Critique of Anthropology*, 32(4), 479–97.

Koster, M. (2014). 'Bridging the Gap in the Dutch Participation Society New Spaces of Governance, Brokers, and Informal Politics'. *Etnofoor*, 26(2), 49–64.

Krugman, P. (2013). 'How the Case for Austerity Has Crumbled'. *New York Review of Books*.

Kuper, L. (1953). *Living in Towns: Selected Research Papers in Urban Sociology of the Faculty of Commerce and Social Sciences*. University of Birmingham: Faculty of Commerce and Social Sciences.

Labour Party (1995). *A Quiet Life*. London.

Lacey, N. (1998). *Unspeakable Subjects: Feminist Essays in Legal and Social Theory*. Oxford: Hart.

Lacey, N. (2008). *The Prisoners' Dilemma: Political Economy and Punishment in Contemporary Democracies*. New York, Cambridge: Cambridge University Press.

Lacey, N. (2010). 'Differentiating among Penal States'. *British Journal of Sociology*, 61(4), 778–94.

Lacey, N. and Soskice, D. (2015). 'Crime, Punishment and Segregation in the United States: The Paradox of Local Democracy'. *Punishment & Society*, 17(4), 454–81.

Lammy (2017). *Lammy Review: Final Report. An Independent Review into the Treatment of, and Outcomes for, Black, Asian and Minority Ethnic Individuals in the Criminal Justice System*. London.

Lawler, S. (2000). *Mothering the Self: Mothers, Daughters, Subjects*. London: Routledge.

Lawler, S. (2005). 'Disgusted Subjects: The Making of Middle-Class Identities'. *The Sociological Review*, 53(3), 429–46.

Lazar, S. (2004). 'Personalist Politics, Clientelism and Citizenship: Local Elections in El Alto, Bolivia'. *Bulletin of Latin American Research*, 23(2), 228–43.

Lazar, S. (2008). *El Alto, Rebel City: Self and Citizenship in Andean Bolivia*. Durham, North Carolina: Duke University Press.

Lazar, S. (2017). *The Social Life of Politics: Ethics, Kinship, and Union Activism in Argentina*. Stanford, California: Stanford University Press.

Lazarus-Black, M. (2001). 'Law and the Pragmatics of Inclusion: Governing Domestic Violence in Trinidad and Tobago'. *American Ethnologist*, 23(2), 388–416.

Lerman, A. and Weaver, V. (2014). *Arresting Citizenship: The Democratic Consequences of American Crime Control*. Chicago, Illinois: University of Chicago Press.

Lewis, J. (1992). 'Gender and the Development of Welfare Regimes'. *Journal of European Social Policy*, 3, 159–73.

Lewis, J. (2002). 'Gender and Welfare State Change'. *European Societies*, 4(4), 331–57.

Lewis, P., Newburn, T., Taylor, M., Mcgillivray, C., Greenhill, A., Fraymon, H., and Proctor, R. (2012). *Reading the Riots: Investigating*

England's Summer of Disorder. London School of Economics and Political Science and *The Guardian*.
Lindquist, J. (2015). 'Of Figures and Types: Brokering Knowledge and Migration in Indonesia and Beyond'. *Journal of the Royal Anthropological Institute*, 21, 162–77.
Loader, I. (1997). 'Policing and the Social: Questions of Symbolic Power'. *British Journal of Sociology*, 48(1), 1–18.
Loader, I. (2005). 'The Affects of Punishment: Emotions, Democracy and Penal Politics'. *Criminal Justice Matters*, 60(1), 12–13.
Loader, I. (2006). 'Fall of the "Platonic Guardians"'. *The British Journal of Criminology*, 46(4), 561–86.
Loader, I. (2008). 'The Anti-Politics of Crime'. *Theoretical Criminology*, 12(3), 399–410.
Lubet, S. (2017). *Interrogating Ethnography: Why Evidence Matters.* New York, Oxford: Oxford University Press.
MacKinnon, C. (1989). *Towards a Feminist Theory of the State.* Cambridge, Massachusetts: Harvard University Press.
Malik, S. and Nwonka, C. (2017). 'Top Boy: Cultural Verisimilitude and the Allure of Black Criminality for UK Public Service Broadcasting Drama'. *Journal of British Cinema and Television*, 14(4), 423–44.
Malinowski, B. (1926). *Crime and Custom in Savage Society.* London: Routledge & Kegan Paul.
Mckenzie, L. (2015). *Getting By: Estates, Class and Culture in Austerity Britain.* Bristol: Policy Press.
Mckenzie, L. 'Brexit is the Only Way the Working Class can Change Anything'. *The Guardian* (15 June 2016).
Macpherson, C. B. (2011). *The Political Theory of Possessive Individualism: Hobbes to Locke.* Oxford: Oxford University Press.
Meares, T. (1997). 'Charting Race and Class Differences in Attitudes Towards Drug Legalization and Law Enforcement: Lessons for Federal Criminal Law'. *Buffalo Criminal Law Review*, 1, 137–74.
Meares, T. and Kahan, D. (1998). 'The Coming Crisis of Criminal Procedure'. *Georgetown Law Journal*, 86, 1153–84.
Meek, J. (2014). 'Where Will We Live: The Housing Disaster'. *London Review of Books*, 36(1), 7–16.
Merry, S. E. (1990). *Getting Justice and Getting Even: Legal Consciousness among Working-Class Americans.* Chicago, Illinois: University of Chicago Press.
Merry, S. E. (1996). 'Gender Violence and Legally Engendered Selves'. *Identities*, 2(1/2), 123–48.
Merry, S. E. (2006). *Human Rights and Gender Violence: Translating International Law into local Justice.* Chicago, Illinois: University of Chicago Press.
Merry, S. E. (2009). 'Relating to the Subjects of Human Rights: The Culture of Human Agency in Human Rights Discourse'. In: *Law*

and Anthropology: Current Legal Issues (pp. 385–407). New York, Oxford: Oxford University Press.

Miller, D. (1988). 'Appropriating the State on the Council Estate'. *Man*, 23(2), 353–72.

Miller, L. (2008). *The Perils of Federalism: Race, Poverty, and the Politics of Crime Control*. New York, Oxford: Oxford University Press.

Miller, L. (2013). 'Power to the People: Violent Victimization, Inequality and Democratic Politics'. *Theoretical Criminology*, 17(3), 283–313.

Miller, L. (2016). *The Myth of Mob Rule: Violent Crime and Democratic Politics*. New York, Oxford: Oxford University Press.

Mogey, J. (1956). *Family and Neighbourhood: Two Studies in Oxford*. Oxford: Oxford University Press.

Mollona, M. (2009). *Made in Sheffield: An Ethnography of Industrial Work and Politics*. New York, London: Berghahn Books.

Morgan, R. and Smith, D. (2017). 'Delivering More with Less: Austerity and the Politics of Law and Order'. In: A. Liebling, S. Maruna, and L. McAra (eds), *Oxford Handbook of Criminology* (6th edn) (pp. 138–62). Oxford: Oxford University Press.

Morgan, S. and Maskovsky, J. (2003). 'The Anthropology of Welfare "Reform": New Perspectives on U.S. Urban Poverty in the Post-Welfare Era'. *Annual Review of Anthropology*, 32, 315–38.

Muehlebach, A. (2016). 'Anthropologies of Austerity'. *History and Anthropology*, 27(3), 359–72.

Mulcahy, L. (2001). 'The Possibilities and Desirability of Mediator Neutrality: Towards an Ethic of Partiality?' *Social and Legal Studies*, 10(4), 505–27.

Mulcahy, L. and Summerfield, L. (2001). *Keeping it in The Community: An Evaluation of the Use of Mediation in Disputes Between Neighbours*. London: Statutory Office for Nuffield Trust.

Murray, C. (1996). 'The Emerging British Underclass'. In: C. Murray and R. Lister (eds), *Charles Murray and the Underclass: The Developing Debate* (pp. 23–52). London: IEA Health and Welfare Unit in association with *The Sunday Times*.

Mutsaers, P. (2014). 'An Ethnographic Study of the Policing of Internal Borders in the Netherlands'. *British Journal of Criminology*, 54(5), 831–48.

Narotzky, S. (2016). 'Between Inequality and Injustice: Dignity as a Motive for Mobilization During the Crisis'. *History and Anthropology*, 27(1), 74–92.

Narotzky, S. (2017). 'Illiberal Capitalism and the Multiple Crisis of the Democratic State. Washington DC: Conference Paper given at *American Anthropological Association Meeting*.

Narotzky, S. and Goddard, V. (eds) (2017). *Work and Livelihoods: History, Ethnography and Models in Times of Crisis*. New York, Abingdon: Routledge.

Navaro-Yashin, Y. (2002). *Faces of the State: Secularism and Public Life in Turkey*. Princeton, New Jersey: Princeton University Press.
Navaro-Yashin, Y. (2006). 'Affect in the Civil Service: A Study of a Modern State-System. *Postcolonial Studies: Culture, Politics, Economy*, 9(3), 281–94.
Newburn, T. (2007). '"Tough on Crime": Penal Policy in England and Wales'. *Crime and Justice*, 36(1), 425–70.
Newburn, T. (2008). 'Introduction: Understanding Policing'. In: T. Newburn (ed.), *Handbook of Policing* (pp. 1–12). Cullompton: Willan.
Norrie, A. (1993). *Crime, Reason and History: A Critical Introduction to Criminal Law*. London: Weidenfeld & Nicolson.
Nugent, D. (2012). 'Commentary: Democracy, Temporalities of Capitalism and Dilemmas of Inclusion in Occupy Movements'. *American Ethnologist*, 39(2), 280–3.
Ong, A. (1996). 'Cultural Citizenship as Subject-Making: Immigrants Negotiate Racial and Cultural Boundaries in the United States'. *Current Anthropology*, 37(5), 737–62.
Orloff, A. (1993). 'Gender and the Social Rights of Citizenship: State Policies and Gender Relations in Comparative Research'. *American Sociological Review*, 58(3), 303–28.
Paley, J. (2008). *Democracy: Anthropological Approaches*. Santa Fe, New Mexico: School for Advanced Research Press.
Palomera, J. and Vetta, T. (2016). 'Moral Economy: Rethinking a Radical Concept'. *Anthropological Theory*, 16(4), 413–32.
Patenam, C. (1988). 'The Patriarchal Welfare State'. In: A. Gutenam (ed.), *Democracy and the Welfare State* (pp. 231–61). Princeton, New Jersey: Princeton University Press.
Peay, J. (1999). 'De Profundis: Criminology at the Water's Edge'. In: G. Dingwall and S. Moody (eds), *Crime and Conflict in the Countryside* (pp. 184–202). Cardiff: University of Wales.
Peston, R. (2017). *WTF: What Have We Done? Why Did it Happen? How Do We Take Back Control?* London: Hodder & Stoughton General Division.
Pratt, J. (2007). *Penal Populism*. New York, London: Routledge.
Putnam, R. (2004). *Bowling Alone: The Collapse and Revival of American Community*. New York: Simon & Schuster.
Ramsay, P. (2010). 'Overcriminalization as Vulnerable Citizenship'. *New Criminal Law Review*, 13(2), 262–85.
Ramsay, P. (2012). *The Insecurity State: Vulnerable Autonomy and the Right to Security in the Criminal Law*. Oxford: Oxford University Press.
Ramsay, P. (2016). 'A Democratic Theory of Imprisonment'. In: A. Dzur, I. Loader, and R. Sparks (eds), *Democratic Theory and Mass Incarceration* (pp. 84–113). Oxford: Oxford University Press.
Rapport, N. (2002). *British Subjects: An Anthropology of Britain*. Oxford: Berg Publishers.

Ravetz, A. (2001). *Council Housing and Culture: The History of a Social Experiment*. New York, London: Routledge.
Razsa, M. and Kurnik, A. (2012). 'The Occupy Movement in Žižek's Hometown: Direct Democracy and a Politics of Becoming'. *American Ethnologist*, 39(2), 238–58.
Reay, D. and Lucey, H. (2000). '"I Don't Really Like it Here but I Don't Want to be Anywhere Else": Children and Inner City Council Estates'. *Antipode*, 32, 410–28.
Reeves, M. (2014). *Border Work: Spatial Lives of the State in Rural Central Asia*. Ithaca, New York: Cornell University Press.
Reiner, R. (2007). *Law and Order: An Honest Citizen's Guide to Crime and Control*. London: Polity.
Reiner, R. (2010). *The Politics of the Police*. Oxford: Oxford University Press.
Reynolds, F. (1986). *The Problem Housing Estate: An Account of Omega and its People*. Aldershot: Gower.
Rhodes, J. (2010). '"Unfairness" and Justifications for the British National Party'. *Ethnicities*, 10(1), 77–99.
Roberts, S. (2013). *Order and Dispute: An Introduction to Legal Anthropology*. New Orleans, Luisiana: Quid Pro Books.
Rogaly, B. and Taylor, B. (2009). *Moving Histories of Class and Community: Identity, Place and Belonging in Contemporary England*. Basingstoke: Palgrave Macmillan.
Rose, N. (1996). 'Governing "Advanced" Liberal Democracies'. In A. Barry, T. Osborne, and N. Rose (eds), *Foucault and Political Reason: Liberalism, Neo-Liberalism and Rationalities of Government* (pp. 37–64). London: Routledge.
Rossner, M. (2013). *Just Emotions: Rituals of Restorative Justice*. Oxford: Oxford University Press.
Savage, M. (2000). *Class Analysis and Social Transformation*. Milton Keynes: Open University Press.
Savage, M. (2015). *Social Class in the 21st Century*. London: Penguin.
Savage, M. (2016). 'The Fall and Rise of Class Analysis in British Sociology, 1950–2016'. *Tempo Social*, 28(2), 57–72.
Savage, M., Bagnall, G., and Longhurst, B. (2001). 'Ordinary, Ambivalent and Defensive: Class Identities in the Northwest of England'. *Sociology*, 35(4), 875–92.
Scheper-Hughes, N. (1992). *Death Without Weeping: The Violence of Everyday Life in Brazil*. Berkeley, California: University of California Press.
Scott, J. (1985). *Weapons of the Weak: Everyday Forms of Peasant Resistance*. New Haven, Connecticut: Yale University Press.
Scott, J. C. (1998). *Seeing like a State: How Certain Schemes to Improve the Human Condition Have Failed*. New Haven, Connecticut: Yale University Press.

Shah, A. (2010). *In the Shadows of the State: Indigenous Politics, Environmentalism, and Insurgency in Jharkhand, India*. Durham, North Carolina: Duke University Press.

Shah, A. (2012). '"The Muck of the Past": Revolution, Social Transformation, and the Maoists in India'. *Journal of the Royal Anthropological Institute*, 20(2), 337–56.

Shore, C. and Wright, S. (2003). 'A New Field in Anthropology: Towards an Anthropology of Policy'. In C. Shore and S. Wright (eds), *Anthropology of Policy: Critical Perspectives on Governance and Power* (pp. 3–31). New York, London: Routledge.

Shore, C. and Wright, S. (2011). 'Conceptualising Policy: Technologies of Governance and the Politics of Visibility'. In C. Shore, S. Wright, and D. Pero (eds), *Policy Worlds: Anthropology and the Analysis of Contemporary Power* (pp. 1–26). Oxford: Berghahn.

Simon, J. (2007). *Governing through Crime: How the War on Crime Transformed American Democracy and Created a Culture of Fear*. New York, Oxford: Oxford University Press.

Skarbeck, D. (2014). *The Social Order of the Underworld: How Prison Gangs Govern the American Penal System*. New York, Oxford: Oxford University Press.

Skeggs, B. (1997). *Formations of Class and Gender: Becoming Respectable*. London: SAGE.

Skeggs, B. (2004). *Class, Self, Culture*. London: Routledge.

Skeggs, B. (2011). 'Imagining Personhood Differently: Person Value and Autonomist Working-Class Value Practices'. *The Sociological Review*, 59, 496–513.

Skeggs, B. and Loveday, V. (2012). 'Struggles for Value: Value Practices, Injustice, Judgement, Affect and the Idea of Class'. *The British Journal of Sociology*, 63, 472–90.

Smith, K. (2012a). 'Anxieties of Englishness and Participation in Democracy'. *Focaal: Journal of Historical and Global Anthropology*, 62, 30–41.

Smith, K. (2012b). *Fairness, Class, and Belonging in Contemporary England*. London: Palgrave Macmillan.

Smith, K. (2017a). '"Don't Call the Police on Me, I Won't Call Them on You": Self-Policing as Ethical Development in North Manchester'. In: J. Symons and C. Lewis (eds), *Realising the City: Urban Ethnographies in Manchester* (pp. 187–202). Manchester: Manchester University Press.

Smith, K. (2017b). '"You Don't Own Money, You're Just the One Who's Holding It": Borrowing, Lending and the Fair Person in North Manchester'. *The Sociological Review*, 65(1_suppl), 121–36.

Stack, C. (1974). *All our Kin: Strategies for Survival in a Black Community*. New York: Basic Books.

Steinberg, J. (2006). *Thin Blue: The Unwritten Rules of Policing South Africa*. Johannesburg, South Africa: Jonathan Ball.

Steinberg, J. (2016). 'How Well Does Theory Travel? David Garland in the Global South'. *The Howard Journal of Crime and Justice*, 55(4), 514–31.

Stewart, H. 'UK Politics Becoming Mired in "Culture Wars", Study Suggests'. *The Guardian* (7 December 2016).

Strathern, M. (1981). *Kinship at the Core: An Anthropology of Elmdon, a Village in North-west Essex in the 1960s*. Cambridge: Cambridge University Press.

Strathern, M. (1992). *After Nature. English Kinship in the Late Twentieth Century*. Cambridge: Cambridge University Press.

Strathern, M. (2004). 'Losing (Out) on Intellectual Resources'. In: *Law, Anthropology, and the Constitution of the Social: Persons and Things* (pp. 201–33). Cambridge: Cambridge University Press.

Super, G. (2016). 'Volatile Sovereignty: Governing Crime through the Community in Khayelitsha'. *Law and Society Review*, 50(2), 450–83.

Swales, K. (2016). *Understanding the Leave Vote*. London: NatCen Social Research.

Symons, J. (2018). '"We're Not Hard-to-Reach, They Are!" Integrating Local Priorities in Urban Research in Northern England: An Experimental Method'. *The Sociological Review*, 66(1), 207–23.

Szombati, K. (2018). *The Revolt of the Provinces: Anti-Gypsyism and Right-Wing Politics in Hungary*. New York, Oxford: Berghahn.

Taylor, B. and Rogaly, B. (2007). '"Mrs Fairly is a Dirty, Lazy Type": Unsatisfactory Households and the Problem of Problem Families, Norwich 1942 to 1963'. *Twentieth Century British History*, 18(4), 428–52.

Thiranagama, S. and Kelly, T. (2009). 'Introduction: Specters of Treason'. In: *Traitors: Suspicion, Intimacy and the Ethics of State-Building* (pp. 1–23). Philadelphia: University of Pennsylvania Press.

Thompson, E. P. (1971). *The Moral Economy of the English Crowd in the Eighteenth Century. Past & Present*. Oxford: Oxford University Press.

Timmins, N. (1995). *The Five Giants*. London: Harper Collins.

Townsend, M. 'Five Years after the Riots, Tension in Tottenham has not Gone Away'. *The Observer* (30 July 2016).

Tuckett, A. (n.d.). 'Britishness Outsourced: State Conduits, Brokers, and the British Citizenship Test'. *Ethnos*.

Tuckett, A. (2018). 'Ethical Brokerage and Self-Fashioning in Italian Immigration Bureaucracy'. *Critique of Anthropology* 38(3): 245-264.

Twyman, J. 'Trump, Brexit, Front National, AfD: Branches of the Same Tree'. *YouGov* (16 November 2016).

Tyler, I. (2008). 'Chav Mum Chav Scum'. *Feminist Media Studies*, 8(1), 17–34.

Tyler, I. (2015). *Revolting Subjects: Social Abjection and Resistance in Neoliberal Britain*. London: Zed Books.

Tyler, K. (2012). *Whiteness, Class and the Legacies of Empire: On Home Ground*. London: Palgrave Macmillan.

Tyler, K. (2015). 'Attachments and Connections: A "White Working-Class" English Family's Relationships with their BrAsian "Pakistani" Neighbours'. *Ethnic and Racial Studies*, 38(7), 1169–84.

Veena, D. and Poole, D. (2004). 'State and Its Margins: Comparative Ethnographies'. In: *Anthropology in the Margins of the State* (pp. 3–33). Santa Fe, New Mexico: School of American Research Press.

Von Benda-Beckmann, K. (2015). 'Social Security, Personhood and the State'. *Asian Journal of Law and Society*, 2(2), 323–38.

Wacquant, L. (2008). *Urban Outcasts: A Comparative Sociology of Advanced Marginality*. Cambridge: Polity Press.

Wacquant, L. (2009). *Punishing the Poor: The Neoliberal Government of Social Insecurity*. Durham, North Carolina: Duke University Press.

Wacquant, L. (2010). 'Crafting the Neoliberal State: Workfare, Prisonfare, and Social Insecurity'. *Sociological Forum*, 25(2), 197–220.

Wacquant, L. (2012). 'Three Steps to a Historical Anthropology of Actually Existing Neoliberalism'. *Social Anthropology*, 20(1), 66–79.

Walker, P. 'Richmond Park Byelection: Tory Brexit Voters Switched to Us, Say LibDems'. *The Guardian* (2 December 2016).

Walkerdine, V. and Lucey, H. (1989). *Democracy in the Kitchen: Regulating Mothers and Socialising Daughters*. London: Virago.

Werbner, P. (2015). *The Migration Process: Capital, Gifts and Offerings among British Pakistanis*. New York, London: Bloomsbury.

Wilde, M. (n.d.). 'Gatekeeping, Militant Care and Moral Economies of Housing in London'. *Ethnos*.

Williams, P. and Clarke, B. (2016). *Dangerous Associations: Joint Enterprise, Gangs and Racism. An Analysis of the Processes of Criminalisation of Black, Asian and Minority Ethnic Individuals*. London: Centre for Crime and Justice Studies.

Young, G. (2016). 'Class-based Punishment? How Legislation to Evict Social Tenants Involved in Riots is Unjust'. *British Politics and Policy at LSE Blog*.

Young, J. (1999). *The Exclusive Society: Social Exclusion, Crime and Difference in Late Modernity*. London: SAGE.

Young, M. D. and Willmott, P. (1957). *Family and Kinship in East London*. London: Routledge & Kegan Paul.

Index

Abrahams, R. 160–61
accumulation by dispossession 44–45
active citizenship 162
  agendas 217–18
  civic society initiatives 29, 168–69
  and consumer–citizen 45–46
  neoliberalism 168
  official explanations for 29
  Park End estate 163–64, 168–69
    community centre 169–70,
      171–72, 176–77, 180, 182–83
  personalization of politics 180
  political brokers 6, 163,
    168–69
  responsibilization
    and participatory
      governance 169
  Thatcherism 194–95
  Third Way politics 165–66, 167–68
  vulnerability to crime 165
actual bodily harm 144
advanced liberalism 17, 116, 134–35
'affluent worker' 66–67
Alexander, C. 14, 18, 114–15,
  206, 218
anthropology
  citizenship 83, 164, 168
  class 191–92, 215
  kinship networks 64
  neoliberalism 191–92, 215
  and personalizing the state 17–18
  policing 141
  policy 164, 168
  political and legal 6–7, 164
    absence of 19
  political ideology and power 15–16
  and state–citizen relations 17
  of United Kingdom 15–16
anti-immigration attitudes 189, 191,
  193–94, 216,
  230–31
anti-social behaviour 222
  coercive policies 112–13, 127
  criminal justice policies 3–4
  evidentiary standard 52
  language of 28, 112, 128,
    134–35, 218, 227–28

  legal definition 115–16,
    154–55, 166
  legislation 115
  local authorities dealing
    with 32–33, 51–52
  New Labour policies 3, 166,
    168
  Park End estate 1
  personalizing 128
  social housing 112
  teams 128–29
Anti-Social Behaviour Act
  (2003) 166
Anti-Social Behaviour, Crime and
  Policing Act (2014) 52–53
Anti-Social Behaviour Orders
  (ASBOs) 7–8, 52, 150–51,
  156, 167–68
apartments 124–25
Arab Spring 214–15
Ascension Trust 31–32
assured tenancies 47–48
austerity politics 3–4, 29–30, 234
  and Brexit 194–95, 196
  and council housing,
    history 34
  defining austerity 222–23
  public sector cuts 199
  and state failure 202, 207
authoritarian
    neoliberalism 214–15
  'authoritarian fixes' 194–95,
    220, 223
authoritarian populism 4, 29–30,
  189, 213
authoritarian voter 193–94
Auyero, J. 99

Bacup, England 64
Barke, M. 206
Barton estate, Oxford 65–66, 69
Baxter v Camden LBC (No 2)
  (2001) 113
Beck, U. 192
'bedroom tax' 103, 196–97,
  198, 222–23
Bell, M. 155

benefits system
  attitudes to complaints 133–34
  benefit officials 126–27,
    217–18
  cheating 108–9
  claiming benefits 53–54, 58,
    88–90, 99, 100, 101, 102, 104,
    108–9, 111–12, 123
  disability benefits 99
  and class 96–97, 107–8, 217–18
  cohabitation 89–90
  contact at time of crisis 122–23
  contemporary policies 107–8
  defining 86–87
  delays and interruptions 199
  disability benefits 117–18,
    196–97, 204–5
  engagement of women with 86–87
  failure to accommodate living
    arrangements 111–12
  form-filling 99–100
  fraud 24, 26, 87, 105
  gender neutrality 87–88, 90, 107–8
  housing benefit 47–48, 86–87,
    100–1, 196–97
  interactions with 28
  means-testing 3–4, 87–88, 89–90,
    91–92, 100–1, 222
  and neoliberalism 57
  officers 49–50
  personalization 103
  playing the system 87, 91–92, 104,
    108–9, 226–28
  post-war period 88
  precarious homes 92
  priority given to individual claimants over couples 89–90, 100
  rules 27–28
  'scroungers' 53–54, 85, 216–17
  state, role of 97
  women 88, 91–97, 98
  see also single mothers; welfare;
    women
Bermondsey, London 146–47
betrayal, sense of 75–76, 81, 83, 194–95, 204, 230–31
  moral betrayal 207
  and New Labour
    government 194–95
  on Park End estate 163–64,
    195–96, 230
  and state failure 75–76, 207
Beveridge, W. 40–41, 90

Big Society 163, 167–68
Bijsterfeld, K. 135
Blackbird Leys estate,
  Oxford 66–67, 68
Blair, T. 50–52, 150
  see also New Labour government
Blunkett, D. 166
Bolivia 187
Borrill, C. 208–9
bottom-up governance 3, 6, 27–28
Bourdieu, P. 15–16, 17, 37–38, 63
Bourgois, P. I. 25–26
Brexit 188, 228–29, 230–31
  anti-immigration attitudes 189,
    191, 193–94, 216
  anticipating result of 2016
    referendum 18, 188
  assumptions around voters 189
  austerity politics 194–95, 196
  characterization of leave voters 4
  crisis of democracy 192, 207
  ethnographic perspective 189
  leave vote 211–12
    characteristics of leave
      voters 189–90
    common portrayals in
      media 188–89
    implications of 29–30,
      188–89
    interpretation of 193–94
    leave campaign 191,
      212–13, 229–30
    motivations for 212
    in Park End estate 211–12
    stigmatizing of leave
      voters 230–31
    and turnout 189–90
  moral dimensions 213–14, 215
  motivations of electorate 189
  and Park End estate 188, 189–91,
    195–96, 211–12, 213–15
    austerity politics 196
    state failure 203–7
  popular authoritarianism 4, 29–30,
    189, 194
  punishment, attitudes of voters
    to 193–94
  referendum result 3–4, 188,
    213–14, 215
  remain vote 188–89
  state failure 202
  and xenophobia 189, 191,
    213, 230–31

see also electorate, British; United Kingdom
Britain see United Kingdom
'broken windows' theory 50–51
Bruff, I. 195, 214–15, 219–20
budgetary control 45–46
building quality, poor 114–15, 116, 125–26, 133–34
bureaucracy 18
  documentation, benefits 99–100
  modes of control 38–39
  Weberian legal–bureaucratic state, personalizing of 17–18
  withdrawal practices 126–27
Burney, E. 39–40, 115–16

Caldeira, T. 142–43
Cameron, D. 167–68
capitalism 40–41
  liberal 4–5
  state-controlled 44–45
  welfare capitalism 70–71
care
  children in 150–51
  codes of 126
  daily responsibilities and commitments 59–60, 79–80, 96–98, 230, 231
  ethics of 109, 218
  expectations for 79–80, 81
  family responsibilities/childcare 58–59, 76–77, 97–98, 100, 104, 230
  gendered practices 68–69
  government failing to honour duties of 29–30
  informal networks/support 27, 61–62, 65, 78–80, 234
  moral framework 30
  mutual relations of 64
  paternalistic 68–69, 204
  sociological perspective 60–61
  state care 69
  top-down control and bottom-up care 27–28
  see also welfare state
CCTV 54–55
Census (2011) 43–44, 48–49, 86–87
citizen–consumer see consumer–citizen
citizen–state relations see state–citizen relations
citizen–worker see worker–citizen

Citizens' Advice Bureau (CAB) 176–77
citizenship
  active see active citizenship
  anthropology 83, 164, 168
  'bad' citizen 27, 59–60, 81, 138–39, 226
  boundaries of 56
  'citizen-as-crime-fighter' 38, 52, 56, 115
  claims to 80
  consumer–citizen see consumer–citizen
  custodial 37, 141–42
  deserving citizens see deserving citizens
  differential citizenship patterns, United States 141–42
  gap between citizens' expectations for support and police performance 28–29
  good citizen see good person/citizen
  idealized citizen see idealized citizen
  informal 168
  'law-and-order state' and vulnerable citizen 65
  marginalized citizens 5–6, 26–27, 84, 216–17, 230–31
  middle-class citizens see middle-class citizens
  moral union between citizens and state 16, 65, 204, 225–26
    attack on 71
  nuisance disputes and vulnerable citizen 113
  and personhood 16, 59–60
  productive citizen 88–89
  'proper citizen' 59–60
  as punishment 4, 220
  restriction of access to 46–47
  righteous person and rightful citizen 27
  rightful 57
  social 87–88, 90
  state–citizen relations see state–citizen relations
  voter–citizen 191, 194
  vulnerable citizens see vulnerable citizens
  worker–citizen see worker–citizen
  working-class citizens see working-class citizens
  worthy citizen 46, 56

civic initiatives 29, 168–69
civil servants, professional
    10–11
Clarke, B. 221–22
class
    absence of as form of positive
        identity 63
    anthropology 191–92, 215
    apartheid/segregation 40,
        42–43
    and being a good citizen/person 59–
        61, 82–83, 225–26, 230
    and benefits system 96–97,
        107–8, 217–18
    Bourdieu on 15–16, 17, 63
    class division 40–41
    denial of 194
    inequalities 4–5, 22, 26, 63, 91,
        117, 164, 220–21
    intra-class conflicts 15–16
    and kinship 62–63
    paradox of 63
    sociological perspective 15–16,
        60–62, 82
    and state 12–14, 15–16, 19
        benefits system 91
        'class apartheid' 40
        coercion/control 4–5, 6–7, 9–10,
            13, 15, 19, 26–27, 40–41,
            111–12, 216, 218–19, 220,
            222–23, 224–25
        council housing 33–34, 35,
            38–39, 40–41, 42–43, 44, 51,
            55–56, 57
        support from 69
        see also benefits system;
            welfare state
    traditional categories 193–94
    see also middle-class citizens; under-
        class; working-class citizens
'classical' industrial neighbour-
    hoods see neighbourhoods
clientelistic politics 187
Coalition government 34–35, 85, 197,
    210, 222–23
coercive governance 4–6, 9–10, 19,
    218, 222
    anti-social behaviour 112–13, 127
    and ethnographic paradox 30
    Park End estate residents as subjects
        of 59–60
    and working-class citizens 5, 9–10
Coffield, F. 208–9

cognitive deficit model 224–25
collective punishment 221–22
Comaroff, J. and J. 37, 56
communal areas, neglect of 28, 114–
    15, 117, 124–26, 127, 129–30
community centre, Park End estate 1–
    2, 15–16,
        19–20
    active citizenship 169–70, 171–72,
        174–75, 176–77, 180, 182–83
    campaigns against closure 21–22
    change 181
    closure 21–22, 182–83
    committee 180
    and council 180
    fieldwork/research 19–20, 59
    funerals 162
    hiring of space 174–75
    management 169–70, 180–82
    meetings 169–70, 171–72
    and regeneration 21–22
    running of 180, 181–82
    see also Park End estate
community-centred perspective 15–16
community policing 32, 51–52
    see also police community support
        officers
        (PCSOs)
complaints
    housing 114–15, 124–25
    NAG meetings 171–72
    neighbours, trouble with 68, 129,
        133, 135
    nuisance 116, 135
    see also building quality, poor;
        council housing; disrepair and
        failure to maintain properties;
        housing; social housing
connectedness
    claims to 24
    and personhood 79–80
consent
    and government 13–14
    informed 23–24
    for 'law and order' 5–6, 12–13
    policing by 31–32, 139–40, 142–43
    popular 17, 19, 154–55,
        224, 227–28
    for state power 194
    tacit 180
conspicuous consumption 66–67
consumer–citizen
    and active citizen 45–46

as dominant model of
citizenship 88–89
idealized citizen as *see* idealized
citizen
and iron law of liberalism 48
respectability 34, 38–39
vigilantism 142–43, 157–58, 159,
160–61, 184, 186, 226–27
and women 88
see also citizenship; worker–
citizen
control
bureaucratic modes 38–39
culture of 10, 11–12, 36–37
by state *see* state control
Cooper-Knock, S. J. 226–27
coordinated market economies
(CMEs) 11–12
correctionalist justice, post-war
ideal 36–37
council housing
alleged moral obligations of
tenants 42
British 38–39
building quality, poor 114–15, 116,
125–26, 133–34
case study of 14
and citizenship 6, 39
communal areas, neglect of 28,
114–15, 117, 124–26,
127, 129–30
complaints about 114–15, 116,
124–25, 133–34
crime-breeding grounds, seen
as 53–54
daily life *see* daily life
disrepair and failure to maintain
properties 28, 114–15, 117,
124–25, 127
eviction of tenants 52–53,
150–51, 198
'ghettos', council estates
depicted as 61
history 26–27
language of 'estates' 35
'law and order' on post-industrial
estates 15
and 'law-and-order' state 34,
38, 49–50
material decline 115
name 14
owner-occupied estates 46–47
policies 41–42

political history 31
post-war period 14, 34, 38–39, 44,
65, 70–71, 82–83,
113–14
privatization 33–34, 46–48, 50
'problem estates', seen
as 48–50, 53–54
rent payments 38–39
right to buy 46–47, 114–15
secure tenancies 47–48, 117–18
selective policies 41–42
signs placed by local
authorities 1–2
single mothers and access to council
houses 90–91
and social democracy 36–38, 39–40
state-building 34, 38–40
'state on council estate' 64
tenants, heterogeneity of 15–16
tenants turned into agents of
policing 115
terminology 26–27
vulnerable citizens, prioritization in
allocation 46
waiting lists 42–43
'walls in people's heads' 75–76
and welfare state 14, 40–41
withdrawal practices 126–27
see also Barton estate, Oxford;
Blackbird Leys estate, Oxford;
Omega estate, Midlands; Park
End estate
councils *see* local authorities
Crime and Disorder Act
(1998) 52, 115–16
Crime and Public Order Act
(1998) 140–41
Crime Prevention Injunctions
(CPIs) 167–68
Crime Reduction Programme 140–41
Criminal Behaviour Orders
(CBOs) 167–68
criminal law/criminal justice policies
'anti-politics of crime' 192–93
changes in policy-making 8–9
council estates seen as crime-
breeding grounds 53–54
criminal as prototypical
outsider 10–11
death penalty 193–94
exclusionary policies 38
Governing through Crime
(Simon) 11

criminal law/criminal justice policies (*cont.*)
  informal networks of control, United States 168
  joint enterprise 144
  moving beyond 220
  nuisance disputes 7–8, 113
  paradoxes of 8
  petty crimes 7–8
  public whipping of criminals 193–94
  punitive and populist turn in 4
  repeat offenders, targeting 31–32
  state–citizen relations 37
  'tough on crime' agenda of New Labour 50–51, 137–38
  victims of crime 7–8
  see also Anti-Social Behaviour, Crime and Policing Act (2014); Crime and Disorder Act (1998)
crisis
  contact with benefit system at time of 122–23
  of democracy 3–4, 5
    and Brexit 192, 207
  of political representation 194–95
  of state 5
critical junctures 191–92, 212–13
Crouch, C. 192–93
culture of control 10, 11–12, 36–37
curfews 7–8
curriculum vitae (CV) writing, assistance with 58, 79–80, 174–75, 204–5
custodial citizenship 37
Cutteslowe Wall, Oxford 40

daily life 18, 27, 61, 85, 110
  care responsibilities 59–60, 79–80, 96–98, 230, 231
  community life 22, 27, 29, 32–33, 54, 127, 128–29, 148
  hazards encountered in 136–37
  kinship networks 64, 71, 82–83, 230
  neighbourhoods 61–62, 133–34
  police protection 143
  state relations 15–16, 27–28
  struggle for security and survival 1, 5–6, 16, 17–18, 109, 168–69, 177, 217–18
  violence and threats 136–37
  women 22, 28, 48–49, 61, 86–87, 88, 91–92, 108–9, 111–12, 121–22, 126, 174–75
Damer, S. 41–42
Davey, R. 100–1, 226
de-industrialization 27
de Tocqueville, A. 4–5
democracy/liberal democracy
  contested term 8
  crisis of 3–4, 5
    and Brexit 192, 207
  disenchantment with 218–19
  failures of 189–90
  'golden age' of British social democracy 4–5, 9–10, 37–38, 220
  illiberal turn 5, 8–9, 13–14, 30
  implications of state–citizen relations for 29–30
  inception of liberal democracy in nineteenth century 4–5
  post-democracy accounts 192–93, 195, 228
  regulation of working-class family 87–88
  social democracy *see* social democracy
  support for anti-democratic measures 8–9, 160
  working-class family as antithesis of freedom 9
  'zombie democracy' 192, 193–94, 195
dependency
  language of 49–50
  and single mothers 49–50
deservingness 34, 41–42, 44
  dominant models 61
  language of undeservingness 59–60
  state categories/criteria 59–60, 82–83
  and 'undeserving' working-class 42–43
Desmond, M. 133–34
  Evicted 23–24
Dickens, C. 39–40
dis-identification 64
disability benefits 117–18, 196–97, 204–5
dispossession 191–92
disrepair and failure to maintain properties 28, 114–15, 117, 124–26, 127, 129–30

Index

domestic abuse 144–45
drug dealing 141, 172
Duggon, M. 202–3
EastEnders (BBC soap) 77–78

Edwards, J. 64
electorate, British
  apathy 131–32, 192
  authoritarian voter 193–94
  choices 229–30
  downward trends in electoral participation 190–91, 192
  ethnographic perspective 189
  motivations when voting 189, 212
  turnout 189–90, 210
  voter–citizen 191, 194
  withdrawal behaviour 3–4, 18, 183–84, 189–91, 192–93, 195–96, 210–11, 213–14
  see also Brexit
Elmdon village 73–74
emic theories
  political 195–96, 231
  state failure 18–19
  streets and police encounters 145–46
emotions 224–26
Engels, F. 39–40
environmental health officers 130–31
environmental suffering 116, 135
Ericson, R. V. 11, 192–93, 228–29
estates, language of 35
  see also council housing; Park End estate
ethics
  of care 109, 218
  of fieldwork 23
  Victorian 45–46, 165–66
ethnographic perspective 5, 6–7, 13
  and British electorate 189
  brokerage relations 163–64
  doing ethnography, defining 25–26
  ethnographic paradox 30, 224
  fieldwork, conducting 22
  and governance 38
  illiberal turn, in liberal democracy 8–9
  literature on Britain 77–78
  policy and law 87–88
  revisions 18–19
  state–citizen relations 216, 218, 223

'trouble' of tenants 134–35
violence and threats 137, 160
European Union, British referendum vote to leave (2016) *see* Brexit
Evans, P. 162–63, 168–69, 184–85, 194–95
eviction of tenants 52–53, 150–51, 198
'excess', figures of 90–91
exclusionary policies 15
Exclusive Society (Young) 11, 36

Family Allowance 41
family/nuclear-family homes 27–28, 87, 93, 95, 157–58
  see also home; male breadwinner model; nuclear family model
far-right politics 191, 215, 229–31
Fassin, D. 34–35, 37–38
Fetzer, T. 194–95
fieldwork
  approaches to 22
  balanced view 26
  data collection 20, 24–25
  difficult issues 24–25
  ethics of 23
  friendships 24, 25–26
  introductions 22
  and 'law and order' 3
  in marginalized place 19
  presentations 24–25
  and stigmatizing of Park End residents 74–75
  trust issues 22, 23–25
  see also ethnographic perspective; Park End estate
Firth, R. 15–16
fixed penalty notices (FPNs) 173–74
Fordism 63, 82–83
Foucault, M. 17, 164
Free Workers Party (FWP) 183–86, 212

Gallo, Z. 11, 230
gang injunction orders 7–8
gangs, racialized images of 53–54, 61
'garden cities' 40
Garland, D. 10–11, 36, 166–67
  Culture of Control 10
gender inequalities 45–46, 85–86, 91, 107–8, 117

see also gender neutrality; inequalities; women
gender neutrality 87–88, 90, 107–8
gentrification 46–47
Geschiere, P. 81
Gillies, V. 90–91, 96–97
Goffman, A. 226
  On the Run 23–24
Goldthorpe, J. 66–67
good governance 168–69, 205–6
good person/citizen
  attempts to be 204
  and 'bad' citizen 27, 59–60, 138–39, 226
  and class 59–61, 82–83, 225–26, 230
  defining/understanding what it means to be 6, 9–10, 27, 60–61, 82, 100, 225–26
  failure to be 81
  'good' mothers 100
  moral expectations 134–35
  Park End residents 59, 207
  primary status of being 83
  see also citizenship
governance
  bottom-up 3, 6, 27–28
  coercive *see* coercive governance
  and ethnographic perspective 38
  good 168–69
  'law and order' 38–39, 55–56
  participatory 169, 217–18
  social 4–5, 34, 37–38, 42–43, 116
  technocratic 4
  top-down 3, 5–6, 27–28
Governing through Crime (Simon) 11
Graeber, D. 48
Grisaffi, T. 17–18, 187, 214–15
group savings schemes 67
Gutierrez-Garza, A. 109

Hall, P. 11–12
Hall, S. 139–40, 194–95
Hanley, L. 40, 75–76
Harrell-Bond, B. 66–67, 68–70
Harrison, E. 206
Harvey, D. 44–45
Heath, E. 45
hegemonic worldviews 17
Hills, J. 45

historical perspective 13, 19
  political history of council housing 31
  post-war period *see* post-war period
Hobbes, T. 147, 160–61, 228
  see also Leviathan
Hoggart, R. 85–86, 207
Hojer-Bruun, M. 14
home
  affording of own 46
  broken 94–95
  care of 77
  family/nuclear-family homes 27–28, 56, 82–83, 87, 93, 95, 157–58, 222
  home-centred living 65–66
  home-oriented culture 65–66
  and homelessness 73
  maintaining 77
  meaning of 77
  ownership of 34, 46, 48–49, 51, 56, 57, 220–21
  precarious homes 47–48, 92
  rented properties 48–49, 52–53, 94–95
  repossession of 143–44
  'respectable' council homes 41–42
  social relations 64
  social tenancy homes 226
  spaces of 76–77
  and street violence 137–38
  see also council housing; housing; social housing
Hornberger, J. 142–43, 155
housing
  'classical' industrial neighbourhoods, destruction of 40–41, 51, 61–62, 65, 68, 72–73
  council estates *see* council housing; Park End estate
  discretionary payments 199–201, 204–5
  disrepair and failure to maintain properties 28, 114–15, 117, 124–25, 127
  mandatory standards in public housing 113–14
  precarious homes 47–48, 92
  private sector 40
    ownership 46, 56, 57

rented properties 47–49, 50, 86–87, 113–14, 120, 122–24, 133–34, 198–99, 200, 217–18
'problem estates' *see* 'problem estates'
public housing projects, Chicago 135
publicly owned, provided by third-sector organizations 47–48
punitive policies 109
slums 39–40, 42–43
social *see* social housing
substandard conditions 47–48
tenement block 40
see also housing associations; housing authorities, encounters with; neighbourhoods
Housing Act (1980) 46–47
housing associations 32–33, 47–48, 110, 111–12, 125–26, 129
social housing 114–15, 128–29
housing authorities, encounters with 110
anti-social behaviour, personalizing 128
nuisance disputes and vulnerable citizen 113
troubled neighbourhoods 117
unresponsiveness 129
see also housing associations
housing benefit 47–48, 86–87, 100–1, 196–97
housing developments 14, 39–40
see also council housing; Park End estate; social housing
Housing (Homeless Persons) Act 1977 46
housing inspectors 70–71
Housing of the Working Classes Act (1885) 40
Howe, L. 73–74
Hyatt, S. 34–35, 38–39, 45–46, 50, 52, 115, 116, 168
hypermoralization 90

idealized citizen
homeowners 34, 46, 56
interpretations of 34
as male white breadwinner 16, 34, 41–42, 56, 87–88
of neoliberal policy 45–46, 52
post-war notions, revision of 45–46
worker–citizen/consumer–citizen as 7–8, 38, 44–46, 50, 52, 87–88, 197, 220–21

illiberal turn, in liberal democracy 5, 7, 8–9, 13–14, 30
illness, long-term 41
immigrants 41
imprisonment
increasing use of 8
rates in United Kingdom 7–8
incident diaries 129–30
individual responsibility, shift to 115, 165
industrial action 45, 208–9
Industrial Revolution 39–40
inequalities
class 4–5, 22, 26, 63, 91, 117, 164, 220–21
and crime 220–21
gendered 45–46, 91, 107–8, 117
neoliberalism 45–46
power 102–3
single mothers 91
structural 167–68
see also class; middle-class citizens; neoliberalism; single mothers; working-class citizens
inflation 45
Insecure Society (Ericson) 11
interviews
with council residents 72–73, 103–4, 107
with local authorities 49–50
oral history 68–69
with single mothers 107

joint enterprise 144
Joyce, P. 34–35
The State of Freedom 37–38
juvenile court, retribution in 8

Kalb, D. 63, 212–13
Kelly, T. 13–14, 81
Keynesianism 38, 197, 220–21
kin/kinship 5–6, 9–10, 16, 22–23, 65
class 62–63
communities 15–16
fictive 24
households 104–5
kinship entities 224–25
members 22–23, 97, 104–5, 108–9, 204–5
networks 64, 71, 82–83, 230
relations 16, 71, 82–83, 96, 97–98, 121, 230

Koch, I. 13–14, 15–16, 18–19, 29, 35, 37, 41, 60–61, 94–95, 109, 112–14, 116, 141–43, 145, 163–64, 177, 179–80, 183–84, 187, 189, 195, 197, 220, 222–23, 230–31
Koster, M. 168–69
Kuper, L. 65–66

Labour Party
  attitudes to 209–10
  inability to respond to various issues 194
  'law and order' 50–51
  neglect of traditional support base 194–95
  traditional voter base, reducing of 51
  see also New Labour government
Lacey, N. 8, 51–52
  The Prisoners' Dilemma 11–12
laissez-faire government 40–41
Lammy Review (2017) 141
landlords
  private 47–48
  social 111–12, 115, 133–34, 135, 140–41
late modernity 11–12, 15, 192, 223
'law and order'
  assumptions of public views on 4, 11–12
  consent for 5–6, 12–13
  controlling of vulnerable and poor 138–39
  cross-party consensus 140–41
  enforcement of policies 52–53
  expansion of 26–27, 33–34, 220–21, 224
  governance 38–39
  and New Labour government 3, 194–95, 223
  overall trend 7–8
  personalization 153
  policies 3–4, 5–6, 7–8, 192–93
  on post-industrial council housing 15
  questioning of state policies 5–6
  shift towards/turn to 5, 8, 10–11, 34–35, 36, 51, 55–56, 57, 82, 223
  social housing 52–53
  United Kingdom policies 7–8
  and New Labour government 3
  vulnerable citizen and 'law-and-order' state 50
  and welfare 34–35
  see also 'law-and-order' state
'law-and-order' state 9–10
  and council housing, history 34, 38, 49–50, 55
  policy shifts 74
  and post-war welfare state 38
  turn to 34
  and vulnerable citizen 50
  see also 'law and order'
law enforcement officials 32, 51–52, 54
Lawler, S. 61–62
Lazar, S. 187
Lerman, A. 37, 207–8
Leviathan 141, 219–20, 228
  see also Hobbes, T.
liberal democracy *see* democracy/liberal democracy
liberal market economies (LMEs) 11–12, 44–45
liberalism
  advanced 17, 116, 134–35
  cosmopolitan liberals 193–94
  in England 48
  internationalist liberals 193–94
  iron law of 48
  moral dimensions 215
  see also democracy/liberal democracy; neoliberalism
Loader, I. 10–11, 192–93, 228–29
local authorities
  anti-social behaviour, dealing with 32–33, 51–52
  assumptions of 64
  and austerity politics 199–200
  collaboration with 21–22, 31
  and council housing 1–2, 14, 40–41, 46, 56, 222
  cutting of funds 24–25, 177–78
  and drug dealing 172
  enforcement powers 41–42, 51–52, 115–16, 183–84
  failure to maintain neighbourhoods 28, 117, 129–30

interviews with
  officials 49–50, 131–32
law enforcement officials employed
  by 32, 51–52
and neighbour 'trouble' 131–32
outsourcing of social housing
  duties 111–12
Park End estate 42–43
paternalistic attitudes of 38–39
post-war builds 47–48
'regeneration'
  agendas 21–22, 182–83
requests for help from 69, 82–83
selective housing policies 41–42
signs placed by 1–2
slums, clearance of 40
as social landlords 111–12
standards 47–48
see also disrepair and failure to
  maintain properties; housing
  associations; neighbourhoods;
  neighbours
Local Government, Planning and Land
  Act (1980) 114–15
London, East End 79
London riots (2012) 202–3
Lucey, H.
  Democracy in the Kitchen 91

MacKinnon, C. 107–8
maintenance, lack of *see* disrepair and
  failure to maintain properties
male breadwinner model 17
  collapse of model 107–8
  idealized citizen and respect-
    ability 16, 34, 41–42,
    56, 87–88
  see also gender inequalities; gender
    neutrality; women
marginalized citizens 5–6, 26–27, 38–
  39, 84, 195, 216–17, 230–31
Marshall, T. H. 14, 208–9
Maskovsky, J. 34–35
material neglect 28, 117
Meadowell, North Shields 206
means-testing 3–4, 87–88, 89–90,
  91–92, 100–1
Meares, T. 141–42
media, liberal 4
Merry, S. E. 128–29
middle-class citizens
  and punitive turn 10–11

quests for standards of 67
and working-class citizens 26–27
migrants 39–40, 43–44
Miller, D. 64–65
Miller, L. 37–38, 137–38,
  141–42, 220–21
'mob rule' thesis 4, 189, 224
miner strikes (1972) 45
misogyny 87–88
misrecognition 63, 64
model citizen *see* idealized citizen
modernity
  late 11–12, 15, 192, 223
  second 192
Mogey, J. 65–66, 67, 68–69, 70
Mollona, M. 64, 70–71, 76–77,
  89–90, 104–5
monetary policies 4, 45–46
moral distancing 74
moral personhood 57, 60–61, 80,
  83, 91–92
moral statecraft 228
Morgan, S. (2003) 34–35
'mosquitos' (technical devices) 54–55
motherhood 85–87
  'good' mothers 100
  see also single mothers
Mulcahy, L. 114–15, 135

NAGs *see* Neighbourhood Action
  Groups (NAGs)
Narotzky, S. 13
National Health Service (NHS) 40–41
Navaro-Yashin, Y. 99–100
needs-based housing policies 15
neglect, material 28, 117
Neighbourhood Action Groups
  (NAGs), meetings 166–67,
  169–70, 174
  complaints 171–72
neighbourhood policing initiatives 7–
  8, 32–33, 51–52, 54
  see also police
neighbourhoods
  action groups 54
  aspirations 27
  'classical' industrial
    destruction of 40–41, 51, 61–62,
      65, 68, 72–73
    in London 79
    social character of 68
    daily life neighbours, 61–62

neighbourhoods (*cont.*)
  destitute/socially abandoned 5–6
  'gang-infested,' perceptions of 54, 137
  maintaining of homes and social relations 77
  marginalized 38–39
  moral boundaries in 68–69, 70
  networks of support 65, 78–79
  under New Labour 53–54
  nostalgia for social relations, questioning 68
  police power 32–33
  poor urban 142–43
  post-industrial portrayal 3
  safeguarding 38
  shift from neighbourhood-centred to family-centred estates 65
  social housing 28
  spaces of 76–77
  troubled 117
  United States, African–American citizens in 141–43, 207–8
  see also housing; neighbourhood policing initiatives; neighbours
neighbours
  complaints about 68, 129–30, 133, 135
  daily engagement with 133–34
  mistrust between 112
  relations with 28, 117
  trouble with 111–12, 113, 117, 128–29
    nuisance disputes 28, 111–12, 113
    in Park End estate 28, 39–40, 117
  see also neighbourhoods
neoliberalism 9–10, 11, 18–19, 26–27
  and active citizen 168
  anthropology 191–92, 215
  authoritarian 214–15
    'authoritarian fixes' 194–95, 220, 223
  and authorities 55–56
  consumer-oriented notions of citizenship 38
  idealized subject of neoliberal policy 45–46, 52
  inequalities *see* inequalities
  moral duty 165
  shift to 220–21

  state–citizen relations 33–34
  and vulnerable citizen 194–95
  and welfare benefits 57
  and world history 63
  see also liberalism
Netherlands, the 168
networks of support 64, 65, 78–79
  see also care; kin/kinship networks
New Labour government
  active citizenship 163, 166
  anti-social behaviour policies 128, 166, 168
  dissatisfaction with 183–84
  eviction, powers of 52–53, 150–51
  idealized citizen 56
  imprisonment rates 7–8
  and 'law and order' 3, 194–95, 223
  law enforcement officials under 32, 51–52, 54
  neighbourhood policing initiatives 7–8, 32–33, 51–52, 54
  neighbourhoods under 53–54
  'new deal' 88–89
  and political theories 57
  replacement by Coalition government (2010) 34–35, 85, 197, 210, 222–23
  tenants turned into agents of policing 115
  'tough on crime' agenda 50–51, 137–38
  turn to policies of 194–95
  voting into power (1997) 51–52
  see also Blair, T.; idealized citizen; Labour Party
Newburn, T. 8
Newhaven, Sussex 206
noise 114–15, 116
Northern Ireland
  unemployment in 73–74
'Notice Seeking Possession' 52–53
nuclear family model 4–5, 16
  council housing, history 41–43, 44, 56
  demise of nuclear family 61–62, 64, 71
  respectability 113–14
  and single mothers 87
  tenants' aspirations for nuclear family homes 82–83
  see also family/nuclear-family homes; home; male breadwinner model
Nugent, D. 51

nuisance disputes, with neighbours 111–12
  coercive policies 112–13
  complaints about 135
  language of nuisance 28, 128, 134–35
  noise 114–15, 116
  policies 222
  vulnerable citizens 113
  see also neighbours

Occupy movement 214–15
Omega estate, Midlands 71–72
Onley, S. 189
opinion surveys 224–25
Organisation for Economic Co-operation and Development (OECD) 7–8
'otherness' 15
  blaming of others 73–74
  and change 73
  and council housing, history 36–37
  respectability, racial and sexual 'others' outside bounds of 75–76
  single mother as 'other' 73
  see also middle-class citizens; working-class citizens
overcrowding 39–40
Owen, O. 226–27

paradox
  of class 63
  different kind of 216
  empirical 8
  ethnographic 30, 224
  EU referendum 190–91
  punitive *see* punitive paradox
parenting orders 144–45
Park End estate 1, 22–23
  active citizenship 163–64, 168–69
  attitudes of residents towards researchers 21, 22, 24–25
  benefits, claiming *see* benefits system
  betrayal, sense of 163–64, 195–96, 230
  and Brexit *see* Brexit
  changes in community (1980s) 73
  children, treatment of 75
  community centre *see* community centre, Park End estate
  construction 43
  cramped conditions 125–26
  cul-de-sacs 1–2
  daily life *see* daily life
  design 1–2
  development in the 1950s 43
  engagement with electoral politics 195–96
  ethnic and racial composition 43–44
  experiences of residents, research implications 5
  fences 2
  good person 6, 18, 27, 83
  grievances, expression of 128–29
  growth of 43–44
  homeless people, housing of 73
  as Labour Party heartland 42–43, 208–9
  and local authorities 42–43
  material neglect 28, 117
  migration into 43–44
  Neighbourhood Action Groups (NAGs), meetings 166–67, 169–70, 171–72, 174, 177
  neighbours, trouble with 28, 39–40, 117
  one-way road system 1–2
  original location 43
  Parish council 7, 172, 177–78
  party politics, disenchantment with 208–10
  police force 143
  population 43–44
  postcode 75
  'problem estate,' seen as 48–50
  refuse, dumping of 2
  responsibilization 166–67
  single mothers on 91–92, 102–3, 107–8, 111–12, 113, 123, 143–44, 158, 201–2, 222
    precarious homes 92–97
  social governance 42–43
  stigmatizing of 43, 74–75, 81–82
  street pastor initiative *see* street pastor initiative
  swap list 75
  'Them' and 'They', talk of 206–7
  troubled neighbourhoods 117
  violence and threats in 49–50, 137–38, 143, 145, 147–48, 158, 159–60, 232–33
    violent image of Park End estate 49–50

Park End estate (*Cont.*)
  vulnerable citizens living
    in 1–2, 49–50
  waiting lists, housing 42–43
  see also council housing; housing; neighbourhoods; working-class citizens
Park End housing development (southern England)
  fieldwork *see* fieldwork
park rangers 32–33
Parker Morris standards 113–14
participation society, the Netherlands 168
participatory governance 217–18
  and responsibilization 169
partnerships 29, 55
  private–public 128
paternalism
  attitudes of officials 41–43
  housing management 70–71
  post-war 39, 56, 70
  welfare state 88, 204
  and worker–citizen 39
patriarchal power 91
PCSOs *see* police community support officers (PCSOs)
PCT trust 31–32
penal populism 8–9
personalization 17
  anti-social behaviour 128
  benefits system 103
  conceptual framework 6, 18, 19
  daily acts of 91–92
  defining 6, 18
  'law and order' 153
  of police 137–38
  of politics
    in active citizenship 180, 187
    and Brexit 190–91
  selective 109
  top-down and bottom-up attempts to personalize the state 3
  of Weberian legal–bureaucratic state 17–18
  of welfare state 108–9
  by working-class citizens 9–10
personhood
  alternative understandings of 82–83, 218
  broad aspects of 22–23
  and citizenship 16, 59–60
  claims to 81–82
  and connectedness 79–80
  everyday 190–91, 195–96
  good person 6, 18, 27, 83
  legitimate 84
  local 24, 60–61, 64–65
  moral 57, 60–61, 80, 83, 91–92
  narratives 79–80
  ordinary 29–30
  'political ontologies of the self' 60–61, 83
  'proper person' 59–60
  punishment 138–39
  self-reliance 16
  and state 91–92
  understandings of 82–83
  values 64–65
  and women 204–5
philanthropists 40
platonic guardianship 10–11
police
  'biggest gang of all', portrayal as 148
  community policing 32, 51–52, 140–41
  consent, policing by 31–32, 139–40, 142–43
  establishment of British force 139
  expanded policing 138–39
  expectations of 137
  extension of power 51–52
  fear of by women 152
  helicopters 32–33, 54–55
  internal problems 139–40
  legitimacy, questioning 139–41
  military-style policing 139–40
  neighbourhood policing initiatives 7–8, 32–33, 51–52, 54
  Park End force 143
  perceptions of 148
  personalization of 137–38
  police community support officers *see* police community support officers (PCSOs)
  policing, crime and security as a collective public good 139
  role in containing serious crime 137
  'spectacles of police power' 32–33
  targets of 221–22
  as threats 217–18
  'zero tolerance policing' strategies 50–51
  see also streets and police encounters

police community support officers
  (PCSOs) 32–33, 140–41, 152,
  170, 171, 172–74
Police Reform Act (2002) 140–41
political brokers 6, 163–64, 168–69
  activities 186
  community champions as 174, 186
  see also active citizenship
political statecraft 228
politics
  'anti-politics of
    crime' 192–93, 228–29
  austerity *see* austerity politics
  'bread and butter' 29, 163–64,
    180, 217–18
  clientelistic 187
  crisis of political
    representation 194–95
  and dispossession 191–92
  emic theories 195–96, 231
  far-right 191, 215, 229–31
  of lawfare 37
  localized 191–92
  moral and political statecraft 228
  party politics, disenchantment
    with 208–10
  personalization of
    in active citizenship 180, 187
    and Brexit 190–91
  'political ontologies of the
    self' 60–61, 83
  of welfare 37
  see also Brexit; democracy/liberal
    democracy; electorate, British;
    political brokers; political
    statecraft
Poor Law 88
popular authoritarianism and
  Brexit 4, 29–30, 189, 194, 213
popular punitivism 13
  and state authority 5, 224
populism
  authoritarian 4, 189, 213
  exclusionary/inclusionary 13
  penal 8–9
populist punitiveness 8–9
post-industrial neighbourhoods 3,
  15, 32–33
post-war period
  benefits system 88
  community studies 71
  correctionalist justice, post-war
    ideal 36–37

council housing 14, 34, 38–39, 44,
  65, 70–71, 82–83, 113–14
  demise of post-war welfare state,
    in UK 45
  paternalism 39, 56, 70
  political economy of 82–83
  reformers 88
  social citizenship 90
  social contract 41, 44–45
  social insurance 87–88
  social security system 88
  in United Kingdom *see* United
    Kingdom
  welfare state 14, 15, 38
  working-class citizens 34
Pratt, J. 8–9
precarious homes 47–48, 92
private–public partnerships 128
privatization 44–46, 194–95
  of council housing sector 33–34,
    46–48, 50
'problem estates', council estates seen
  as 48, 53–54
  and Park End estate 48–50
'problem families' 70
productive citizen 88–89
prostitution 95
public, assumptions concerning
  and state's own logics of
    punitiveness 11–12
  views on 'law and order' 4, 11–12
  views on punishment 8
public-sector cuts 3–4
punishment
  assumptions of public views on 8
  attitudes of Brexit voters to 193–94
  austerity reforms as form of 201–2
  citizenship as 220
  collective 221–22
  crisis of state legitimacy 11
  ethnographic paradox 30
  personhood 138–39
  policing 141, 160–61
  popular punitivism and state
    authority 5, 224
  popular support for 160–61
  and state–citizen relations 221–22
  welfare state 37–38
  see also police; punitive paradox;
    punitive turn
punitive paradox
  versus ethnographic paradox 30
  macro-accounts of 13–14

punitive paradox (*Cont.*)
  making sense of 6–7
  and punitive turn 10
  support for anti-democratic measures 8–9, 160
  see also paradox
punitive turn
  and council housing 36
  ethnographic perspective 8–9
  explaining 10
  narratives 8–10
  paradox of 10, 30, 218–19
  policing, expanded 138–39
  state-centric accounts of 62–63
  within criminal justice policies 4
punitivism
  popular 13, 30
    and state authority 5, 224
  populist punitiveness 8–9, 216
  punitive paradox 10, 30, 218–19
  state's increased reliance on 218–19
  state's own logics of punitiveness 11–12
  welfare systems 109
  see also punishment; punitive turn

racism
  accusations in personal relationships 154–55
  exclusion, racialized 113–14
  gangs, racialized images of 53–54, 61
  prejudices 68
  racialized practices 45–46
Ramsay, P. 52, 57, 165, 167–68
  The Insecurity State 11
redistribution, demand for 109
referendum of 2016 *see* Brexit
regeneration
  agendas 21–22, 182–83
  and Park End estate community centre 21–22
rehabilitation 36
Reiner, R. 139–40
rent officials 70–71
rent payments 38–39
respectability
  case study 143–44
  defining 41–42, 56
  expansion of categories 53–54
  families 113–14
  homeowners 34, 46, 56
  and male white breadwinner 34, 41–42, 56
  and morality 67
  racial and sexual 'others' outside bounds of 75–76
  state categories 82–83
  worker–citizen/consumer–citizen 34, 38–39
  working-class citizens 70–71, 74
responsibilization 45–46, 166–67
  and participatory governance 169
restorative justice 11–12, 224–25
restructuring plans 180
retribution 4
Reynolds, F. 48, 71–73, 114–15
Richmond Park, West London 189–90
right to buy (council tenants) 46–47, 114–15
riots 52–54, 118, 139–40
  London riots (2012) 202–3
  in Park End estate 203, 206–7
Rogaly, B. 69, 70
Rooney, W. 95
Rose, N. 116
Rossner, M. 224–25

Savage, M. 62–63
Saxton, C. 40
Scheper-Hughes, N. 95–96
Scott, J. 39–40
second modernity 192
secure tenancies 47–48, 117–18
security gap 137–38, 141–42, 143, 160
self-policing 142–43
sentencing
  harsher nature of 8
  mandatory 3–4
  minimum sentencing-laws 8
service charges 126–27
Shah, A. 13–14, 214–15
Simon, J. 11, 192–93, 228–29
single mothers
  access to council houses 90–91
  alternative accounts 87
  as anti-citizens 90–91
  austerity politics 201–2
  and benefits system 27–28, 85
  case law 113
  and dependency 49–50
  figures of 'excess' 90–91
  Housing (Homeless Persons) Act 1977 46
  images of 53–54, 72–73, 104–5, 106

Index 271

inequalities 91
interviews with 103–4, 107
men, views of 95–96
narratives 96–97
as 'other' 73
on Park End estate 100–2, 107–8, 111–12, 113, 123, 143–44, 158, 201–2, 222
  benefits system and consumer–citizen 91–97
  playing the system 87, 91–92, 104, 108–9, 226–28
  and rising underclass 71
  and state–citizen relations 102
  stigmatizing of 86–87
  and street pastor initiative 32
  terminology 86–87
  trope of 91, 112–13
  working hours, menial service sector 97
  see also women
Skeggs, B. 63, 74, 91, 222
slums 39–40, 42–43
  clearance schemes 40–41, 65
social citizenship 87–88, 90
social class see class; middle-class citizens; working-class citizens
social contract 41, 44–45, 90–91
  and violence 139, 160–61
social democracy 4–5, 9–10, 11
  and council housing, history 36–38, 39–40
  'golden age' 4–5, 9–10, 37–38, 220
social governance 4–5, 116
  and council housing, history 34, 37–38
  Park End estate 42–43
social housing 5, 16, 28, 111–12
  anti-social behaviour 112
  dependence of tenants on landlords 135
  environmental suffering 116
  expansion to include vulnerable categories of people 46–47
  housing associations 114–15, 128–29
  'law and order' policies 52–53
  materiality 112–13, 114–15
  outsourcing of duties 111–12
  providers 217–18
  and single mothers 103
  tenants as fighters of crime 134–35
  withdrawal practices 126–27
  and worthiness 46
  see also council housing; housing
social insurance 40–41
  and means-testing 90
  post-war period 87–88
social landlords 111–12, 115, 133–34, 135, 140–41
Social Security and Housing Benefits Act (1982) 47–48
social security system 88
sociology
  class 15–16, 60–62, 82
  political ideology and power 15–16
  of United Kingdom 15–16
Soskice, D. 11–12
Sparks, R. 142–43, 148, 224–25
state
  authority of, and popular punitivism 5, 224
  and benefits system 97
  and class 12–14, 15–16
    benefits system 91
    'class apartheid' 40
    coercion/control 4–5, 6–7, 9–10, 13, 15, 19, 26–27, 40–41, 111–12, 216, 218–19, 220, 222–23, 224–25
    council housing 33–34, 35, 38–39, 40–41, 42–43, 44, 51, 55–56, 57
    support from state 69
    see also benefits system; welfare state
  control by see state control
  crisis of 5
  defining 6
  everyday forms of engagement with 6–7
  expectations of support from 69
  failure of 18–19, 75–76, 202
    and betrayal 75–76, 207
    emic theories 18–19, 84, 229–30
  history of council housing as history of state-building 34
  law-and-order state see 'law-and-order' state
  logics of punitiveness 11–12
  moral and political statecraft 228
  moral union between citizens and state 16, 65, 204, 225–26
    attack on 71
  patients of 111–12

state (*cont.*)
  personalization of *see* **personalization**
  and personhood 91–92
  'replacing the man' 85–86, 97
  'right' and 'left' hands 37–38
  state-building and council housing 34, 38–40
  state–citizen relations *see* **state–citizen relations**
  top-down and bottom-up attempts to personalize 3
  violence and threats by 157–58
  Weberian legal–bureaucratic, personalizing of 17–18
  see also **welfare state**
state–citizen relations 4–5
  and anthropology 17
  assumption of state as sole arbiter of citizenship, questioning 60–61
  complex forms 142–43
  council housing, history 33–34, 35
  in criminal justice interactions versus social welfare programmes 37
  and daily life 15–16, 27–28
  engagement 18–19
  ethnographic perspective 216, 218, 223
  everyday forms of engagement 227–28
  gendering of 85–86
  implications for liberal democracy 29–30
  and personalizing the state 6, 17
  political theory 6–7
  post-war history 82
  and punishment 221–22
  and single mothers 102
  state–citizen–market relations 222–23
  see also **social contract**
state coercion *see* **coercive governance**
state control
  capitalism 44–45
  and class 4–5, 6–7, 9–10, 13, 15, 19, 26–27, 40–41, 111–12, 216, 218–19, 220, 222–23, 224–25
  classed nature of 111–12
  council housing, history 34–35, 38–39, 44–45

popular punitivism and state authority 224
  of vulnerable and poor 138–39
  welfare state 35
  see also **coercive governance; police; state**
Steinberg, J. 13, 142–43
Stoke Newington, London 234–35
stop-and-search powers 54–55
Strathern, M. 67, 73–74
Straw, J. 50–51
street pastor initiative
  characteristics of street pastors 31
  launch of scheme 31–32
  making sense of 33–34
  repeat offenders, targeting 31–32
  and single mothers 32
street wardens 32–34, 51–52
streets and police encounters 136
  emic category, streets as 145–46
  perceptions of police 148
  policing, crime and security as a collective public good 139
  violence and threats 143
strike action 45, 208–9
symbolic violence 63, 74
Symons, J. 21, 49–50, 181–82

tax credits 88–89
Taylor, B. 69, 70
technocratic governance 4
Tenant Management Organizations (TMOs) 115
  see also **council housing**
Thatcher, M./Thatcherism 15, 71, 220–21
  and active citizen 194–95
  and council housing, history 45–47, 51
  images of 194
  individual responsibility, shift to 115, 165
Thirangama, S. 81
third-sector organisations 33–34, 47–48
Third Way politics
  active citizenship 165–66, 167–68
Thompson, E. P. 13
Together (Home Office Campaign) 166
top-down governance 3, 5–6, 27–28
tower blocks 124–25
trade union movements 40–41, 51, 208–9, 210, 218–19

Turkey 18
Turnbull, G. 206
Tyler, K. 219–20

UKIP 215
underclass
  images of 71
  rise of 61–62
  single mothers 71
  see also class
unemployment 45
  long-term 41
  in Northern Ireland 73–74
United Kingdom
  anthropology of 15–16
  benefits system 88
  establishment of British police force 139
  ethnographic literature 77–78
  'law and order' policies 7–8
  liberal market economy (LME) 11–12, 44–45
  liberalism in England 48
  London riots (2012) 202–3
  miner strikes (1972) 45
  New Labour government *see* New Labour government
  policy reforms 10
  Poor Law 88
  poor urban neighbourhoods 142–43
  post-industrial neighbourhoods 3, 15, 32–33
  post-war period 36–37, 39–40, 44, 56
    demise of post-war welfare state 45
  punitive dimensions of democracy 7–8
  referendum of 2016 *see* Brexit
  sociology of 15–16
  see also benefits system
United States
  African–American citizens 141–43, 207–8
  custodial citizenship 37, 141–42
  differential citizenship patterns in 141–42
  informal networks of crime control 168
  liberal market economies (LMEs) 11–12
  policy reforms 10
  poor urban neighbourhoods 142–43

post-war state 38
public housing projects, Chicago 135
'welfare queen' 90–91
universal credit 86–87
utopian projects 39–40

values
  value accrual, alternative processes 76
vigilantism 142–43, 157–58, 159, 160–61, 184, 186, 226–27
violence and threats
  daily life 136–37
  'do or get done' 147
  domestic abuse 144–45
  ethnographic perspective 137, 160
  extra-legal violence 141–42
  informal violence 141–42
  legitimate violence 84
  London riots (2012) 202–3
  in Park End estate 49–50, 137–38, 143, 145–48, 158, 159–60, 232–33
  reputation for 146–47
  by state 157–58
  streets and police encounters 143
  symbolic violence 63, 74
voters, British *see* Brexit; electorate, British
vulnerable citizens
  active citizenship 165
  assumptions regarding 57
  'citizen-as-crime-fighter' 38, 52, 56, 115
  information sharing 31–32
  and 'law-and-order' state 50
  and model citizens 115
  and neoliberalism 194–95
  nuisance disputes 113
  in Park End estate 1–2, 49–50
  prioritization of in allocation of council housing 46
  responsibility for structural problems shifted onto 17–18
  see also citizenship

Wacquant, L. 37–38, 141, 146–47
Walkerdine, V.
  Democracy in the Kitchen 91
Weaver, V. 37, 207–8
Weber, M. 84
welfare
  council housing, history

welfare (*Cont.*)
 broader focus on policies 37–38
 'law and order' 34–35
 politics of welfare 37
 social welfare programmes versus criminal justice 37
 strong policies 44–45
 versus lawfare 223
 paternalistic policies 204
 punitive systems 109
 recipients of 58, 151–52, 226
  austerity politics 199–200, 201–2
  material neglect 117
  playing the system 87, 91–92, 104, 108–9, 218, 226–27
  single mothers 86–87, 89–90, 100–1
 reforms 85
 see also benefits system
welfare state 5
 and austerity politics 197
 and council housing 14, 40–41
 dependence of women on 91–92
 dominant policies 27
 emergence of 40–41
 officials 49–50
 paternalistic 88
 personalization of 108–9
 post-war 14, 15, 38
  demise of in the UK 45
 punishment 37–38
 state control 35
 see also benefits system; social housing; state
welfarism 36–37
 welfarist consensus 10–11, 139
Wilde, M. 109
Williams, P. 221–22
Willmott, P. 15–16, 65, 79
withdrawal, electoral participation 3–4, 18, 183–84, 189–91, 192–93, 195–96, 210–11, 213–14
women
 of Afro-Caribbean descent 43–44
 authority figures, contact with 48–49
 benefits system 88, 91–97, 98–88
 collaborative nature of relationships 107
 and consumer–citizen 88
 daily life 22, 28, 48–49, 61, 86–87, 88, 91–92, 108–9, 111–12, 121–22, 126, 174–75
 dependants of husbands, seen as 41
 exclusion, gendered 113–14
 independence from men 96
 men using information against 105–6
 paternalistic attitudes to 38–39
 single mothers *see* single mothers
 status 41
worker–citizen
 idealized citizen as *see* idealized citizen
 and post-war paternalism 39
 respectability 38–39
 see also citizenship; consumer–citizen; worker–citizen
working-class citizens
 'affluent worker' 66–67
 authentic model 62–63
 common-sense, portrayal of 194
 community-centred perspective 15–16
 daily life 18, 58, 61
  state relations 15–16, 27–28
 grievances, expression of 128–29
 home-oriented culture 65–66
 housing developments for 14
 images of imagined lack 61
 and middle-class citizens 26–27
 moral denigration 61–62
 personalization by 9–10
 in post-war decades 34
 regulation of 87–88
 respectability 70–71, 74
 social contract, provision of council housing as 14
 social governance 4–5, 34
 and state coercion 5, 9–10
 'undeserving' 42–43
 see also council housing; respectability
worthy citizen 46, 56

xenophobia, and Brexit 189, 191, 213, 230–31
Young, J. (**1999**) 11, 36
Young, M. D. (**1957**) 15–16, 65, 79
youth services 32–33

'zombie democracy' 192, 193–94, 195